ETHICS AND SPIRITUALITY AT WORK

ETHICS AND SPIRITUALITY AT WORK

Hopes and Pitfalls of the Search for Meaning in Organizations

Edited by Thierry C. Pauchant

Quorum Books
Westport, Connecticut • London

Library of Congress Cataloging-in-Publication Data

Ethics and spirituality at work : hopes and pitfalls of the search for meaning in
organizations / edited by Thierry C. Pauchant.
    p.   cm.
    Includes bibliographical references and index.
    ISBN 1–56720–562–3 (alk. paper)
    1. Management—Religious aspects—Congresses. 2. Work—Religious
aspects—Congresses. 3. Business ethics—Congresses. I. Pauchant, Thierry C.
BL65.W67 E88   2002
174—dc21   2002017940

British Library Cataloguing in Publication Data is available.

Library of Congress Catalog Card Number: 2002017940
ISBN: 1–56720–562–3

First published in 2002

Quorum Books, 88 Post Road West, Westport, CT 06881
An imprint of Greenwood Publishing Group, Inc.
www.quorumbooks.com

Printed in the United States of America

The paper used in this book complies with the
Permanent Paper Standard issued by the National
Information Standards Organization (Z39.48–1984).

10 9 8 7 6 5 4 3 2 1

The editor and publisher gratefully acknowledge permission for use of the following material:

Chapter 6, copyright © 2002 Ouimet-Cordon Bleu Inc.

Excerpts in Chapter 11 reprinted from Simone Weil's *Oppression and Liberty* (Amherst:
University of Massachusetts Press, 1973). Copyright © 1958 by Routledge and Kegan Paul.
Reprinted by permission of University of Massachusetts Press, Routledge and Kegan Paul,
and Editions Gallimard.

Excerpts in Chapter 11 reprinted from Simone Weil, *The Need for Roots: Prelude to a Declaration of Duties towards Mankind.* (London: Routledge and Kegan Paul, 1949). Reprinted
by permission of Routledge and Kegan Paul.

Contents

Preface

This book is an exploration of the promises and dangers of the new corporate God rush. If the twentieth century started with the famous California gold rush, today's executives and employees alike are rushing for the divine in their work. As indicated in Chapter 2, studies suggest that 92 percent of U.S. executives wish to resolve the basic paradox between material life and metaphysics, consumerism and spiritual values, gold and God.

For once, corporate America agrees with academia. At the close of last century, the December 1999 cover story of *Business Week* was entitled "Religion in the Workplace: The Rise of Spirituality in Corporate America"; and at the first twenty-first-century meeting of the Academy of Management, the official scientific research group was created on "management, spirituality, and religion." Is it possible that "In God we trust" is becoming a powerful ideology that could overthrow our current "In Gold we trust"? Will the MBA's motto "Me Before Anyone" be replaced by "Meaning Before Anything"?

Many popular writers will answer these questions positively. For them, the spiritual quest, the search for God or for the spirit, will be the one that will cure our infatuation with gold and glory, the two other "G's" that Georges Bernanos identified as the human curse since the beginning of time.

I am sympathetic to this view. While I find books such as *Jesus CEO* or *Chicken Soup for the Soul at Work* too simplistic, I view them also as an expression of our longing for something more, as a beginning of an answer to the existential question asked by this twenty-five-year-old Silicon Valley millionaire "Is this all there is?" The same question arose after the September 11 tragedy as Americans searched for meaning.

But these popular accounts also have their shortcomings: Most of them confuse the spiritual quest with the search for personal identity or even with the wish to be protected by a loving community, two tendencies that Abraham Maslow viewed as "defensive needs." Further, these accounts often present the spiritual path as providing unambiguous answers in our complex world. Quite different in intent, the world's major spiritual traditions have all emphasized that the spiritual quest is a courageous encounter with the mystery of the world—never a final destination, but a journey without end. Last, these popular accounts rarely examine the dark side of the pseudospiritual quest, which could also lead, in the political arena of organizations, to the use of our body, mind, and soul for the idolatry of these lesser gods that are engaged in the search for gold and glory.

Thus, this book is a critical journey: "critical" in that it attempts to look both at the promises and dangers offered by the integration of ethical and spiritual values at work; "journey" in that it provides many different voices for approaching the spiritual realm. This is not to say that the book does not offer any concrete lessons. The five cases included in the book, written by leaders of organizations in different sectors, present five different strategies for integrating ethical and spiritual values at work (banking, food, public management, healthcare, and education). Although these cases are interesting and provide some concrete strategies and tools, they do not exhaust all the different ways that could be used for better integrating ethical and spiritual values at work. Further, they should all be studied to better understand their promises and dangers. I am convinced that the best we can do is document the different strategies used in different organizations, across time, space, cultures, and traditions, for future comparison and evaluation.

While this book has a very practical side, it also offers different ways of conceptualizing the quest for ethics and spirituality at work. This is particularly important as many of the current works available on the subject of spirituality at work lack a conceptual grounding. For example, the Introduction revisits Abraham Maslow's theory of need. While virtually all management students have been exposed to that theory, many are not aware that Maslow warned of the dangers of self-actualization and that he proposed a transcendental need, thus opening the way to spirituality. Also, in the concluding chapter, the Integral Model of Ken Wilber is presented in managerial terms. In my opinion, this model is one of the richest available today for both mapping the promises and dangers of ethics and spirituality at work, and for assisting with their development in a healthy way.

Last, between the theory chapters and the more practical ones, there are three chapters of dialogues. These dialogues took place during the first Forum on International Management, Ethics, and Spirituality at the École des Haute Études Commerciales (HEC) in Montreal, the oldest and largest business school in Canada. It was organized by FIMES, a network organization whose goal is the better integration of ethical and spiritual values in the workplace (www.hec.ca/fimes). These dialogues offer yet another way for exploring these aspirations at work. Definitively unstructured, vagabond in nature, and wandering in their quest, dialogues are often disconcerting to read as they offer a glimpse behind the curtain of sequential logic. I am convinced that with poetry, the arts, and the divers spiritual practices, the diffuse form of dialogues can sometimes better approach the formless nature of spirit.

As this book has been previously published in French, American readers can benefit from the reactions it has triggered in both North America and Europe. The critics have been unanimous in stating that the book is extremely rich, sometimes profound, and that the subject needs further inquiry. I fully agree with these commentaries. Considering the lack of scientific studies conducted on this subject, the integration of spiritual values in organizations is, today, still mostly a research endeavor. As a reader you will gain from this book many insights useful in the practice of management and leadership; and yet, you will also end up with several deeper questions. This is, perhaps, one of the signs that a genuine spiritual quest is active in our world of organizations.

Acknowledgments

I would like to warmly thank Roger Berthouzoz, J.-Robert Ouimet, Jean-Marie Toulouse, and Maurice Villet for the long conversations we had together in preparation for the first Forum on International Management, Ethics, and Spirituality (FIMES). I would also like to thank the collaborators who were enthusiastic in their response to our invitation to be contributors to this forum and who offered comments on the first version of this book: Claude Béland, Yves Benoît, Vera Danyluk, Michel Dion, James Hurley, Solange Lefebvre, Ian I. Mitroff, and Peter Sheldrake.

Both the first forum and this book would not have come to life without the diligent work of Kariann Aarup, Maguelone Boë, Denis Cauchon, Virginie Lecourt, and Nathalie Morin, research assistants at FIMES. I thank you for your sincere commitment and for your enthusiasm. Many other people have also devoted their time and talent to the forum and to the preparation of this book: Alexis Descollonges, Sylvain Bossé, Daniel Carroué, Marlène Charland, Louis Chauvin, Yannik Chauvin, Benoît Cherré, Consuelo Garcia de la Torre, Roger Marcaurelle, Patrick McNamara, Linda Néron, Charles Perreault, Emmanuel Raufflet, Angelo Soares, Frances Stober, and Céline Thérieault. Thanks to Jacqueline Avard for her facilitation of the forum and to Kim Gosselin for his inspiring music.

I would also like to thank the 200 or so people who have participated in the forum and those who have contributed to the dialogues that have been transcribed in this book, as well as Eric Valentine at Quorum Books.

Finally, I cannot help being reminded of the precious support of Yves Bériault, André Descoteaux, Yves Moreau, and their communities.

I thank you all from the depth of my heart. Together, we organized a conference and produced a book that answers a real and profound need for managers and their employees. I also enjoyed dialoguing, learning, and working with you for a cause that extends beyond us as individuals and inspires us.

Introduction: Ethical and Spiritual Management Addresses the Need for Meaning in the Workplace

Thierry C. Pauchant

Integrating ethics and spirituality into all facets of management and leadership of organizations has become an urgent need expressed by managers themselves. How to reconcile economic value and ethical or spiritual value becomes the fundamental question. This is a fascinating, serious, and slippery subject. The potential pitfalls are numerous: Ethics can devolve into legalism, dogmatism, or abusive moralization; spirituality can lead to fundamentalism, archaic superstitions, or the growth of abusive sects; both ethics and spirituality can be coopted to manipulate people, employees, and managers as a way to maximize profits.

Yet introducing ethics and spirituality into the workplace, the first more rational, the second more transcendent, could meet a fundamental human need: a need for meaning, a need for integration, a need for establishing roots, a need for transcendence.

In this introduction, I propose several reasons why the integration of ethics and spirituality is sought today by many people, while also proposing strategies for avoiding certain pitfalls. After presenting some of the reasons behind the present crisis of meaning in organizations, I describe the positive and less positive ways in which people generally react to crises. I then suggest that four major trends support the idea that introducing ethics and spirituality in the workplace is not just another management fad but rather that it meets a deep and lasting need. I conclude by presenting the chapters of the book.

THE QUEST FOR MEANING AT WORK

This book is a pragmatic and concrete response to the expression of a need for meaning. This need is expressed by a growing number of people working in organizations worldwide. This search for meaning is felt by employees, managers, upper and senior management, leaders, consultants, professors, and students. It is a need that is generic to the human condition but is particularly felt in today's workplace.

As I have already suggested in a previous work on this subject, this search for meaning is not the exclusive purview of the marginal, the forgotten, the poor, the unemployed, the sick or the dying.[1] Employees, managers, upper management, and corporate leaders who have succeeded, according to social convention, also feel it.

Numerous factors are associated with this search for meaning.[2] In a broad sense several changes have contributed to an increased sense of insecurity in the general population and to the upending of traditional paradigms that gave meaning to their world and their lives. We can refer to problems of international security, the rise of terrorism and dogmatism—as exemplified by the September 11 tragedy, the appearance and growth of AIDS and the ecological crisis. We can also point to the decline of the influence of traditional religion in the West, which provided people with guidance, or to the increased realization that the dream of a scientifically and technologically based Edenic society in the year 2000 is far from being fulfilled. Other observers have attributed this increased quest for meaning to the fact that a large portion of our Western population—the baby-boomers—is aging and that these people are now faced with the prospect of the end of their lives.

Other factors have also created upheaval in the institutional and economic worlds: increased unemployment, fiercer competition, an increased rate of change, major restructuring, and corporate scandals. We are also faced with the reality of increases in bankruptcies, budget cuts and corporate mergers, increases in industrial accident impacts and the constant push for more and faster—with, of course, fewer resources. A number of managers and employees are also feeling squeezed at work and are questioning the restrictive conditions to which they must submit. These restrictions—this fragmentation of reality—includes the often abusive technocratic rationalizing present in numerous organizations; the supremacy of "economism" in strategic and managerial decisions; or the rise of backroom political maneuvering that directs certain corporate activities to the advantage of a small number of people.

In order to survive in these organizations, many people must put aside their most profound ethical and spiritual values and aspirations such as the respect of people and of the natural environment. Numerous studies also show that in the United States, South America, Europe, and Asia, many people who are still working have seen their work hours increase since World War II but with an actual decrease in wages.[3] In the last fifty years the work situation has deteriorated for a great number of people. Consequently, the gaps and inequalities have increased between those who work too much and those now without work, between the so-called "information" professions and the more traditional ones, and between so-called "developed" and "developing" countries.

The negative effects of this lack of meaning are also diverse and worrisome: increased stress, burnout, and other psychological problems; a rise in dependence on drugs, alcohol, and tranquillizers such as Prozac; workaholism; increase in spousal abuse; sexual and psychological harassment in the workplace; an increase in suicides, violence, and school drop-outs among our youth; idealization of abusive charismatic leaders; a frantic search for magical managerial solutions or tools; and so forth.

I should not, of course, paint too bleak a picture of the situation. I do not want to suggest that working for a corporation is necessarily devoid of meaning. Science, technology, industry, and business in general have certainly contributed to numerous improvements in our lives. Think, for example, of the increase in life expectancy, the development of democracy, the abolition of slavery, and the increase in material comfort, at least in certain parts of the world. We could also mention progress in the fields of medicine, food production, transportation, computer sciences and telecommunications, to name only a few sectors. In addition, many people still find meaning in their work, especially if it brings them a sense of self-realization and accomplishment, and coincides with their deepest values, as we shall see in this book. The increase in individualism in our societies or of this "self-centeredness" as some have referred to it, is not necessarily negative. It also means a salutary enfranchisement from political, religious, and other dogmatic systems of the past, and the possibility to critically exercise one's personal judgment.

As the well-known philosopher Charles Taylor has so aptly pointed out, our situation in modern societies bears the stamp of greatness and misery: Our time is at once one of unequalled possibilities and major problems; whence the experience of a profound malaise, of ambivalence between hope and despair, whence the search for meaning.[4]

To give another example, Rollo May, one of the founders of humanist psychology, has also proposed that our current malaise stems from ambivalence. In particular, he insisted that the world of only a short time ago that supplied existential meaning to its inhabitants had undergone a radical transformation, and now lacked a new worldview. We need only think of the major changes in transportation, telecommunications, domestic comforts, and goods and services made available in the past fifty years.

THE CRISIS OF MEANING AND THE MEANING OF THE CRISIS

The experience of a crisis, of a traumatic experience or of a recurring malaise—we refer here to a "crisis of meaning" or a "crisis of belief" as stated by Solange Lefebvre in this book (see Chapter 3)—moves people to action. My colleague, Ian I. Mitroff, and I have suggested in our works on crisis management that these people often use three generic strategies in action.[5]

The first strategy consists of doing "more of the same thing." This strategy partially explains the rise of corporate orthodoxy and an increase of fundamentalist thought. In management, this strategy can lead to arbitrary budget or personnel cuts; to a hardening of managerial positions that were already quite autocratic; to the mind-set of "always more with fewer resources"; or to the increase of an even colder, more impersonal, more rigid technocratic logic. Estelle Morin, an industrial psychologist, provides a good description of this "more of the same" strategy that varies according to the personality type of the managers who adopt it and that often leads to increasingly absurd situations because of their extremism.[6] In a similar fashion, the organizational theorist Danny Miller has suggested that inordinate use of traditional business functions—marketing, production, finance, or research and development—can lead to a decline of these organizations.[7]

The second strategy consists of an "escape into anything." Where in the first strategy people became relatively conscious of the problem but remained tied to one or several unique solutions, the purpose of using this second strategy is to become as unconscious as possible of the traumatic situation. This escape can take many shapes such as the consumption of drugs, alcohol, tranquillizers, or headlong flight into sex, money, or workaholism. It can also lead to a scapegoat phenomenon through an increase in violence toward a person or group perceived—wrongfully—as responsible for the trauma, as well as promote racism and terrorism. This strategy can also become a frantic search for a magic solution such as the blind idealization of a charismatic leader, the latest fad in managerial tools or a guru.

This escape can also lead people to join a sect. The West has witnessed a dramatic increase in the number of sects and their members all increasing within the workplace. In France, for example, where in 1982 there were an estimated 150,000 disciples and sympathizers, today that number is thought to be more of the order of at least 260,000. One remembers the downfall of the Church of Scientology, in France, which brought about the creation of a parliamentary commission on the issue of sects, as well as the massacre of the Order of the Solar Temple in Switzerland and Canada, the attack in the Tokyo metro by the Aoum sect, or the collective suicide of the Heaven's Gate sect in the United States. Of course not all sects are dangerous and some help their members to attain real, profound, and beneficial self-realization that is not an escape but a temporary salutary refuge. My comments are more directed at abusive sects that manipulate their disciples in a demagogical fashion and often have negative, if not dramatic effects.

Where the first defense strategy led to amplification and the second to escape from a trauma or malaise, the third strategy is rather a learning process that leads to a transformation.[8] A fundamental reason makes this strategy the most difficult of the three: It requires courage, discipline, and a great deal of effort. In this strategy there is no denial of the crisis: The experience, while traumatic, is transcended and leads to a transformation of the person allowing them to actualize new values, new behavior, and a new level of consciousness. I will return to this subject.

Several of the contributors to this book refer to the need for a crisis as an initiator of a voyage on the pathways of ethics and spirituality. These people will go as far as to propose that happiness is not only the absence of trauma but that the experience of suffering itself, without going so far as idealizing it, can also hold happiness. We will see that individuals who have attained a certain level of maturity can grow as much through the experience of suffering as through that of joy, a character trait that Abraham Maslow discovered in so-called "actualized" persons.[9] But this strategy requires true courage of personal transformation and a rigorous and sustained effort, often in the context of a therapeutic and/or spiritual discipline. I will also come back to this important subject.

For now, I would like to say, and this is quite encouraging, that many individuals in business organizations are already actively engaged in the pursuit of their personal transformation, attempting to formalize their search for meaning, having the courage to learn from their experiences of joy and of suffering. Stated differently, if the existentialists Paul Tillich and Rollo May have insisted on "the courage to be" and "The courage to create," there exists also a courage to learn.[10] In this book, Peter Sheldrake and James Hurley, who describe an interesting learning experience in a business school (see Chapter 9) refer to the courage to teach.[11]

INDICATORS OF THE NEED FOR ETHICS AND SPIRITUALITY IN THE ORGANIZATIONAL WORLD

I started this introduction by saying that this book is a response to the search for meaning. I have suggested, based on both positive and negative yet concrete manifestations, that this search is very real for many managers. Even the defensive strategies used to respond to this quest for meaning, amplification or escape, are concrete indications that many people in the workplace are seeking, are sojourning, and need assistance in redirecting their quest toward less destructive means.

Other indicators suggest that more and more employees and managers want to include ethical and spiritual values in their workplaces. I will define these two concepts at a later time. At this point, I would like to introduce four of these indicators: the increased preoccupation with ethics in the workplace; the upholding of a certain religious belief or the existence of a spiritual renewal; the rise of experimentation with the concepts of ethics and spirituality in the workplace; and the greater presence of information on spirituality and spiritual education.

An Effervescent Need for Ethics in the Workplace

To affirm that business ethics is in demand would be to state a truism. We've come a long way since Chester I. Barnard, CEO in the AT&T group and renowned theorist of administrative sciences published, in 1958, possibly the first seminal article on business ethics.[12] Today a study cites that almost two-thirds of corporate recruiters in the United States consider honesty and personal integrity as fundamental qualities of a prospective employee. The Conference Board has also insisted that honesty, integrity, and moral values are basic requirements for all employees.[13] The importance of trust, integrity, and morality in an increasingly global, complex, paradoxical, and ambiguous world has recently also been stressed by experts and influential authors like Warren Bennis, Charles Handy, and Daniel Yankelovich.[14]

A sign of the times, wide-ranging scientific literature exists on the subject of business ethics. We have witnessed the appearance of several scientific and professional journals and a number of research and training centers or institutes have opened worldwide.[15] Many businesses and organizations of all types have adopted diverse codes of ethics or of deontology, and consulting firms such as Price Waterhouse Coopers or KPMG are providing support services in this area.

A shift to applied ethics can also be observed in ethical research in the workplace. We thus now refer to differentiated fields such as bioethics, business ethics, environmental ethics, international ethics, political ethics, ethics in scientific research, and social ethics, to name only a few. Each of these specialties attempts to respond to the specific demands of its field.

In a shrinking world of increased opening of markets and globalization, ethical principles are no longer derived solely from an individual's personal values, or from a single philosophical, religious, or cultural tradition. The tendency is to seek an international synthesis. Increasingly, ethics are also proposed as an integral part of organizational strategy, broadening the debate and making ethical considerations as present at the top of the hierarchical order as they are in everyday business operations.[16]

Echoing certain themes presented in this introduction—employment crisis, crisis of meaning, ecological crisis, crisis of belief—numerous authors have proposed that ethics in business, in organizations, and in society in general are no longer a desire or a luxury but a strategic imperative. The titles of their works are eloquent: *The Ecology of Commerce* by Paul Hawken;

Leadership for the Common Good; Tackling Public Problems in a Shared-Power World by John Bryson and Barbara Crosby; *Earth in the Balance: Ecology and the Human Spirit* by Al Gore; *For the Common Good* by Herman Daly and J. Cobb; *For People and Profit* by Kazuo Inamori; *Just Rewards* by David Olive; *The Executive Compass: Business and the Good Society* by James O'Toole; *Greening Business, Profiting the Corporation and the Environment* by Paul Shrivastava; *The Moral Commonwealth* by Philip Selznik; *In Pursuit of Principle and Profit* by Alan Reder; or *In Search of Meaning* by Thierry C. Pauchant and Associates.

John Dalla Costa's book, *The Ethical Imperative*, is possibly one of the best recent works to illustrate why ethics have become a strategic imperative. In his book the author proposes that, in a world where the economy has become global, ethics concern us all: producers and consumers, investors and regulators, presidents and employees. His example of Nike is particularly edifying. Although this corporation's dramatic growth can be seen as an international success story and an apt model having outpaced giants like Adidas, its exploitation of employees and subcontractors' employees in Korea and China has been exposed and condemned by the international community. Nike, a powerful corporation, was forced to conduct an internal audit and introduce changes under the supervision of Andrew Young, ex-ambassador to the United Nations.

This case is particularly interesting because it shows that a global economy produces systemic effects, a recurring theme in this book. It is essential to note, for example, that for years, Nike denied its immoral practices—just like many other firms before it. It is only after exposure of these practices by different interest groups or stakeholders that Nike was finally coerced into modifying its activities. Included in these groups were human rights organizations, media such as *Newsweek* and NBC, consumer groups, diverse Canadian and American churches, and finally, the shareholders themselves. This is a perfect demonstration that the imperative of an organizational ethic, in an increasingly interconnected and systemic world, is a strategic necessity. Dalla Costa says it well:

Although ethics flow from deep personal beliefs, the value of an ethical commitment is realized only in its effect on others and on society. This has always been true, but because of the global economy and global sensibility, the gulf between self and society has never been greater. Ours is the paradox of "universal intimacy" in which the ethical construct is no longer limited to "I" and "thou", or "us" and "them", but now must embrace the most comprehensive of "we".

In practice this means that Nike's failings are our failings. When workers are abused in faraway plants it is we—the ones who wear the shoes and buy the imagery and worship the athletes—who are sullied by the unfairness. This is the guilt of being informed, the inescapable responsibility of participating while knowing. In the heyday of consumption, buying was a party, and more buying the objective. There were no worries about deforestation or landfills or sweatshops. Now nearly every purchase carries with it some consciousness of consequence.[17]

And yet, despite this real effervescence around questions of business ethics and the increased awareness brought about by these activities, the majority of corporate codes of ethics of the last twenty years have limited themselves to issues which, though quite relevant, are rather limited in scope: questions of gifts and privileges, conflicts of interest, falsification or leaking of data, unfair competition, or adherence to norms and regulations.[18] The politically correct and the legally correct remain major concerns in many corporations while much academic work still centers on bickering among the different philosophical schools. In the conclusion of this book I will revisit this important topic of the ethical imperative, proposing that this leads us to the difficult task of creating a planetary ethic.

UPHOLDING RELIGIOUS BELIEFS OR THE EXISTENCE OF A SPIRITUAL RENEWAL

In our Western societies where separation of church (in this book, the word "church" is used generically and does not imply a particular religious tradition) and state is a reality, where materialism and rationalism have triumphed, faith in a universal spirit is nevertheless predominant. In North America, 84 percent of Canadians are believers; in the United States, 95 percent of Americans believe in a supreme being.[19] In this book (see Chapter 2), Ian I. Mitroff reports, based on a recent survey, that these ratios are identical for managers and business leaders. These statistics will lead him to conclude that the lack of incorporation of spiritual values at work stems not from a lack of faith or belief in a transcendent reality but rather is a result of people's fears and uncertainties about themselves and others and a lack of familiarity with the diverse tools and methods applicable in this area. Another survey, dating from the end of the 1980s, suggested that 65 percent of top managers regularly attended church, temple, or synagogue services compared to the nonmanagerial national average of 40 percent.[20]

The data available on this subject clearly show that belief in a god or supreme power or being is a majority position in most countries of the world whether it be the three Americas, Africa, Australia, or certain parts of Europe. The major exception is Eastern and Central Europe where a decline of belief has been observed with the exception of a few countries like Spain, Italy, and Portugal.[21] In Table I.1 I have indicated the percentages, for a few countries, of people who have declared themselves believers.[22] But stating one's belief in no way ascertains that this has an effect on people's everyday lives and more particularly on their workplace activities or behavior. I have therefore also indicated the percentage of people who affirm that their faith does have a concrete effect on their lives. The middle

Table I.1
Percentage of Beliefs and Their Importance in Daily Life

Country	Belief in God	Importance in life Evaluation from 5 to 10[**]	Importance in life Evaluation from 7 to 10[**]
Sweden	45%	37%	19%
France	62	50	27
Denmark	64	40	18
The Netherlands	64	53	33
Norway	65	47	28
Japan	65	59	20
Belgium	69	61	39
Britain	78	59	36
West Germany (Former)	78	60	39
Israel	79	DNA[*]	DNA
Australia	79	DNA	DNA
New Zealand	80	DNA	DNA
Spain	86	73	49
Portugal	86	75	57
Austria	88	DNA	DNA
Italy	89	79	62
Canada	89	80	62
United States	96	87	74
Poland	97	94	87
Ireland	98	90	73
Philippines	99	DNA	DNA

See M. Doggan (1995), "Le déclin des croyances religieuses," who presents a synthesis of three international studies dating from the early 1990s. These trends are confirmed by other studies from the mid-1990s.

*DNA: Data not available.

**From 1 "not at all" to 10 "totally"

column shows the percentage of people who state that the effect of their belief ranges from average (starting at 5 on a scale of 1 to 10) to really fundamental. The last column indicates the percentage of people who declare that their faith has a very important or primordial effect on their daily lives.

These statistics and surveys teach us several fundamental things:

- There are important differences between countries. For example, where 90 percent of Americans say their belief in a superior being affects their daily lives (and therefore their work), this percentage falls to 80 percent in Canada, 60 percent in Britain, 50 percent in France, and less than 40 percent in Sweden.
- These beliefs aren't always related to a religious education. Though 20 percent of Americans admit to no religious education, 96 percent state they are believers. Similarly, where 78 percent of Japanese say they have no religious education background, 65 percent admit to links with Buddhism or Shintoism. Inversely, where 80 percent of French respondents refer to a religious education only 62 percent say they believe.
- Finally, if the general tendency in the world is a major belief in a transcendent power, including mainstream religions, fundamentalist trends, spiritual movements, New Age thinking, and so on, a decline in this belief can be observed in a specific part of the world; that is, Eastern and Central Europe, notwithstanding a few exceptions.

We must, however, be careful with these data. These surveys often ask whether the person believes in God or not, which can imply an association to a particular institution such as a church, a temple, or a synagogue, thus leading people to answer by the negative. In addition, the question can exclude certain populations such as Buddhists who do not believe in a god. We will see in greater detail in this book that managers radically differentiate between religion and its institutions and spirituality.

Though a decline has been observed in Europe, it must be noted that certain aspects of spirituality have not been included in the data presented. France is a typical example. In this republican country the practice of Catholicism has decreased, although the importance of Christ, his person, and his life is on the rise. In this country—as well as in many others—the thirst for god[23] (also the title of an important magazine), is palpable, expressed in a multitude of ways, from a general search for meaning in one's life to belief in a certain personal fate, from belief in the existence of a supreme being to that of extraterrestrials, all of which can lead to religious practice in traditional churches, adherence to abusive sects, to esoteric movements, or to an individual spiritual practice. There has also been an exodus by the millions to other religious traditions. Buddhism, described as a "Godless religion," provides a striking example. Estimates today refer to 2 million recent Buddhist adepts in France and up to 5 million in the United States. The success of numerous books or films on the subject, such as *Little Buddha* or *Seven Years in Tibet*, echoes this growth.

The importance of spirituality in our Western societies has also been identified by the trend analyst Faith Popcorn in her survey on social trends as the factor that could be the most influential at the start of the third millennium.[24] She refers to this trend as a need for roots, one of philosopher Simone Weil's favorite expressions. Weil already referred to this as a pressing need in 1941, more than sixty years ago. I will present some of Simone Weil's views on spirituality at work later in this book (see Chapter 11).

These statistics support a recurring theme of this book: an important difference between adherence to a particular religion and a more general spiritual belief. But these numbers also hide differences in the deepest needs that motivate people in the workplace and in society in general: their need for meaning, their need for roots. Meaning can be sought through different values and values can be subject to different interpretations. A recent study on values in the United States allows us to better identify these differences. This study of 1,036 adults divided the population into three groups: the Modernists, the Traditionalists, and the Transmodernists.[25]

People in the first and largest group (47 percent of the adult population in the United States or 88 million people) are called Modernists. These people embrace the present. Personal success, consumerism, materialism, rationality, and technology are important values. These individuals can be religious and/or spiritual but of the three groups they are less involved in volunteer work, civil society, and have the lowest rates of charitable donations. This group represents the dominant social trend.

The second group, Traditionalists, is made up of 29 percent of adults or 56 million people. These people are characterized by a certain nostalgic view of the past: small town, family, clear gender roles, work, a sense of community, traditional religion. A quest for traditional values makes them a countercultural force, opposed to the dominant position of the Modernists.

The third and final group represents 24 percent of adults or 44 million individuals. This group is more difficult to identify since it attempts to draw new pathways for the future, to create a new myth, as suggested earlier by Rollo May. Different labels have been suggested for this group: Transmodernists, Integrals, cultural creatives. This group also forms a countercultural force, critical of modernity but without the call for a return to traditional values of the past. These individuals are more particularly concerned with authenticity, personal development, and spirituality and are sympathetic to communitarian, feminist, and ecological ideologies. They are more open than the other two groups to different experiences and viewpoints, more tolerant of ambiguity and uncertainty. Of the three, this group has the greatest number of activists.

The differences in values that characterize these three groups influence the type of spirituality the individuals seek: Modernists will gravitate toward a religion or spirituality that brings them concrete and personal benefits; Traditionalists are more wary of new spiritual movements and tend to condone a return to mainstream, often orthodox religion; Transmodernists are suspicious of traditional religions and tend to look for new forms of spiritual expression.

It would be tempting to conclude, along with the initiator of this survey, that this last group is the rising cultural force that will lead society to a better future. Transmodernists have even been seen by some as the "culture of hope."[26] It would even be tempting to conclude that the need for integration of ethics and spiritual values in the workplace stems mainly from this group. It is true that it proposes alternatives for the management of our organizations and for the economic system as a whole. But it seems to me that to idealize this group and to consider it the "potential savior of humanity and of the planet" is far-fetched. It is likely that a person could belong to more than one group at once, to different degrees, and that these three groups, Modernists, Traditionalists, and Transmodernists, use the three defense and/or integration strategies previously mentioned; that is, amplification, escape, and transformation. My argument—and new research should be conducted on this subject—summarized in Table I.2, suggests nine general trends in the quest for meaning of individuals in the workplace. I will only address a few of these trends.

It seems entirely possible, for example, that Modernists and Traditionalists would be attracted by the first strategy of amplification, endorsing "more of the same," Modernists by affirming current social values, and Traditionalists by invoking traditional values. But these two groups are also capable of renewal; the first, for example, by the advent of a new and revolutionary scientific discovery contributing to material progress, and the second, through a reinterpretation of fundamental doctrines.

Similarly, if Modernists and Traditionalists can use the second strategy, escape or flight, through fundamentalism, violence, or cynicism, Transmodernists can also be attracted by this path: They are more open than the other groups to new experiences and viewpoints, and some in this group are attracted to the so-called esoteric or occult sciences.

Having lived in California for ten years, I met several people in the New Age movement, who scurried from conference to conference, retreat to

Table I.2
Nine General Trends in the Search for Meaning at Work

Strategy adopted when faced with a crisis	Dominant values of the group		
	Modernists	Traditionalists	Trans-modernists
Amplification	1	4	7
Escape	2	5	8
Transformation	3	6	9

retreat, in search of strong sensations, of instantaneous illumination. While claiming the experience of a real breakthrough that would have a profound influence on their future lives, quite often, at best, the only result was a certain mastery of a few new concepts that they could now proudly share with others, or, at worst, indebtedness, illness, or other dramatic consequences. I was, at the time, a doctoral student, and I remember how some of these people expressed disdain at the scientific mind. Totally absorbed by the views of such authors as Helena Blavatsky, Edgar Cayce, or Georges Gurdjieff, they failed to recognize that true scientific research also includes a deep respect for the mysterious, the inexplicable, the divine.[27] New Age thought can become dangerous when it is transformed into an ideology that locks people into a syncretic view of the world. It would be informative to know precisely what percentage of Transmodernists, compared to Modernists and Traditionalists, become disciples of abusive sects that promote "escape into anything."

It is not my intention to deny the potential social or global contributions of Transmodernists. I simply want to make relative the hopes that some have for this group. Nor do I want to condemn New Age disciples. I also met some very sincere, authentic, and mature individuals who, through this movement were going through replenishing experiences of transformative growth. Some New Age techniques are based on traditional practices of proven efficacy in spiritual development if they are practiced diligently, under supervision, and for many years. These contemplative practices include the practice of silence and prayer, different forms of meditation, martial arts, yoga, or Zen.[28]

Based on these considerations it is not at all evident that the present interest in spirituality in society in general or at work is the purview of a single type of individual, or that it is a new spirituality or even a spiritual renewal. To complicate things—which indicates the pressing need for scientific research on this topic—other studies suggest that some of the values promoted by the spirituality-at-work movement (a sense of responsibility, a feeling of interconnectedness to others and nature, the respect of certain limits, the importance of spiritual practice, and so forth) were already shared by a large number of people in the United States at the close of the last century.[29] These studies suggest that we are neither in the advent of a new age nor in the renewal of an old age. I will come back to this topic in the conclusion of this book.

THE RISE OF EXPERIMENTATION WITH THE CONCEPTS OF ETHICS AND SPIRITUALITY IN THE WORKPLACE

Despite managers' reservations and fears referred to earlier and presented in this book, a growing number of senior managers and corporate leaders have already started experimenting with ethics and spirituality in their organizations. Some of the most famous mentioned in this book include Ben &

Jerry's, The Body Shop, and Tom's of Maine. These firms have come to bolster the ranks of those organizations that have had spiritual management processes for years given their original links to religious groups or communities. One can mention, for example, The Salvation Army, World Vision, or the YMCA. Other organizations have also been described by their CEOs as incorporating spiritual principles. This is the case, for example, of Michelin in France, Marriott International in the United States, or Svensk Filmindustri in Sweden.[30]

To provide a few other examples, the following companies have either instituted certain internal mechanisms to encourage a spiritual quest or have actively participated in conferences on the subject: Aetna Life Insurance Company, AT&T, Aveda, the Bank of Boston, Bell Canada, BioGenex, Boeing, Carlisle Motors, Cascade Communications, Cirrus Logic, Deloitte & Touche, Digital Equipment, Elf Aquitaine, Esprit, Ford, Gillette, Goldman Sachs, Hydro-Ontario, KPMG, Lotus Development, Lucent Technologies, Medtronic Inc., Motorola, Nortel Networks, Odwalla, Pizza Hut, Raytheon, The Royal Bank, ServiceMaster Company, Shell Oil, Southwest Airlines, Starbucks, Stonyfield Yogurt, Sun Microsystems, Taco Bell, Timberland, U.S. Young President Organization, Wal-Mart, the World Bank, and Xerox Corp.[31] Asian firms have also developed spiritual approaches mostly inspired by Buddhism: Kyocera Corporation, Mitsutoyo Company, the Miyazaki Bank, and Yasuda Mutual Life Insurance.[32]

In this book, six CEOs, presidents, directors, or general managers of well-known and respected firms confirm this openness to ethics and spirituality in organizations: the president of a financial institution with more than 40,000 employees (Desjardins); the CEO of a mid-size company in the food sector (Ouimet–Cordon Bleu Inc.); the president of a municipality of more than 1.8 million people (the Montreal Urban Community); the director of a 250-bed hospital (the Anna–Laberge Hospital); and two directors of business schools responsible for more than 10,000 students each (HEC Montreal, Canada, and the Royal Melbourne Institute of Technology, Australia).

The Increase of Information and Training in Spirituality

The final indicator of the importance of this need for spirituality in business is the increase in the means of information dissemination and training in this area. Consulting firms and training and research centers such as The Advantage Group, le Centre Entreprise de Ganagobie, Empowerment Plus, Inner Work Company or Livelihood Inc., have responded to increased demand by specializing in the spiritual accompaniment of organizations. Numerous associations have appeared, sometimes accompanied by the publication of a newsletter and offering their members an e-mail address and elaborate Web sites. The association for spirit at work lists these resources (www.spiritatwork.com). A number of conferences, seminars, and colloquia have also been organized around this topic in Acapulco, Austin, Texas, Boston, Mexico City, Montreal, Toronto, and Washington, D.C., to mention only the most recent events in North America.

Many books have also been published around this issue. The following are only a few: Helen Alford and Michael Naughton, *Managing as if Faith Mattered*; Kenneth Boa, *Wisdom at Work*; Richard Barrett, *Liberating the Corporate Soul*; Jerry Biderman and Michale Whitty, *Work and Spirit*; Lee Bolman and Terrence Deal, *Leading with Soul*; Alan Briskin, *The Stirring of Soul in the Workplace*; Jimmy Carter, *Sources of Strength*; Tom Chappel, *The Soul of a Business and Managing Upsidedown*; Debashis Chatterjee, *Leading Consciously*; Richard Chewing et al., *Business through the Eyes of Faith*; Ann Combs, *The Living Workplace*; Jay Conger and Associates, *Spirit at Work*; Diane Dreher, *The Tao of Personal Leadership*; Matthew Fox, *The Reinvention of Work*; Charles Handy, *The New Alchemists*; Dee Hock, *Birth of the Chaordic Age*; Shinichi Inoue, *Putting Buddhism to Work*; Roger Harrisson, *Consultant's Journey*; Jack Hawley, *Reawakening the Spirit in Work*; Les Kaye, *Zen at Work*; James Liebig, *Merchants of Vision*; Ian I. Mitroff and Elisabeth Denton, *A Spiritual Audit of Corporate America*; Gary Moore, *Spiritual Investment: Wall Street Wisdom from the Career of Sir John Templeton*; Russ Moxley, *Leadership and Spirit*; Michael Novak, *Business as a Calling*; Carol Osbourn, *Inner Excellence at Work*; Perry Pascarella, *Christ-Centered Leadership*; John Renesh, *Spirit and Leadership in the 21st Century*; Lewis Richmond, *Work as a Spiritual Practice*; Anita Roddick, *Body and Soul* and *Business as Unusual*; Lance Secretan, *Reclaiming Higher Ground*; Deborah Ann Smith, *Work with What You Have*; William Torbert, *The Power of Balance*; Peter Vaill, *Spirited Leading and Learning*; and David Whyte, *The Heart Aroused*.

Conscious of the importance of this demand, several North American publishers specialized in management works have recently published special collections on this subject. This is the case for Berrett-Koehler, Doubleday, Currency, Fides, Jossey-Bass, and Quorum Books.

If these publications have all been released recently, they join the ranks of a multitude of others on the same subject published since World War II that were previously often considered as bizarre, deviant, and more often proposed in *sotto voce* in the hallways of management faculties or business schools. The following in particular come to mind: *A Holy Tradition of Working*, from the works of Eric Gill, published in 1983; *The Human Condition* by Hanna Arendt, 1958; *The Working Condition* by Simone Weil, 1951; *Good Work* by E. F. Schumacher, 1979; *Higher Creativity* by Willis Harman and Howard Rheingold, 1984; *The Self-Organizing Universe*, by Eric Jantsch, 1980; *The Tao of Leadership* by John Heider, 1985; *Zen and Creative Management* by Albert Low, 1976; and, let us not forget *Zen and the Art of Motorcycle Maintenance* by Robert Pirsig, 1974, and *The Road Less Traveled* by Scott Peck, 1978.

The theme of spirituality at work, just as that of ethics, is currently quite popular and provides numerous business opportunities. Seminars featuring the most prominent authors and gurus in the area can cost as much as $1,000 per day plus expenses. A recent evaluation of the North American market for New Age business publications puts it at more than $1 billion annually. Televangelists rake in over $3 billion annually in the United States. One of the largest networks, the Trinity Broadcasting Network (TBN), based in the Los Angeles suburbs, broadcasts 700 religious programs throughout the planet, increasing its market share through aggressive marketing and an efficient communications strategy. *Psychology Today*, the popular magazine, spared no effort to announce, on their cover, that even Madonna, the very symbol of the "material girl," has found her spiritual path.[33] Even advertisers increasingly use spiritual themes to reach their target audiences. Thus, Apple uses the Dalai Lama's photo to invite us to "think differently"; Banana Republic's clothing is presented on mannequins sitting in the lotus position; Evian invites us to drink the "eternal life force"; Ford offers its Ranger to get us to the mountain top where we can find "eternal wisdom"; Lancôme's latest beauty product is the Hydra Zen; and Xerox uses monks to sell us its photocopiers.[34]

In this domain, where charlatans rub elbows with authentic individuals, where exploitation and demagoguery exist alongside the sincere and the profound, it is little wonder that many managers dare not speak too much of spirituality at work. They are also wary of encouraging their people to participate in a program that could do them harm and possibly bring their liability into play. Some businesses have already been pointed to for having members of abusive sects in their ranks. The cases of Hydro-Quebec in Canada and Pacific Telesis in California are but two examples. Both of these saw several of their upper managers involved with sects: the first with the Order of the Solar Temple and the second with the Charles Krone group.

Given the proliferation of literature on the topic it has become increasingly difficult for a novice to recognize serious works. A number of authors appear to want to profit from this authentic need for meaning and for anchoring for their personal benefit. Many works, for example, encourage their readers to use pseudospiritual values in order to increase profits, work less, or have more fun. These concepts are sometimes used in the workplace to attempt to increase employee motivation and productivity.

It is also important to mention two very popular books published in the early 1980s that targeted a wide audience but were also very influential among managers: *The Turning Point* by Fritjof Capra and *The Aquarian Conspiracy* by Marilyn Ferguson. The common thread in these two works was the attempt to link recent discoveries in quantum physics to the development of levels of consciousness, a notion I will address later. Fritjof Capra made a direct connection between quantum theory and the reality of actual spiritual experiences. Marilyn Ferguson, for her part, started from recent discoveries in the area of consciousness development and established parallels with modern theories of physics. Both authors also addressed, each in their own way, the issue of the influence of spirituality on our societies, more particularly culture, values, health, education, politics, economics, and business.[35] The 1990s saw the appearance of similar works linking quantum physics to levels of consciousness and dealing with society in general as well as management and leadership. The most famous are probably those of Danah Zoar and Margaret Wheatley.[36] These attempts are related to other efforts that deal less with spirituality but try to link management of organizations to another source, a purportedly emerging new science. Different authors give different names to this new science, using expressions such as chaos theory, complexity, autopoïesis, emerging structures, dissipative structures, systemic thought, nonlinear dynamics, artificial life, auto-organization, and numerous others.[37]

It would be interesting to have a clearer understanding of the various sources or traditions—religious, spiritual, intellectual, scientific, cultural, and so forth—that managers, open to spirituality in the workplace, identify with. Unfortunately, I know of no studies in this area. Marilyn Ferguson conducted such a study in the public at large for the writing of her book, a book that wavers between rigorous science and New Age ideology: Her survey questionnaire dealt with 185 respondents identified as "Aquarian conspirators."[38] A list of their most influential authors allowed the identification of these individuals' intellectual tradition. The four most cited authors in order of importance were the following: Pierre Teilhard de Chardin, Carl G. Jung, Abraham Maslow, and Carl Rogers—whom we will meet in this book. Other key authors were also identified: Gregory Bateson, Kenneth Boulding, Martin Buber, Ruth Benedict, Albert Einstein, Erich Fromm, Willis Harman, Hermann Hesse, Alfred Korzybki, Jay Krishnamurti, Margaret Mead, Thomas Merton, Swami Muktananda, D. T. Suzuki, Paul Tillich, Heinz von Foerster, Allan Watts, and Alfred North Whitehead.

Although 81 percent of respondents declared to no longer be active in the religion of their childhood, they confirmed their participation in the following spiritual practices (in order of decreasing popularity): Zen, yoga, the Christian mystical tradition, Tai-chi, psychosynthesis, Jungian psychoanalysis, Tibetan Buddhism, Transcendental Meditation, Sufism, transactional analysis, and Kabala.

This list is informative and it would be important to make a current one in order to identify less credible and more suspect traditions and sources. For example, respondents to Ferguson's survey also listed practices and authors like the EST movement or John Lilly who were or still are quite controversial. I will propose a strategy to help distinguish a healthy from a less healthy spiritual attraction.

CONFUSION BETWEEN THE PREPERSONAL
AND TRANSPERSONAL LEVELS OF CONSCIOUSNESS

Ken Wilber, renowned author in the field of consciousness and founder of the Integral Institute in the United States, has proposed an interesting categorization to distinguish between healthy and less healthy attractions to spirituality. Authors in this book state that a common trait among managers open to spirituality in the workplace is a need for a "feeling of fusion." This feeling stems from a need to feel connected to others, to the world, to nature, to the universe, to the divine; to feel that there exists some sort of world order, some finitude, a sense of the immanent, a destiny; to not feel one's deepest values as fragmented and to realize harmony, a better fit among one's personal life, life at work, and society in general.

Wilber distinguishes between two types of fusion and insists that, though radically different, they are often confused. He believes one type of fusion eventually leads to unhealthy situations whereas another type allows individuals to attain the highest levels of consciousness to which human beings are capable. He therefore points to the dangers of what he has called the confusion between the prepersonal and transpersonal levels.[39] To understand this confusion it is necessary to grasp the basics of the complex process of consciousness development described by Ken Wilber, particularly the prepersonal, personal, and transpersonal levels.[40]

The prepersonal level is the first level of consciousness described by Wilber. This level represents the preconscious, preverbal world dominated by biological and emotional impulses. This is, for example, the world of the newborn dominated by physiological and emotional needs of security, nutrition, and affection. The differences between the internal and external worlds have not been incorporated and the newborn feels as one with, or undifferentiated from, its external environment. At this stage, cognitive or moral abilities have not emerged.[41]

Applying Wilber's theory to the world of organizations, the quest for prepersonal fusion can bring an individual or group to idealize, for example, an authority figure, to adhere to dogmatism and fundamentalism, to lose oneself in the sensorial realm or to seek unrestrained acquisition of material goods, including an unchecked quest for short-term profits. This need for prepersonal fusion can also lead to the elaboration of impulsive and unthought-out strategies, to the exclusive use of indoctrinating training and education, or to individualistic strategies favoring and encouraging organizational or personal competitiveness. This need can also lead to an attitude of "I am the world" or "we are the world" with the belief that it is perfectly natural to exploit the world, be it financial, human, social, or ecological. This attitude has been exemplified in the business world by the saying "What's good for GM is good for the world." There is a good deal of scientific literature on the pathologies that this prepersonal fusion can instantiate in individuals who are no longer newborns, which describe the symptoms and potential clinical treatment.[42] At the organizational level various descriptions have been suggested for firms in this situation: "the neurotic organization," "corporate decline," "the shadow of organizations," or "the crisis-prone organization."[43]

However, despite numerous potential pitfalls, we must not forget that the prepersonal level has an important role. It is the level of the basic forces of nature from which stem the life-force and vital energy that are absolutely essential for consequent development of the world and of consciousness. This level is also the locus of creation, of creativity, of innovation in the material sphere, an essential element for all humans and organizations. The danger is not in the existence of this level but of the possibility that individuals' or groups' consciousness development will be arrested at that level.

The second generic level of consciousness development described by Wilber is the personal level. This is the world of ideas, concepts, reason, cognition, language, and morality. It is also the level where an individual develops his or her own personality and differentiates between "I" and the external world. This stage leads to autonomy, individuality, self-esteem, self-realization, and humanism.

In the organizational world, this level allows the use of reason, of the scientific method and of the different technological or conceptual tools we use. This level can also be credited for the humanist trend in management, a trend promoting freedom, creativity, self-realization, democracy, and ethics in business.

Recent authors have blamed humanism for several of our fundamental social problems.[44] Without going into details it is important to state that some of the founders of the modern humanist movement have also expressed certain reservations in its regard. They have suggested that personal development, though an essential step, is but one stage of human development. Abraham Maslow, one of the most famous founding fathers of the humanist school in psychology, education, and management, but also—and this is not a well-known fact—one of the initiators of transpersonal psychology, has stated the same thing. Maslow is possibly the author who has best described what he calls "metapathologies," that can occur if the personal development level is not integrated and surpassed, if an individual remains too attached to this "need for actualization" and doesn't succeed in transcending it.[45]

Maslow stated in 1968 the following:

Humanistic Psychology . . . is now quite solidly established as a viable third alternative to objectivistic, behaviorist psychology and to orthodox Freudianism. . . . There is work to be done here, effective, virtuous. Satisfying work which can give rich meaning to one's own life and to others. . . . I should say also that I consider Humanistic, Third Force Psychology to be transitional, a preparation for a still "higher" fourth Psychology, transpersonal, transhuman, centered in the cosmos rather than in human needs and interest, going beyond humanness, identity, self-actualization. . . . Without the transcendent and the transpersonal, we get sick, violent, and nihilistic, or else hopeless and apathetic. We need something "bigger than we are" to be awed by and to commit ourselves to in a new, naturalistic, empirical, non-churchly sense, perhaps as Thoreau and Whitman, William James and John Dewey did.[46]

Warren Bennis, the influential author in management and leadership has also recently proposed the following:

What's missing at work, the root cause of the affluenza syndrome, is meaning, purpose beyond one-self, wholeness, integration. . . . The underlying cause of organizational dysfunctions, ineffectiveness, and all manner of human stress is the lack of a spiritual foundation in the workplace.[47]

The third level of consciousness described by Ken Wilber is the transpersonal level. As its name indicates, this level does not deny the existence of the person, the preceding level, but incorporates it and transcends it just as the personal level had done for the prepersonal. This level is the most difficult to describe. Where the first level is dominated by the forces of nature, the concrete and material, and the second level is the source of the mind and humanism, of mature intellectual and emotional capacities, this third level is spiritual. In this sense, spirituality means to be "spirit-conscious." It relates to an openness to intuition, to compassion, to transcendence, to grace, to the divine. Individuals who have attained this stage of development or who at least are close to it after a long process that can last a lifetime, transcend their own individuality, and emphasize the inherent interconnections that they experience daily between themselves, others, nature, the universe, and the divine.

Less material than the first and less mental than the second, this level of conscience can only be approached, conceptually, through paradoxical and poetic statements. This detracts in no way from its reality but limits the possibility of discussing it in unambiguous terms. Essentially this level transcends the intellect and is born of a subjective experience quite often attained only after extended and patient spiritual practice like, for example, the Christian spiritual exercises of Ignatius of Loyola, or the Hindu integral yoga of Shrî Aurobindo.[48]

It is too early to predict the contribution of this level to the practice of management and leadership in organizations. The books on spirituality at work mentioned previously provide an initial answer. A great deal of research and experimentation is still necessary to better grasp the specific contribution that this transpersonal level can make to the workplace. In order to be effective and long lasting, this contribution must incorporate but also transcend that of humanism. The humanist contribution springs, at least in part, from the second level of consciousness development, the personal: It refers to responsibility and personal integrity, respect of others and the gift of self, to justice and ethics, equity, solidarity and morality, democracy, and so forth.[49] Nevertheless, if the transpersonal realm must bolster the pursuit of these humanist values, they must also bring to the workplace new practices. The following is a short list of possible contributions:

- The creation of tools and approaches that promote economic, ethical, and spiritual enrichment through work
- Production of industrial goods, services, and information that can actually become food for the spirit
- The quest for aesthetics and beauty in management
- The use of silence, intuition, meditation, contemplation, or prayer in the decision-making process
- Encouraging people to pursue their vocation(s) or to give free reign to their enthusiasm at work
- The development of mental and physical health through spiritual practices
- Invention of industrial processes respectful of human dignity and the sacred origins of nature
- Redefinition of work such as to allow spiritual growth through one's work
- The use of archetypes and sacred rituals in management
- The development of love of others and of forgiveness in managerial practices
- The elaboration of new views of the world of organizations and of the economy that promote hope for people
- The creation of a true spirit in business that transcends all traditional administrative functions as well as organizational culture and strategies
- The development of faith, hope, and of a state of attentiveness or mindfulness to complex problems and the capacity to meet the numerous paradoxes of management and leadership with great subtlety
- Recognition of a philosophy of suffering—without idealizing it—that allows the advent of grace

It seems quite clear that the notions presented—spiritual riches, food for the soul, aestheticism, contemplation, meditation and prayer, vocation, enthusiasm, sacred rituals, anchoring, corporate spirit, forgiveness, faith and hope, and grace—are not only humanist but stem mainly from the spiritual level of conscience.

Now that the levels of consciousness proposed by Ken Wilber have been summarily defined, we can address the confusion that exists between the different types of fusion. In the quite simplified generic model proposed earlier, two stages of development animate this feeling of fusion with the world: the prepersonal and the transpersonal. At the intermediate level of the personal stage, the individual is fairly well differentiated from other people and the world in general and seeks less this fusion but rather the development of personal creativity and of his or her individuality.

Though in both cases we refer to fusion, prepersonal fusion, and transpersonal fusion, they are, in effect, fundamentally different in nature: The first happens before the appearance of personality, of consciousness, of reason, and of morality and is governed by archaic impulses. These impulses are very intense, nonsubtle needs that are not easily manageable even when individuals in these situations invoke spiritual and/or religious themes. Conversely, the second occurs after the appearance of self-identity and personality that it transcends, being motivated by a more mature, subtle, and complex need for connection to others and to the world.

There is another basic difference between these two types of fusion. Transpersonal fusion emanates from and transcends the personal level; it neither cancels it out nor denies it. This implies that the mature individual who feels the need for spiritual fusion can also appeal to reason, common sense, morality, humanism, and a more mature emotionality acquired at the personal level. By definition these possibilities do not exist for the person moved by a prepersonal desire of fusion. This desire is then not motivated by the transcendence of one's individuality but by a need for security found in the haven of a primitive world. Since the desire does not emanate from the personal stage, it is virtually impossible to counter the potential dangers of adherence to dogmatic ideologies, to abusive sects, or of immoral or criminal behavior.

It thus becomes essential to find rigorous means of determining whether the desire for fusion with the world stems from the prepersonal or transpersonal levels of conscious development. The differences between the prepersonal and transpersonal could greatly affect the incorporation of spiritual and ethical values in management and in the workplace. It therefore seems essential to undertake a program of scientific studies of these stages of development, taking into consideration the richness of the models developed by authors like Wilber, all the while realizing that they must be refined.

In order to ensure that the reader realizes the dangers of presenting only summary descriptions of the levels of consciousness development, I have summarized the twenty different levels discussed by Wilber in Figure I.1.[50] The circles in the diagram differentiate among the generic prepersonal, personal, and transpersonal levels.

As this figure shows, the prepersonal starts at the sensory–physical stage and ends at the reptilian stage; this stage permits access to the personal consciousness level and ends at the logical-vision stage; and this second stage gives access to the transpersonal level and proceeds to the non-dual stage. The circles drawn in this figure are an attempt to symbolize the transcendent relationships established between the levels, indicating that the expressions "permits access" and "ends" are relative. The more primitive prepersonal level does not end at the personal level but is transcended by this level which incorporates, then makes it more complex; similarly, the

Figure I.1
Levels of Consciousness and Their Links to the "Psychic Aspirations" and the Different "Moral Senses"

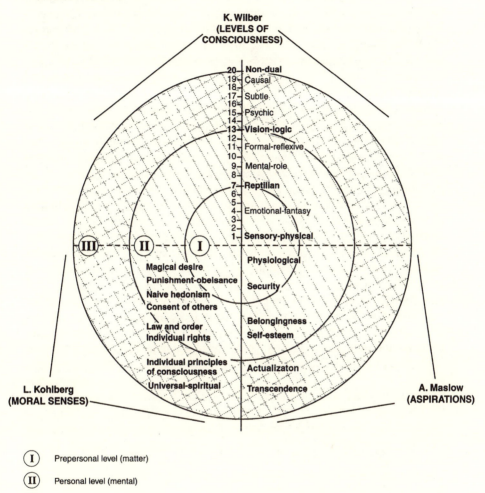

(I)	Prepersonal level (matter)
(II)	Personal level (mental)
(III)	Transpersonal level (spiritual)

personal level does not end at the transpersonal level but the latter incorporates it and makes it more complex as well.

I have also included in this figure the relationships between these levels of consciousness with Abraham Maslow's "theory of needs" with which all management students are familiar. I have also indicated in this figure Kohlberg's "stages of moral development" which proposes different types of ethics depending on the level of consciousness.[51] Although Maslow is well-known in management it is often presented in a stunted version. The theory is most often simplistically presented as a linear, five level pyramidal hierarchy where a person will automatically move from the satisfaction of inferior to superior needs (See Figure I.2). Not only does this approach not do Maslow's theory justice, it also prevents us from seeing the subtleties of the relationships between the different levels of consciousness as presented by Wilber. In Figure I.3, I have presented a more adequate view of Maslow's theory replacing the expression "need theory" with "cones of aspirations."[52] The notion of cone of attraction implies that an individual can be dominated by one or more attractions, the "cones" guiding his or her perceptions of reality and actions within that reality. The image of a cone suggests that, like a marble that would have slipped to the bottom of the cone, an individual is relatively limited by his or her attraction to one or several cones. As Maslow himself so clearly stated, each need or cone of attraction "organizes or even creates external reality," driven by biological and psychological processes.[53]

I have placed the sign of the Tao at the bottom of each cone to indicate that each attraction can lead to either positive or negative effects. An attraction to the biological, for example, can be very natural or healthy and leads the body to nourish itself but it can also lead to bulimia. I also included in this figure the level of transcendence, the sixth, but often forgotten attraction proposed by Maslow. Finally, I have used the letters of the alphabet ("A," "AB," "ABC," and so on) to indicate that each "cone of aspiration" contains within it the preceding ones and proceeds in a spiral development. The structure of language helps us to better understand the transcendent

Figure I.2
Abraham Maslow's Hierarchy of Needs: A Linear Perspective

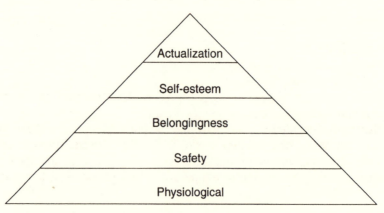

Figure I.3
Abraham Maslow's "Cones of Attraction"

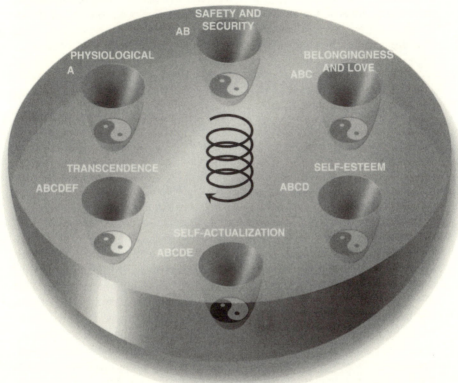

character of each level as referred to by Abraham Maslow and Ken Wilber: Where a lower level has only one or two levels, the higher levels have several letters allowing for increased complexity. Stated otherwise, if Shakespeare's play *Hamlet* can represent the realm of transcendence, it is quite evident that without the existence of the letters of the alphabet Shakespeare could not have written this masterpiece. This is the sense in which a more complex level incorporates but complexify the preceding levels.

It can't exist without them but it is capable of complexity not attainable by the first: Words are made up of letters, sentences of words, paragraphs of sentences, paragraphs of concepts, civilizations of concepts, and so on.

Finally, Maslow, like Wilber, insisted that these levels should not be considered individually but as a whole, a gestalt, if we are to avoid, as the psychology of attributes has done "that one attribute . . . engenders but one type of action."[54] According to this view, an individual can be inspired 10 percent by the biological level, 20 percent by security, 15 percent by belonging, 40 percent by self-esteem, and so on. Revisiting this same concept of gestalt, Ken Wilber suggested that the divine is also present at the prepersonal level—in nature—but that this level cannot be equated with the divine, thus avoiding the problem of pantheism.

If we regroup the cones of aspirations suggested by Maslow, it becomes easier to grasp the content of the prepersonal, personal, and transpersonal levels described by Wilber. The aspiration suggested by Maslow to physiological needs and needs of security provide a good idea of what these levels imply. An individual—or an organization or culture, referring then in these cases to a "general cultural axis"—will first and foremost be concerned by the physical aspects of his or her life as well as with his or her survival. This level of aspiration corresponds to Wilber's prepersonal level governed by matter and the senses, and to a type of morality regulated by punishment and obedience or by a naïve hedonism according to the stages of moral development proposed by Kohlberg (See Figure I.1).

In the same manner, an individual attracted by needs of belonging and self-esteem corresponds to Wilber's personal level. This individual will be more preoccupied with acceptance by the group, affirmation of his or her identity, emphasizing his or her originality, and so on. Morality is, in this case, more informed by peer approval, the law, and individual rights. The 1948 declaration of human rights stems, for example, from this level. In Kohberg's model, morality and ethics at this level will be strongly influenced by a conventional view; that is, group value and the cultural gestalt.

Finally, aspiration for self-realization and transcendence as described by Maslow corresponds to Wilber's transpersonal level. Morality at this level will be based not on others and values but on principles derived from personal conscience and from the spiritual realm; that is, a postconventional view.

I certainly hope that these explanations—though brief and often quite technical—will help in the understanding of the various levels of consciousness presented by Wilber. It should be emphasized that many other authors have also proposed these levels.[55] I will return to this model in the concluding chapter of this book. I would now like to conclude this chapter by presenting the chapters of this book.

THE BOOK'S FORMAT, CONTENT, AND TARGET AUDIENCE

The book is divided into three sections. The first part is analytical. It describes the field and lays down the groundwork. The second is practical and presents five experiments conducted within various organizations. The third part is inspirational, suggesting new pathways.

The first part addresses the need for, and the challenges to, the integration of ethics and spirituality into the workplace. In Chapter 1, Jean-Marie Toulouse suggests that this is one of six complex issues that managers throughout the world are faced with today. In Chapter 2, Ian I. Mitroff presents the results of a first detailed survey conducted in the United States on spirituality at work. In Chapter 3, Solange Lefebvre discusses the various connotations of the concepts of values, ethics, spirituality, and religion. Chapter 4 presents a collective dialogue on these themes.

The second part is a presentation by five organizational leaders from different fields on how ethics and spirituality have been integrated into their organizations. These are Claude Beland from the banking sector in Chapter 5; J.-Robert Ouimet from the food sector in Chapter 6; Vera Danyluk from a public organization in Chapter 7; Yves Benoît from the health sector in Chapter 8; and Peter Sheldrake and James Hurley from a business school in Chapter 9. Chapter 10 is a collective dialogue on these cases and the issues that arose from them.

The third part proposes three directions for the future incorporation of ethics and spirituality into the economic system, management and work in general. In Chapter 11, Thierry Pauchant proposes the vision of worker-philosopher Simone Weil regarding the spiritualization of work. In Chapter 12, Roger Berthouzoz calls for the use of a systemic view in management, a recurring theme in this book; and in Chapter 13, Michel Dion examines the similarities and differences among the Jewish, Christian, and Islamic views of the economy. Chapter 14 is the collective dialogue around these pathways.

In the concluding chapter, I suggest that every managerial action or decision presupposes a certain view of truth, goodness, and beauty, based on Ken Wilber's systemic views, and I propose a model for distinguishing between the hopes and the dangers triggered by the introduction of ethics and spirituality at work. I also draw several general conclusions on the ground covered by the book.

This book is primarily directed to employees, professionals, managers, trainers, consultants, and organizational leaders in a variety of disciplines and sectors. It can also be useful to professors, researchers, and students interested in management and organizations. The direct style and concrete examples make it valuable in management, consultation, and training; its theoretical framework, scientific basis, and detailed references and sources make it useful in education and research in universities, management faculties, and business schools, in a field that still lacks rigorous research.

PART I

THE NECESSITY AND CHALLENGES OF INTEGRATING ETHICS AND SPIRITUALITY IN MANAGEMENT

In this first part of the book, the necessity and the challenges of the integration of ethics and spirituality in management are presented. In Chapter 1, Jean-Marie Toulouse suggests that this integration is a major problem encountered by today's managers. In Chapter 2, Ian I. Mitroff presents the results of a detailed survey. In Chapter 3, Solange Lefebvre discusses the connotations associated to the notions of values, ethics, spirituality, and religions. Chapter 4 presents a collective dialogue on these themes.

A close look at each era of our history reveals how we were able to identify the appropriate measures necessary to reach the institution's goals; to accomplish its mission. That same historic review will also demonstrate that in the more than ninety years of our existence, four fundamental values emerged. These values are the following: our rootedness in our sphere of activity, the internationalization of our action, the pedagogical innovation, and the balance between specialized and general education.

You have probably noted that innovation, particularly pedagogic innovation, is of major importance to us; whether it is the early use of cinematic projection in 1910 to teach geography or correspondence courses to teach professional bookkeeping in the 1930s, or the use of audio–visual techniques toward the end of the 1970s, or the intensive use of new information technologies since 1996 in our new building; this school has always tried to be innovative.

You probably also noted, I'm sure, the last of the four values mentioned earlier. Here is an excerpt of a text presented to the assembly of professors, September 9, 1998: "The fourth value represents the balance between specialized and general education. Our programs have always tried to respect this balance. We made sure to maintain this balance when recently revising our programs."

On a daily basis, businesses and managers are confronted with issues and problems that surpass technical limits or practical considerations. I am referring to values, ethics, and issues of social justice. I also question the role of business people in this society; what is expected from them, their long-term motives versus short-term concerns. A school like HEC, aspiring to a balance between specialized and general education, should always find the way to prepare its students to confront those realities when they enter the workforce and during their entire professional lives.

This forum on management, ethics, and spirituality mirrors our deepest values. It responds to some of our deepest concerns. It is a worldwide innovation: Never before have we joined together, in a conference, the words "management," "ethics," and "spirituality." Moreover, those who dreamed of this project never imagined it happening in a management school, an administration faculty, or even less at HEC. This forum addresses this balance between specialized and general education in an exemplary fashion and is marvelously in line with international tendencies.

I will linger on this forum's relevance to the concerns of the business community and internationalization, as these are the most complex issues. In Canada, and practically in every country, businesses are at the heart of an exceptional fluctuation. They must deal with problems and events often related to the market's globalization and internationalization; fluctuation in markets (those who witness the fluctuations of the stock market will understand what this means); affirmation of national, regional, and religious identities; the emergence of new information technologies; the massive circulation

of specialized information (e.g., the Internet); the decisive role of technological education in the capacity to be competitive; and the collapse and
experimentation associated with traditional roles, particularly those associated to women, men, professionals, and young people.

In that fluctuation, businesses learned to manage; they learned to improve their functioning, their management structure; they learned how to
maintain human values at the heart of management, how to manage important mergers, with their advantages, disadvantages, and risks; and they learned
to live with fragility and vulnerability. No business, even the biggest, is
totally protected from storms. They learned to balance resources, costs, and
advantages. During that period, they also realized that some issues were
easier to resolve than others. They need reflection, discussion, and probably fundamental research. At my nomination as the director of HEC, I
summed up six critical issues. They are as follows:

1. *Structures*. Certainly, the pyramidal model is not the only one. Businesses talk
   about virtual structures. They talk about networks, horizontal organizations,
   associations, partnerships, and concentration. Beyond restructuring, reengineer-
   ing, flattening structures, and pyramidal reversal, businesses are now elaborat-
   ing a somewhat new notion of business practices. However, no one so far has
   the answer as to which model will dominate, or even if a particular model will
   exist.

2. *Management*. While observing how some businesses operate, we realize that
   managing doesn't mean finding mechanisms that will postpone judgment or the
   need to choose. Managing means working with others in trust and collaboration
   in order to carry out a project. Businesses often ask management schools to
   assist them in educating future managers. They ask us to enlighten them in the
   management exercise and to prepare today's young students to become
   tomorrow's managers and leaders.

3. *Efficiency and decline*. Businesses are short of the traditional resources to manage decline or to increase efficiency. They have cut expenses, reduced jobs, and
   dismissed people. What's left to do? This issue is very acute in the public
   sector. How can we really manage an organization when resources are not
   available? Businesses are profoundly concerned with these issues. They seek
   answers and, every day, they realize that textbook solutions don't work.

4. *Environment*. Environment is a complex issue. Some businesses try to address
   it, others are in denial, some merely work on their public image, while others
   wait for it to pass. Businesses expect management specialists to provide new
   concepts, new approaches, and new concrete and realistic work tools to address
   that issue.

5. *Entrepreneurship*. On that issue, I want to remind you of an article in *Business
   Week*, published in the first issue of 1993, "How Entrepreneurs Are Reshaping
   the Economy and What Can Big Companies Learn."[1] I think that a school like
   HEC must see that its students develop their sense of entrepreneurship, regardless of their professional field.

6. *Values and ethics*. The teaching and practice of management is not possible without talking about values and ethics. These questions are raised around concrete actions: firing, relocation of production sites from one country to another, remuneration, investment choices, the action priorities for short-term gains, and so on. All those questions take us back to values, ethics, and spirituality, which inspired this forum's theme.

I think that these few elements demonstrate how this forum fits into the continuity of our concerns. To finish, I would like to wish you all a good forum, a good dialogue, and a great stay among us and, when this book is completed, good reading on these fundamental issues.

2

Spirituality at Work: The Next Major Challenge in Management

Ian I. Mitroff

EDITOR'S NOTE

In this chapter, Ian I. Mitroff, an influential management scholar and a renowned consultant, presents the results of one of the first scientific studies on spirituality at work. The study that he has recently conducted includes 230 managers and top executives in the United States. Many of the results are counter to what common knowledge would have us expect. We learn, for example, that 92 percent of managers would like to include spiritual principles in their organization but that they refrain to do so for different reasons including the lack of practical examples and models, their need to stay critical and not to be associated with the New Age trend, or the wish to be respectful of themselves and others. As another example, while these managers perceive differently the notions of spirituality and religion, all of them agree that more spirituality at work would allow them to live a more integrated and more systemic life as well as allow their organization to become world-class. Last, we learn from this important research some of the conditions and processes required to develop a more spiritual or ethical organization. This includes, for example, the need of a crisis for starting the process of transformation; the need of a higher ethical plane and very different rules; or the need to challenge the traditional view that spiritual matters are only personal and to instead consider that they need to be institutionalized as well. The chapter concludes by providing a typology of the different paths that could be taken by organizations for transforming themselves and discloses the moral outrage experienced by the author by the lack of scientific research conducted on this paramount subject.

I would like to report here some of the results of a study I have recently conducted with my colleague Elizabeth Denton on the subject of spirituality in the workplace. As far as I know, this is the first systematic study conducted on this important subject from a management point of view. The fact that no extensive studies have been conducted in management science on this subject is itself indicative of the problems existing in the field of management in general and in the management research community in particular. I will come back to this subject at the end of my presentation. I will first describe the research we have conducted, next its major results, most of them counter to common expectations, and I will present a typology of the different paths an organization could take to become more spiritual or ethical.

THE STUDY

I am a professor and researcher in a business school. I am also a consultant for all kinds of organizations, private, public, government, or associative. I work primarily in the field of crisis management but, for the past year along with my colleague Elizabeth Denton, I have been interviewing scores of managers and executive in all kinds of business as to what spirituality means for them.

We have conducted this study not only to better describe what spirituality is in the context of work but, more important, how it is concretely practiced. I do not have the time here to go into all the details of this study. I will try to just give you its essence. For those who wish to dig into detail we have published a book on these results.[1] We interviewed and collected data from a total of 230 managers and top executives for this study, in firms of various natures, be they private, public, or associative. Some of these organizations were traditional utilitarian ones, governed by strict economic values. Others were overly concerned with promoting spirituality and ethical values in business. This allowed us to draw some comparisons between the different types of organizations and to focus on the actual practices and behaviors of organizations that have radically different orientations.

We have drawn our results from two sets of data: from 131 questionnaires returned to us by Fortune 500 firms, and from 99 in-depth interviews with managers and top executives, sometimes including the CEO. For the interviews, we opened up with some basic demographics questions, more so to put people at ease than anything else. We then asked people a host of questions and used different instruments. For example, we asked them what the meaning and purpose of their work was; how fearful they were of losing their job and what amount of downsizing their organization had gone through; how their work activities contributed to the general meaning in their lives; what the basic values that guided their life were, and so forth.

We also asked for the religious affiliation of the person, their parents, their partners, and if they believed in a deity or in a higher power. We asked them to give us what the term spiritual and religious meant to them. We did not want to give them our definition but we were interested in getting theirs. We also asked how appropriate it was to talk about spirituality in their organization, as opposed to something more abstract such as the notion of "value."

Most important, we asked them if there were processes in their organizations that could foster or enhance spirituality at work. For example, we asked about prayer, how frequently they prayed in general, whether they prayed at work, and if their organization had in place any processes that facilitated prayer. We also asked questions on how they could express deeper emotions during their work activities, and so forth.

Finally, we secured a portrait of each organization through the respondents' perceptions in order to allow us to make comparisons between organizations. We asked them to describe their organization through a number of scales, from "warm" to "cold," "flexible" to "inflexible," "profitable" to "unprofitable," and so forth. We further asked them to rate both religion and spirituality on scales such as "tolerant" and "intolerant," "open minded" and "close minded," "inclusive" and "exclusive," and so forth.

SOME OF THE RESULTS OF THIS STUDY

It is important to report right away that most of our results are surprising or ran contrary to conventional wisdom. Again, I cannot go into all the details here, but will concentrate on what seems to me most important.

The Quasi-Totality of Managers Are in Favor of Integrating Spiritual Values at Work

One of the most important result of this study is that 92 percent of our respondents, out of 320 managers and top executives in various organizations, have a positive view of spirituality or religion and search for ways to integrate them better in their daily work activities. While Jean-Marie Toulouse stated that to better address the problem of values, ethics, and spirituality in management really answered one of the paramount needs of the business milieu (see Chapter 1), he was fundamentally right. Notice that this demand is not made by a minority of managers, nor even their majority, but, more important, by the quasi-totality of them, at least in the United States. Only 8 percent of our respondents had a negative view of these topics in organization.

There Is Actually a Lack of Models and Tools for Integrating Spirituality at Work

To state that 92 percent of our respondents wish to better integrate spirituality at work does not mean that it is easy nor that this wish does not encounter a host of resistance. Our research suggests that there is a deep fear in organizations of actualizing these values in daily work and management activities. People suffer from what I would call a Faustian dilemma: They want to be able to practice their spirituality at work but they do not know of any concrete ways or concrete models that would allow them to do so.

They are also afraid because most of them have already been mocked and humiliated at work repeatedly and in different areas. They realized that if they brought all of themselves to work, including their spiritual ideals, they risk to be mocked even more, the humiliation touching this time the core of their souls.

Another reason why managers and executives are ambivalent to bring up spirituality at work is their wish to stay critical and not to offend their coworkers. Some people restrain themselves from using the "S" words—that is, spirit and soul—because they have been tarnished. Most of our respondents, for example, dissociate themselves from the New Age movement which they consider silly and without credibility. These managers and executive want, on the one hand, to remain critical and not be associated with questionable movements, and on the other hand, to stay respectful of their colleagues.

And yet, despite these difficulties, these managers and executives do not wish to give up the search for spirituality at work. On an individual basis, they search for something bigger than themselves at work and they wish to find ways to live a more integrated life. At the organizational level, they also realize that unless organizations can find ways to tap into this power, no organization could really produce world-class services and products that could benefit mankind and be in harmony with nature.

There Exists a Strong Agreement among Managers on the Notion of Spirituality

Another finding is equally fundamental and counterintuitive. While our respondents used many different words and notions to describe spirituality at work and while they strongly separated the notions of spirituality and religion, a subject to which I will come back later, everybody we have talked to had roughly the same definition of spirituality. All expressed in one form or the other that the number-one concern of spirituality at work is to overcome an experience of fragmentation, to live a more systemic life. Simply put, people in general and managers and top executives in particular do not want to live a fragmented life. They realize that their lives are split into a thousand pieces. Their search for meaning is constant, as Thierry Pauchant and his colleagues have documented in a book bearing that title.[2]

To confine this search to off hours or to one or two days a week is understood as absurd. As one of our respondents stated, "We can come to work for eight hours and they mock us and humiliate our spirit. Then, we are free to go home and repair ourselves in the remaining time."

Further, despite differences in language, just about everybody we talked to affirmed that there exists a higher power: They believe there is meaning and purpose in the universe and that they have been put on earth "to do good." For them, the world is neither absurd nor aimless and, thus, the world of their work should also have meaning and purpose. Another respondent stated, "Spirituality is the fundamental feeling that you are part of and connected to everything, the entire physical universe and all of humanity. . . . We are put here on Earth basically to increase goodness, and not just make money."

Again, it is really outrageous that many of these metaphysical issues and spiritual beliefs have not been seriously studied in the past decades, aside from a few exceptions. We know why: fear, lack of courage, the disdain in positivistic science for metaphysical questions, the separation between the church and the state which assumes that people leave their spirituality behind when they go to work, and many other reasons.

This lack of interest in the issue of spirituality at work becomes even more absurd at a time where more and more organizations search for ways to bring the complete person to work in order to engage their total creativity in a world of increasing globalization. This absurdity is even more evident when one realizes that, increasingly, organizations wish to foster and to gain the commitment and the enthusiasm of their workers, managers and executives alike. We often forget but the word enthusiasm is a spiritual concept. It comes from the Greek *en*, which means "within," and *thuos*, "god." Very literally, to be enthusiastic means to have god or a spiritual force within oneself.

Finally, the fact that despite differences in words and referents, the notion of spirituality is pretty much homogeneous from managers and executives alike means that this notion can be scientifically studied and even measured. I am again in agreement with Jean-Marie Toulouse (see Chapter 1) when he proposed that the issues of ethics and spirituality are among the most important questions to be answered in management. If the issue of spirituality at work can be seen as a soft issue, it is indeed a hard one to address in management. But the question is fundamental for the life of individuals, workers and executives alike, as well as for the well-being of our organizations, our communities, and our fragile planet.

The Spiritual Organization Has Specific Characteristics

A spiritual organization is an organization whose executives, managers, and workers attempt to actualize some spiritual and ethical principles in their daily activities. Despite our current lack of knowledge on the characteristics of these organizations, our pilot study suggests that they are not traditional. If anything, they are hybrid and locate themselves between a not-for-profit and profit-oriented organization. They seem to be a new entity. Ben & Jerry's, headquartered in the state of Vermont, is an example of this different breed. Without, however, idealizing this company, one of the first things that Ben & Jerry's did was to get rid of the idea of a threshold. They stated that no matter how much money they will make, they were going to give more to good causes than traditional businesses do. They knew that if they had established a threshold above which they would give some money away, this would not happen. In that company, 10 cents of each dollar made is given away as a contribution for a better world. This is only an example of the difference existing in spiritual organizations: They attempt to practice at a higher ethical plane; they operate with a different set of rules.

This notion is also evident at the individual level. When asked what gave them meaning at work, our respondents ranked first the possibility "to realize one's full potential as a human being." The second and third reasons were "to do interesting work" and "to work in an ethical organization." The amount of money they made came only in fifth place.

Making money while working is, without question, a paramount condition. This is even more so for somebody living at the level of physical subsistence. But, as Abraham Maslow proposed years ago (see the Introduction), as soon as the level of subsistence is attained, other values become more important. This implies, as our respondents clearly indicated, that spirituality must be practiced for its own sake. Organizations or individuals who embark on the road of spirituality in order to make more money fail in their endeavor. But the inverse maybe true: Organizations that embrace the spiritual path for a question of higher values, and not for greed, can become more profitable, a fundamental paradox. Yet fundamental paradoxes often develop for most important things. This topic of the relationships existing between profit making and the practice of higher values is certainly a topic in great need of further research, but one thing seems clear. The organizations which are the most spiritual are not necessarily the not-for-profit ones. A profit-oriented organization can also be highly spiritual.

A Crisis Is Often Needed for Starting the Process of Transformation

One other important result of our study is the necessity of a crisis in the process of transformation on the path of spirituality. Managers and executive alike do not just wake up one morning and decide that their organization is going to become spiritual because it is just a good thing to do. They need a severe crisis or, most of the time, several major crises that injure them personally. We had already documented this need of a crisis for a process of transformation to start in a previous study conducted in the field of crisis management.³ The example of Tom Chappell, of Tom's of Maine, is a telling example. Tom had become an enormous success: He had the great house, the great car, the trophy wife, and so forth, but he woke up one day and found his life empty. Instead of going to his local therapist, which he could have easily done, he did something even more radical; he went to his local minister. Later he studied at the Harvard Divinity School for two years to find out what was required for a person to become spiritual. He realized that his problem was not just therapeutic; it was more profoundly spiritual. The same thing was realized years ago by Carl Jung for treating alcoholism. The disease from which the alcoholic is suffering is a loss of spirit and soul and for a recovery to begin, a crisis is needed.⁴ In Alcoholics Anonymous's (AA's) terminology, the person has to "hit rock bottom." While it seems that not everyone could reach enlightenment, whatever enlightenment is, in most cases the path has to be started by a major crisis.

In an organization, the crisis has to be more than the loss of money, market, or profits: It has to be a crisis of meaning; it has to become existential. The crisis has to lead to the realization for the individuals involved in an organization—workers, managers, or executives—that the way in which they were running their lives and their business would not guarantee the development of their full potential as individuals.

Managers Perceive Religion and Spirituality Very Differently

The last finding on which I would like to comment here is the difference of perception that exists in organizations between the notions of religion and spirituality. The vast majority of managers and executive in our study strongly differentiate between them. Religion has an extremely negative connotation. It is seen as dogmatic, intolerant, more concerned with organization and less concerned with the individual. Spirituality is sharply opposed to religion, and I have some of the strongest statistical proof on this opposition that I have ever seen in my scientific research career. Spirituality is viewed as open minded, tolerant, and more individually based and not as formal or bureaucratic as religion is.

A FIRST TYPOLOGY OF SPIRITUAL ORGANIZATIONS

One of the most significant findings from our study is that we were able to identify five different models by which organizations could become more spiritual and/or ethical. None of these models to our knowledge had been described extensively and most are even unknown to our respondents. While this typology is still incomplete and needs to be completed by other studies, it could provide people in organizations the models that they, as they told us, are searching for. This typology is derived from the positive and negative views our respondents held about spirituality and religion, as discussed previously.

In Figure 2.1 we have indicated in parenthesis the percentage of our respondents who held a positive or a negative view of spirituality and religion: Thirty percent of the respondents hold a positive view of both spirituality and religion while 60 percent, the majority, hold a positive view of spirituality but a negative view of religion. It is also interesting to note that only a small minority of respondents, 8 percent, hold a negative view of both spirituality and religion, and that only 2 percent of the respondents, while holding a positive view of religion, do not view spirituality in a positive light. It is most important to note, however, that despite these differences, 92 percent of our respondents, managers, executives, or CEOs hold a positive view of either religion or spirituality. These results demonstrate the fundamental importance of spirituality at work and the need for further scientific research on the subject.

From the examples our respondents provided us as well as from our analysis of the burgeoning scientific literature exiting on the subject, we were able to classify some of the different paths an organization can take in order to become spiritual (see Figure 2.1).[5]

Figure 2.1
Different Paths to Becoming a Spiritual or Ethical Organization

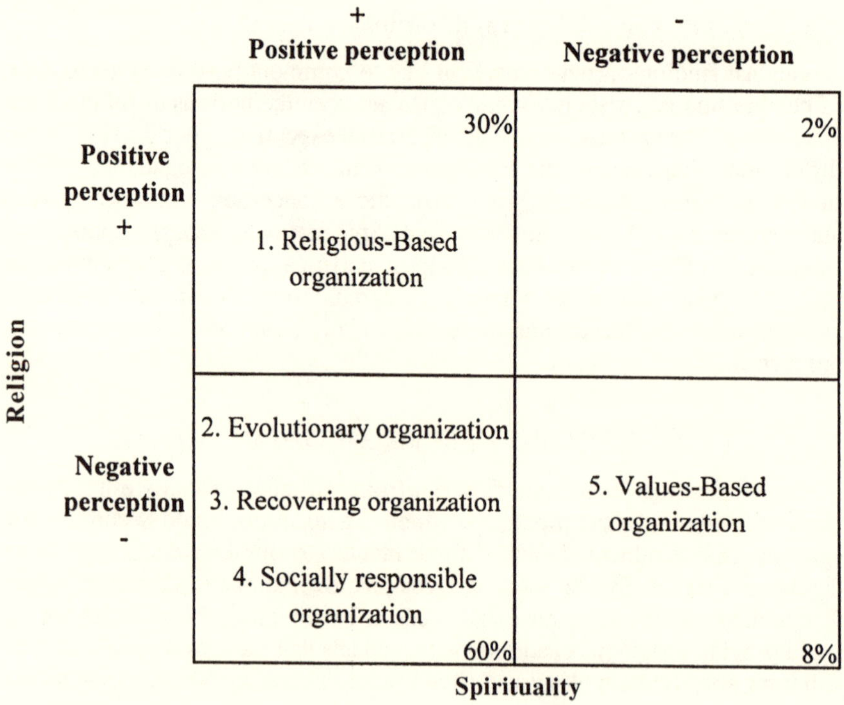

	+ Positive perception	- Negative perception
Positive perception +	30% 1. Religious-Based organization	2%
Negative perception -	2. Evolutionary organization 3. Recovering organization 4. Socially responsible organization 60%	5. Values-Based organization 8%

(Religion — vertical axis; Spirituality — horizontal axis)

The first path, the religious-based organization, spans the top two cases of the typology where religion, spirituality, or both are the sources of basic beliefs and universal values. These organizations can have been created by diverse religious communities or have derived their principles from a specific religious tradition, such as, for example, Ouimet-Cordon Bleu, a Canadian firm operating in the food industry and described in this book (see Chapter 7).

The second path is constituted by three types of organizations: the evolutionary organization, the recovering organization, and the socially responsible organization. While these organizations hold a positive view of spirituality, they do not necessarily follow the specific characteristics of religious norms.

The evolutionary organization is an organization which had been founded on a strong association with a specific religion but which has evolved through time to a more ecumenical position. Tom's of Maine and the YMCA are prime examples. I talked to the chief executive officer of the YMCA in Los Angeles. This CEO stated that the fact that he is Jewish and president of one of the larger chapels of the YMCA is living proof of how ecumenical this organization has become through time. Indeed, for over 150 years, the YMCA transformed itself from a primarily Christian Protestant organization to a more ecumenical or interreligious one.

The recovering organization, the second type of organization on this path, is fascinating. A number of the organizations we went into had most of their senior staff recovering from alcoholism. They were all members of Alcoholics Anonymous. These managers and top executives were trying to apply and adapt the AA principles to the management of their organization. Since they were not organizational specialists, they struggled with this task. However, as they all attended AA meetings, they all had a language for talking about spirituality in nonreligious terms; that is, terms which could be more readily accepted by all their employees. They were learning how to speak about spirituality in soft ways. One of the lessons we have derived from our study is that it seems necessary to develop a specific "spiritual listening" and "spiritual talking" in an organization. This does not mean to become covert or even mysterious about the notion of spirituality, but to develop concepts, processes, and practices which are not offensive to people. While I referred here specifically to alcoholism, the same remarks could be made about drugs, greed, sex, violence, or workaholism.

Finally, the socially responsible organization, the third type of organization in this path, often emerges from the founder's vision, guided by spiritual principles and social values. A prime example of this type of organization is Ben & Jerry's. There, spirituality takes the form of working on the problems of the surrounding society.

The value-based organization is the third generic path that a firm can take in order to become more ethical. In this case, the organization is not founded or driven by religion nor spiritual values. Rather, these organizations are guided by social and/or environmental values that are secular. As an example, one could mention Kingston Technologies, a maker of computer equipment in Orange County.

This typology allows for an initial classification of the different paths an organization could take in order to become more spiritual or ethical. Each path is influenced by the organization's own history and each is a valid path with its own strengths and weaknesses. Each of these models has its own triggering crisis, its own principle of hope, its own sources of wisdom and faith, such as fundamental texts or stories, its own different language and its own mechanisms for setting directions, practices, as well as limiting excess, such as the limit for greed.

One word of caution: The path, in order to last through generations, needs to be institutionalized. This means that spiritual and/or ethical principles need to be concretely applied in all the major components and processes of the organization, such as policies and practices in human resources, finance, marketing, accounting, strategy, leadership, product design and safety, and so forth. The inspiration of a single leader or even a group of leaders, or a family, does not often survive when these individuals are no longer a part of the organization. This leads to another paradox: While spirituality is often viewed as a personal experience, it needs, in order to survive and flourish, to be institutionalized; that is, to transcend one's experience.

CONCLUDING REMARKS

One of my best friends and colleagues at the University of Southern California, Warren Bennis, asked me why I was conducting all these interviews. Most of the findings reported here were already pretty clear after thirty interviews or so, but I was still pursuing them. I responded that this is the way I am experiencing my own spirituality.

The longer I have been in the academic world, the greater my love–hate relationship with it has grown. I regard it as a moral outrage that we have had almost no scientific studies on the subject of spirituality at work despite a few exceptions. I really regard it as morally outrageous that people who have tenure, who are financially and socially secured and protected, do not have the courage to tackle issues like this. They do not assist workers, managers, or executives in the field, who have neither the time nor the training to study these issues. In my mind, this study is important as it has the potential, hopefully, to assist the world in its need for spiritual enrichment. Professors and researchers in business schools have the moral duty to conduct such studies. If they do not, they are not ethical in regard to their own profession. If they do not fully actualize themselves, our natural and spiritual world will remain impoverished.

3

The "Crises of Belief" in Business and the Need for a Dialogue on the Meaning of Work

Solange Lefebvre

EDITOR'S NOTE

In this chapter, theologian and anthropologist Solange Lefebvre retraces the different meanings attributed to the notions of religion, spirituality, and work throughout the centuries. She suggests that a serious dialogue based on these ideas is required to address the "crisis of belief" observed today in business and in society at large. Based on in-depth interviews conducted in the business world, she tackles the taboos surrounding the notions of spirituality and religion in the business world and the negative connotations generally associated with work. She stresses the need for respect and connection pursued by many when confronted with the fragmentation of their life experience, a condition evoked by Ian I. Mitroff in Chapter 2.

Reminding us that happiness is also found in adversity, and that one of the functions of religion and spirituality is to allow people to become aware of their limits—to realize that they are not Gods and Goddesses—Solange Lefebvre proposes that an ethic and spirituality of work must be founded not in an escape from this world, but in the imperative for communal life and a reinterpretation of notion of work itself. She further suggests that the integration of ethics and spirituality in the business world must be supported by very specific policies, like the encouragement of mentors and workplace rituals. Finally, she suggests that the world of business and the economy, which are at the base of vital exchanges, must integrate ethical and spiritual values in this century, during which "progress," as she puts it, "has penetrated our bodies."

One of my great pleasures as a theologian is to meet professionals from outside my field and listen to their own thinking on spiritual and ethical issues, to learn about their practices. Theoretical reflection is constructed from, among other things, the efforts of those in society who are rethinking ethical and spiritual questions.

In the last few months while preparing this presentation, I was inspired by a quote from Sherry Connolly, reported recently in *The Globe and Mail*. As a manager with the Royal Bank, she coordinated a conference in Toronto on the relationship between spirituality and management. She confided "Spirituality is not a common subject of conversation in my workplace. It is not easy."[1] We can examine the reasons for this.

There are many explanations for our difficulty dealing with this question in the workplace. Before considering this issue, my first two points will reflect that recently, ethical and spiritual questions have been pondered in all professional domains. First, I will briefly discuss the distinction people make between spirituality, values, and religion in their own experience and from an historical point of view. After touching on some sources of resistance to spirituality in the workplace, I will question certain common views on spirituality. Given that for ten years I have been working on issues of transmission, solidarity, and tension in intergenerational relationships, I will close on how these relationships challenge communal life.

SPIRITUALITY, VALUES, OR RELIGION:
A HISTORICAL DETOUR

Many people have a very personal definition of these three words: spirituality, value, and religion; to an extent, they will exclude one or another from their vocabulary. It is important to remember that these are very empirical perceptions which reflect very deep-seated tendencies.

As Ian I. Mitroff suggested (see Chapter 2), referring to his inquiry into spirituality in U.S. corporations, and as explained in greater detail in his book, certain subjects interviewed preferred talking about values rather than spirituality.[2] The former seemed less threatening, less emotionally charged and comfortably removed from debates on religious affiliations. This is also the predominant tendency here in the province of Quebec. People talk about values more easily. For the past few years, when I have been invited to speak in various professional milieus, it has been to discuss values. The organizers of this forum debated the issue—"Do we use the word 'spirituality' or 'values'?" This shows just how important words can be. They finally opted for the formula "management, ethics, and spirituality."

For many people, spirituality is clearly distinguished from religion. The first refers to a more subjective, freer experience whereas the second is identified with structures and constraining systems in which the subject or person feels they have little place and almost no freedom to interpret. Generally, the modern individual will declare themselves against institutions. But whether we like it or not, Western history, like all of world history, has been deeply marked by religious questions. As well, even if we prefer discussing values or spirituality, we cannot help but refer to our own religious roots to understand our ethical decisions, our view of the world and of work, our resistance, our choices, and our attitudes.

For example, it is useful to roughly sketch out the importance that questions of spirituality and values have acquired in the last few years. Why are there presently new quests, searches for expression, and new practices as well? The context in which traditional values and spiritualities have developed has profoundly changed.

Let us recall that prewar society, enveloped in the primacy of religion, internalized the values of austerity endemic to a suffering economy. From this emerged a religion of sacrifice based on poverty in a world referred to as "a vale of tears." This was how one gave meaning to the conditions for survival; a certain pessimism reigned. An older person once explained to me that, in the past, when the weather was good they would say "We're gonna pay for it." And "the beyond" represented the promise for a happy life, at last.

The postwar period favored the emergence of more materialistic values as society aspired to prosperity and comfort. Happiness, which had been deferred until after death, was then more sought in the here and now. Little by little, modern aspirations took over from the austere values of the "religion of sacrifice." The values of freedom and well being became more important and a balance was sought between them and older values.

During the 1960s and 1970s, major secular reforms were taking place in many places in the world and new elites were affirming themselves, particularly in business. At the same time, more priority was given to the values of quality of life, the liberalization of morals, and personal and moral autonomy. They expressed themselves as an investment in affectivity and subjectivity: "It has to feel good" and "it has to suit me." These attitudes imply the new spiritual beliefs that emerged in the 1970s: individuality, experience, interiority, emotion, feeling, and the body all become very important. The importance of the actor and performer were affirmed. There was a revulsion for large bureaucratic organizations and the universe invaded by positivist science. It is at this time that the difference between religion and spirituality emerged: Religion designated a coded system of prescribed practices based on a defined credo; spirituality suggested a freer more individual experience, centered around emotion and experience; a spirituality which anyone may live, inside or outside of a religious institution.

At the same time, the family and basic loci of belonging were shaken by this affirmation of the self and sensation. Many parts of the world, as well as here, were influenced by promises of a great future: unlimited economic, social, cultural, and political progress. Criticism or rejection of traditional religion became an emancipation, a reappropriation of the self, of one's life, one's conscience, with an upsurge of new beliefs and new practices.

During the 1980s spiritual values continued to assert themselves under the guise of crises, the word chosen by Thierry Pauchant to begin his book on management entitled *In Search for Meaning*.[3] For example, a major recession in the early 1980s led us to talk about the structural difficulties of integrating young people into the workforce. We were confronted with the limits of the expected progress and the reforms that had been undertaken. We also see new inquiries into the meaning of life, a renewed interest in spirituality, moral examination, and a questioning of values. The values and aspirations of modernity were still strong, economic values became more important but they were tainted by that first recession and the realities of survival that were faced by many. We renewed ourselves in our private and emotional lives. Spiritual searches continued, but they were accompanied by major ethical questions, raised primarily by the economic and environmental crisis.

In this continuum, the 1990s seemed marked by a movement to revise and recompose values, the expression "to integrate the various dimensions of one's life" refers to this. This revision was often expressed in terms of balance: one's daily bread and the depths of the soul, material and spiritual, social issues and personal fulfillment, freedom and responsibility, living in the present and preparing the future, belief, knowledge, and know-how.[4] We tried to rejoin that which has been separated or divided; we attempted to integrate the various dimensions of our life in a search for balance.

To conclude this overview, we should note that the attempt to reconcile rationality, productivity, and techno-science on the one hand and humanist values such as justice, tenderness, and compassion on the other. Everything happened so quickly in the twentieth century: Progress penetrated our bodies. Now, many are standing back and asking where all this is heading. We have given ourselves extraordinary means and tools, but how do we manage them to insure a good and just communal life?

The relationship between technique, management, and meaning concerns everyone. According to a number of texts, lectures, and articles, including the presentation by Yves Benoît in this book (see Chapter 8), hospitals are trying to humanize healthcare. We are trying to redefine learning in our school system where, on a more existential level, we can hear the plea of the seventeen-year-old high school drop-out who spoke to a gathering of professionals and administrators—"Our schools have no soul." In management, there is an attempt to synchronize practice and discourse on the horizon of meaning and ethics. All this speaks of a need to connect.

In this light, allow me to quote an extract of the 1961 encyclical on social justice, *Mater et Magistra*, by Pope John XXIII:

If the whole structure and organization of an economic system is such as to compromise human dignity, to lessen a man's sense of responsibility or rob him of opportunity for exercising personal initiative, then such a system, we maintain, is altogether unjust—no matter how much wealth it produces, or how justly and equitably such wealth is distributed.[5]

In this vain and beyond the workplace, an antiutilitarian current has developed in the last few years in the social sciences which makes us ponder on the "humus" and on the deeper meaning of social relations. For example, we often speak in terms of negotiations and transactions as though we were discussing finance. Jacques T. Godbout represents this trend. In his most recent book, he maintains that the human touch of a society is expressed by the practice of giving in all social interaction. This small, free, "surplus of meaning" goes beyond the mechanical and syndical rule, the obligatory tie, the purely instrumental or functional rapport. Giving is to society what the conscience is to humans, what democracy is to politics. As he has written, "How, by what feat, do the social sciences discuss social relations without using words which describe everyday life: abandonment, forgiveness, sacrifice, love, respect, dignity, atonement, reparation, compassion, all that is at the heart of human relationships which is nourished by giving?"[6]

Against this backdrop, this conference takes on all its contemporary relevance. After these general comments on the relationship between work and spirituality, let us quickly look at why it is difficult to deal with spiritual questions in the workplace.

BLOCKS AND RESISTANCE

Dealing with spiritual questions at work is far from simple. It is actually very difficult, and for many reasons. Let us recall the words of the Royal Bank executive that I quoted earlier: "It is not easy to discuss spirituality in our work places." There are blocks and resistance. Why is it so difficult? Let me offer a few clues.

Taboo and Residue

On the one hand there is the issue of passion: Like politics, religion or spirituality arouses very strong feelings that stem from one's convictions. It is well known that here and in other parts of the world, it is customary to avoid discussing religion or politics at the dinner table, so as not to interfere with one's digestion. Although I use the example humorously, it is nonetheless significant. I believe our challenge is to relearn how to discuss these issues with a healthy understanding of our identity and our convictions, while respecting and welcoming others and their differences. This no easy task, but it would represent a real dialogue on spiritual issues.

It is also difficult to discuss religious issues for historical reasons: First, modernity caused the withdrawal of religion into the private sphere of the family and of the individual. Implicit social norms recognize the right to a diversity of beliefs on the condition that they do not disrupt the social order or constrain individual freedom. To discuss one's spirituality, or one's membership to a religion, even a traditional one, can easily be seen as interference. A person who wants to bring up the subject worries that he or she may be poorly received.

Religion or spirituality have been invested with a certain taboo just as sexuality once was. I mean taboo in the larger sense of a subtle prohibition, unexpressed but which weighs on the members of a society very efficiently. It doesn't look bad to have a spiritual life or to practice a religion but it doesn't look good to talk about it or display it.

In terms of thought, even though we may have evolved, the conviction held by, for example, Emile Durkheim, still lives on: As society progresses religion will disappear. Even considering that numerous debates and the reality of individuals has taken us beyond that, this first idea of modernity perpetuates itself. For many, spirituality or religion is always present and is more than merely a residual phenomenon or a compensation for the anxiety of life and death.

Lack of References

My second point regarding the difficulty of tackling this question is about the lack of references. Ultimately, we have few well established references to help us deal with spiritual questions in the workplace. For example, in Western history, there are two negative aspects that weigh on spirituality at work: First, work has been considered as a very painful thing; second, the day of rest or Sunday (at least for Christians), was the state or space in which one did not work.

In other words, the ancient concept of work has penetrated history pessimistically: Work is not worthy of free man. In the first book of the Bible, Genesis, work is a curse. It is true that in the context of survival agriculture the techniques were rudimentary and consequently work was hard and painful. As well, work was long considered incompatible with the day of rest which was reserved for prayer. Sunday one does not work: Sunday one prays.

Therefore, the spiritual, in the greatest, most noble sense of the word, existed primarily outside work. Its apex was in monastic life. In fact, monks worked a lot; they were involved in the birth of printing, they were great scholars and producers of precious commodities, and so forth. Nonetheless, in the minds of many, the summit of spiritual life, and this is particularly true of Christianity, implied a separation from this world. The Protestant reform sought to enhance the value of secular life, including work, but our ancient roots continue to mark us.

But let us reflect upon a discourse closer to us in time. In 1962, the American Baptist theologian, Harvey Cox, observed that attitudes toward technology and work were directly linked to the religious presuppositions of those making the judgment. The symbols of God, or the ultimate reality of nature and order influenced one's conception of politics, work, and tools.[7] In the same year, the Calvinist theologian, Gabriel Vahanian observed, in a manner of speaking, the opposite: "Technical mastery will necessarily evoke in man the feeling of a different relationship with God, if it does not suppress that relationship altogether."[8] Here, we see the inverse: Rather than the concept of God influencing the vision of work and technique, the latter is causing a revision of the relation to God, or in a larger sense, spirituality.

Cox's observation remains true for individuals who are born and live in societies or milieus suffused by religion: Their religious or spiritual path influences their vision of the world. But in advanced, modern societies—our present society—the opposite is often true. We can access the spiritual domain or live our own tradition from within our condition of worker and citizen. Vahanian has clearly evaluated the distance that separates us from ancient societies that shaped the beginnings of the great religious traditions: The aim of the sacred would have been to escape or change worlds. Inversely, the utopianism of technology, far from fleeing the world, honors it by transforming it. It is no less than a true spiritual revolution.

When presupposing that technique is the framework of the modern and contemporary West, Vahanian does not use technique in the modern sense of technology or applied science, but primarily as the deployment of the Greek *techne* as in "the art of living." Beyond the common instrumental meaning, *techne* is understood as a "human technique, imbued with its own religiosity [whose] application concerns man in his entire being."[9] It is not an addition to the human being but signifies that all that is conceived is done so by humans and consequently includes an ethical dimension.

Beyond these concepts which beg reflection, let us remember that in an advanced modernity like our own, the world and its multiple realities is the grammar of our spirituality, and certainly not the reverse; that is, it is not religion that defines our vision of the world and of work, even if we are still influenced by our sacred heritage.

A challenge, however, remains: To find meaning, create spiritual practices from within our experience of work and management. It is not necessarily pure fabrication; we could draw from our heritage and our traditions but not without interpretation or reformatting.

In its present form, work represents a striking example of this need for reinterpretation. In fact, as I said, it is agricultural work, and the cycles of nature that marked the time of human endeavor. This has given form to many of the traditional spiritual symbols. And the need to escape this world has inspired the loftiest spirituality, with monastic life at its summit. Indeed, many new spiritualities present themselves with a desire to return to nature, to retreat from the world and they are sometimes accompanied by a critique or actual refusal of technology and an industrialized bureaucratic society.

In one of the interviews carried out during my research on transition in the workplace, we asked a supervisor in a high-tech company if there was any spirituality in his milieus. He described one of his colleagues:

In my team of five supervisors there is one we call the great guru because he is always calm; he has taken all these philosophy courses, he sings on his off hours. He always looks calm, poised and the rest of us we always look nervous–stressed. The image that he projects, is like . . . spiritual . . . sometimes, it's funny, we wonder if he's always there or not. Sometimes he comes up with stuff . . . you wonder where he comes from.

What we discover is what many people consider "spiritual": a reality which is elsewhere, a bit removed from reality. It must be said that many traditional images of spirituality evoke retreat: rest, silence, solitude. When we reflect upon the relationship between spirituality and work it makes us search for meaning in secular activities: rapid and serious decision making, the difficult management of money and personnel, daily pressures, the insecurities inherent in competition. We do not intend to negate the spiritual virtues of silence and retreat, of repose and of nature, or of the beauty of temples. But we must also search for these same virtues in human activity.

I will make an analogy to happiness. The common definitions of happiness circulate around the family, the home, and a good worker. Whereas when we dig, we realize that happiness exists outside these common loci: Happiness can be experienced through challenges. I said this to a top school board administrator during a conference. He said "I don't agree. There is no happiness in difficult challenges!" Half an hour later, I asked him, "So Mister director, you were happiest during your fantastic family vacation last summer?" No, he said, it was when I had to put through a major reform. I mobilized the team, we stuck together and we managed to get through it. That was one of the best moments of my life." If happiness is not the greatest where we expect it, the same may be said about the spiritual.

LOOKING FOR A MEANING IN WORK

I think that the wisdom inherited from our ancestors is fundamental even as we continue to research new avenues. I have a great deal of respect for traditions tested by large communities, passed on and transformed through history and put to the test of time. Now, when I examine them, both traditional and new spiritualities want to make sense of the dissatisfaction at the heart of man instead of just denying it.

We live with the feeling of deep divisions, within and between ourselves; we feel the anguish of separations; we aspire to unity or to wholeness. "When we work," said a former professional during a recent interview, "we must put aside much of our tastes, aptitudes and desires. We cannot fulfill all of our dimensions, because the demands of work are incompatible with our artistic or spiritual sides." This sentiment echoes the notion of fragmentation advanced by Ian I. Mitroff (see Chapter 2).

A time for work, a time for rest and reflection we could say. But there is something else. We still tend toward the goals of integration, the harmony of the self and of life, without quite being able to reach them. Now, scientific, medical, and technological advances have made us even more ambitious in terms of our personal sense of wholeness and the harmonization of our existence: We do not deal with ambiguity, doubt, need, or limits very well. The sociologist of religion, Daniele Hervieu-Leger, has accurately noted that modernity produced great aspirations and desires; progress, comfort, material wealth, self-fulfillment, personal evolution. But in the same breath, it is unable to totally satisfy them. The combination of these major aspirations and the powerlessness to satisfy them has given rise to all kinds of new beliefs.[10] The popularity of magic, for example, stems from the desire to find simple answers to all these problems: "Pray to God and make money"; "Practice yoga and you will succeed in business"; "I am God, I can do all," and so forth.

According to a French parliamentary commission report on sects, which attract more and more members of the business and political elite (as hinted at by Thierry Pauchant in the introductory chapter), many individuals currently have a low tolerance for doubt. The commission did not sketch a determined preexisting profile of followers who more often than not correspond to normal criterion. But they do note that a "depressive episode is a factor which seems to favor an attraction to a sect." However, vulnerability is not the predominant factor. What is a predominant factor is an interest in self-improvement, particularly with the scientific and intellectual elite. Why? It appears that these elites have a problem with "the idea of doubt" and consequently are strongly attracted by "a movement that proposes global explanations." What makes these people even more vulnerable, is indeed "their conviction that they are not manipulable."[11] This brings us back to our difficulty in living with our own ambiguities.

Indeed, one of the major roles of religion or spirituality is to enable human beings, who are by nature excessive, who foster grand dreams and high aspirations, to understand the meaning of limitations. That is what is meant by the saying that is engraved in ancient stone: "Know thy self," in other words "Know that you are human and not a god."

WORKING TODAY: A CHALLENGE OF COMMUNAL LIFE

Let us repeat this enlightening phrase, "The worker does not live by bread alone." In the majority of our interviews, participants from all domains reported that they had noticed a deterioration in their attachment to their workplace. Everyone does his own thing; in the anguish of unemployment, job loss, and fierce competition each individual concentrates on his own role, responsibilities, and functions, and leaves little time for socialization. Yet meaning and spirituality emerge from the quality of our relationships to others.

Yet, if we refer to spiritual questions, we can also evoke a type of exaltation of solitude which is evident in much moral and religious thinking. The French thinker, Tvetan Todorov, focuses our attention on certain asocial European philosophical traditions which implicitly postulate that "communal life is not regarded as necessary to man."[12] According to modern philosophers, like Hobbs for example, human beings are constrained to follow the rules of social life, but they are basically egotistical and self-seeking. Society and morals go against human nature: "It is this concept of man, this immoralist concept which has won out over those of the moralists; and it is that which we find working in the most influential political and psychological theories of our day," estimates Todorov.[13] In contrast to this tendency, he considers man as fundamentally social, that he could not exist alone. Seeking their approval, engaging in activities in order to be, act, and live with one another is to accomplish this vital social link.

This very accurate idea illustrates the fact that ethical and spiritual currents exalt solitude and detachment from the group. To my mind, in business and the workplace the imperative of communal life is one of the central challenges of contemporary spirituality and ethics.

I would like to underline the importance of small rituals in caring for and giving meaning to communal life in the workplace and other loci of belonging. Many of our interviewees noted the disappearance of these traditions (parties at restaurants, birthdays, celebrating retirement, and so on). And more important, the welcome of new employees, their initiation, the recognition of acquired experience, the rituals of retirement, have been found to be sorely lacking.

Moreover, we find a humanizing place in the appreciation of models, mentors, tutors, or bosses. At the core of the current crisis, where many are afraid to lose their jobs, we are suspicious of the new guy, indeed we mistrust one another. This does help matters. But one figure can transcend these relationship difficulties; the model or mentor. When we ask people, "Do you have a model in your professional life?" they take on a different tone. They allude to values and sometimes even spirituality. The model is the person who does not feel threatened by another, who is unconditionally welcoming, who is there to lend support during professional difficulties, who guides and opens doors. The model, the mentor, is a person in the organization who has no ulterior motives. I think it is necessary to underline the importance of these experiences which can provide a veritable oasis in today's difficult working life. And often, they are relationships between people of different ages, which can represent an enriching exchange.

CONCLUSION

I will conclude by proposing that at this time, more than a spiritual and ethical crisis, there is a fundamental "crisis of belief." It is very difficult for people, young and old, to believe in one another and in the future. Particularly in business, where you find yourselves on the front lines as it were, there is much you can do in terms of spirituality and ethics to restore this confidence, both interpersonally and collectively. It is a fundamental battle against the pervading despair and skepticism, which are often linked to economic considerations. The economy is nonetheless the basis for vital and significant exchanges between us.

4

Dialogue on Part I

Roger Berthouzoz, Solange Lefebvre,
Ian I. Mitroff, and Thierry C. Pauchant

EDITOR'S NOTE

As suggested in the introduction, a dialogue is much more than a question and answer session for the sake of argumentation and information. Its purpose is not only limited to communication but to the encouragement of self-affirmation and attentiveness to others. More fundamentally, the practice of dialogue allows for the exploration of people's basic assumptions, without necessarily following some logic or a preestablished structure.[1]

In the following dialogue, the reader will be able to detect the questions, hopes, experiences, and anger of participants as well as their despair and pain, successes and joy. The obvious lack of structure in a dialogue seems particularly well adapted to the inherent ambiguity of the integration of ethics and spirituality in management and in the workplace. Its unfolding is sometimes as baffling as the explored subject. This book contains three dialogues. The following one is the first, held at the end of the first session of the forum. It presents some of the comments and questions discussed in an audience of about 200 participants, 140 of which work as consultants, executives, and managers in private and public organizations, governments, and associations, and the remaining 60 being professors and students, mainly in administration.

Participant: I have a question for professor Mitroff. I noticed in your research that you looked at individual values and I was wondering if, by any chance, you have noticed either on an individual or organizational level, an "invisible field" which we could also possibly call an "invisible field of love"?

Ian I. Mitroff: The common underlying ground of all those models of practices of spirituality in the workplace is that every one of them has their own distinct language; they all reach their goals by using different avenues; they use their own texts and specific sources of wisdom for inspiration. Nevertheless, despite its importance, language is not sufficient. What matters is what we call an epiphany or a profound transformation in the individual's life.

Here is an example of an Atlanta-based carpet business called Inner Face. One day, the owner woke up and had an epiphany experience. He realized that his product was toxic and harmful for the environment. Until then, he had considered himself a spiritual person and believed in the notion of connection. He then questioned himself: How can I believe that everything is interconnected and at the same time leave out the consequences of my business activities from my personal life? From that moment on, the company started to test the carpets. To their own surprise, the carpets were made of 2,500 chemical products, 95 percent of them being dangerous for health. The company then started to manufacture carpets using essentially nontoxic products for the environment. More than that, in that company, the consumer who buys carpets does not own them, they rent them. When a carpet is worn out, the company takes it back and recycles it ecologically.

To answer your question, yes it's a "field of love," but that notion is too ethereal and doesn't capture the essential. A spiritual organization manifests itself through concrete actions. My point here is that those who decide to take that path are not philosophers nor academicians. They don't necessarily exist on a theoretical plane. They appreciate the concepts and use a different language, but if their ideas are not operationalized, their business will be worse off. Those who play with words are often cynical. Some people I know bet money on next year's management trend. That's how cynical some are. Yes it's a question of language, but it must be followed by meaningful actions that will transform the organization as a whole. For me, this is the only "field" that really counts.

Participant: My remark here won't be philosophical or theoretical. I would like to discuss the definition of happiness proposed by Mrs. Lefebvre. She proposed that happiness can be going through a difficult period or a crisis. Personally, I can tell you that going through the hardship of losing one of my five senses (sight), I can still feel some happiness.

Solange Lefebvre: I find it important to realize that. I wouldn't want to overly praise suffering or even search for it. But it is true that we dislike suffering. What we don't like in it is the change it creates in us. In my example, I was referring to the mysterious sense of challenge that human beings experience when they have to overcome obstacles, to accomplish what they thought impossible. That's what you are corroborating by your remark because health is a central value for many peoples. You remind us more fundamentally of the proposition I made in my presentation by going even beyond my comments. Thank you very much.

Roger Berthouzoz: That testimony is very important. We should find a way to share what allowed this person to find happiness through that difficult experience. As a theologian and ethicist, I have nothing more to say regarding suffering or loss than it is absurd and has no sense. However, during the experience, there might be a presence; the presence of others, or the other, or the presence of God, enabling and supporting that happiness. I think that when we are able to share the happiness experienced through hardship, it can be very decisive. Then there may be the beginning of a transformation.

Participant: I am pleased to hear us trying to ask questions to which there is no answer. I find our confusion between ethics, spirituality, or religion interesting. Because somehow we don't know what we're talking about and that's interesting. In my opinion, that is why silence helps us feel whole as opposed to empty. Sometimes we try to transcend our differences by trying to see how words could describe them. But that doesn't take us very far. Either we dilute our differences and we disappear completely, or we assert our difference in an integrated manner. What I suggest is to try not to go "beyond" our differences, but rather "underneath them." Even concepts I don't know are within me. A connection exists between the Hindu's and Carl Jung's worlds. Nevertheless, they are unfamiliar to each other. I think we should avoid this confrontation of language and try to find a common ground of silence underlying all discourses. Mr. Belanger lost one of his five senses, leading him to a search for meaning. Even though I didn't go through that same loss, part of me can experience that also. This is a remark that is not necessarily theoretical.

Roger Berthouzoz: I agree with this last comment. However, in a forum like this it is necessary to name the experience. I understand not wanting to talk about spirituality, ethics, or religion, because of their different contexts and connotations. But I think that we should also try, and that is one of our responsibilities in this forum, to communicate that experience to allow people to have access to it. To me, this deals with faith. Not only a theological faith, but faith that leads us to the beginning of life, that source of life, that converging experience with others. Dorothee de Gaza, a father of antiquity, was conveying this very nice image of a spiritual experience by saying that we are in extraordinarily different positions just like on a sphere. If we move from one experience to the other in the sense of religion, we will be very sensitive to the distance and the difference. If we dig, then each of us moves forward in its own experience while getting closer to each other.

Ian I. Mitroff: One of the reasons I find the model I presented interesting, based on how people felt differently about religion and spirituality, is because people have different perceptions about these notions. It doesn't mean we can't talk about them. For some people religion and spirituality are inseparable and for others they are separate. What's an important point is to realize that we can talk about each of these orientations.

In fact, what interested me the most is that just about everybody had pretty much the same definition of spirituality regardless of all the different definitions of spirituality and religion. Everybody had the sense of connection with the universe and the feeling of being a part of it and a sense of a higher power. There is an inherent ambiguity to spirituality but that shouldn't stop us from talking about it or from integrating it into management theory and practice.

What we are trying to talk about in this forum (that no one talks about in other management faculties) is the epistemology of a "management of truth." It is a dangerous notion because we are human beings and we are sometimes mistaken. Yet we need to talk about the "management of spirit." Again, no school of management I know talks about that, and yet every day, in management, we try to manage the truth and to manage the spirit even unconsciously. It is about time we do talk about it because that is what we have been doing throughout history and most of us don't like the consequences of those management actions, neither in business nor in society in general. Work is as much a part of life as spirituality. Spirituality is the fundamental desire to not separate or fragment one's soul into a thousand tiny bits. Spirituality is at the core of management and has been since the beginning of time. We need to be allowed to discuss it.

Thierry Pauchant: I have a question for Ian Mitroff. During your presentation you talked about the lack of courage of many professors and researchers in management schools. Those schools are supposed to train young people as well as managers to better themselves and better the world through their work but we miserably fail to do that. What will it take for those professors to find the courage to accomplish the mission of their institution and their vocation?

Ian I. Mitroff: This is an excellent question and it is at the core of the problem. If a crisis on the individual level is necessary to start on the path of spirituality as expressed by Joseph Campbell in his notion of the myth of the hero—use the expression you want—then we ought to establish learning procedures in business schools that are fundamentally different.[2] No one gets involved in graduate work unless they had a significant failure or crisis in their life. That has to be understood and be the cornerstone of any change. The desire to learn a bunch of desegregated facts, to pursue a career, or do meaningless research—and we have admirably succeeded at that in business schools—must be thwarted. Only a few executive programs attempt to do that. In those programs it is understood that some people are on a search for meaning and that it is necessary to conceive and develop a program that helps them. The Royal Melbourne Institute of Technology is an example that we'll talk about later that attempts to do that (see Chapter 10).

However, most of the programs are—consciously or unconsciously—structured to suppress the spirit of people, to break it. University education and management training is so fragmented that it kills the human spirit. The spiritual path is a search for integration. We owe ourselves different teachers, different programs that will allow for the systemic search of meaning and growth. That transformation could begin when business schools experience a major crisis forcing them to acknowledge their condition.

A final point: How dare we in the academic world in general and in the administration sciences in particular, think that businesses need to restructure themselves radically to survive and compete in the global economy, when this need for transformation is ignored by business schools and the academic world in general? What hypocrisy!

Participant: I work at Dawson College and one of my responsibilities is to act as an ombudsman. In that role, I have to be proactive toward professors who have problems with students. Of course, I question the pedagogical tools, but mostly I question the lack of soul in our programs. As in other establishments, we are victims of an educational system that is highly centralized and autocratic. Even though we are one of the biggest colleges in our area, I am positive that we are not the only people feeling that kind of moral vacuum in which we keep functioning mechanically: Students come and go.

Mr. Mitroff spoke about the lack of spiritual tools. In our organization, we use an approach developed by Lance Secretan, who suggested the notion of higher ground community.[3] He talks about the necessity to act on different levels: First, on mastery, meaning competence; second, on chemistry, meaning tact; third, on delivery, meaning the necessity to attend to a need. When I have to intervene in the school, I never quote Mr. Secretan and I don't talk about love or spirituality. I simply talk about mastery, chemistry, and delivery; this way of conceptualizing things and giving people a language which allows them to act differently has positive results.

We also hold role-playing workshops that we film and view afterward. All this helps and I would like to compare our approach with others in order to improve our work. We really need these kinds of tools to counter the soulessness in our programs.

Participant: This past example struck me. This reminded me of some of Solange Lefebvre's suggestions; for example, she suggested that spirituality is not always where we think it is. It is a great challenge, for example, to find spiritual places. I was observing people during the break; some rushed to their cell phones, seemed nervous, and looked like they were rushing to something, and so on. Why should we talk about spirituality of meditation instead of spirituality of action? We seem to forget that spirituality is not only lived in silence but also in action. But those who move all the time have trouble stopping. Lawrence Freeman has an interesting approach called meditation for the citizen.[4] Meditating in front of a tree is easier, but what to do on a busy street?

Participant: My question is for Mr. Mitroff. In your model showing the perception of religion on one side and on the other the perception of spirituality, you are classifying organizations, not individuals. As we know, the search of spirituality exists primarily within each individual. Also, I feel that each model presented was leading us to a top-down approach. And yet, I would put forth the hypothesis that concrete things happen when people hear the call of self-realization, when they get together and act freely.

Ian I. Mitroff: I found Ken Wilber's work very helpful to address those points (see the Introduction).[5] He has a very interesting framework for talking about spirituality. He distinguishes four different fields within a combining matrix: the inner life, the outer life, the individual, and the society. As mentioned by Solange Lefrebvre, in Western society we mostly associate spirituality to the inner individual life; that is, in only one of Ken Wilber's quadrants. And yet, the systemic level, the outer life and social reality are also important.

Here are some examples. Even if we had an organization where everybody was spiritually fulfilled and enlightened, that would not necessarily make for a spiritual or enlightened organization. For example, even with all their good values, GM's executives produced the Pinto with all its problems. Look at the TWA crash: All the different parts of the business were good but the system as a whole failed. This is why we are talking about systems.

To seriously talk about the social dimensions of spirituality we need to study the actions of an organization in society. This is very important because all of the personal emotional development taught by the New Age movement is individualistic; that is, fragmented, touching only one of

Wilber's quadrants. The individual level—the subjective, inner dimension of the individual—is of course very necessary. But by itself, it won't be able to affect the organizational or societal milieu; that is, the concrete outer world. Spirituality includes all four of Wilber's dimensions.

To answer your top-down question, I agree that the autocratic approach kills the spirit. When you look at the YMCA, it is not a top-down organizational structure. We need new organizational structures. The same is true at the social level. You cannot expect to have healthy people in a sick society. The reverse is also true. The social context has an impact on individual development. In the United States we dream about becoming a healthy society with 220 million guns around. That is absurd. We have to realize that the systemic level includes and at the same time transcends the individual level.

Participant: I would like to share some thoughts with you following Mrs. Lefebvre's suggestion; we are evolving more and more in a world of mobility and communication. Recently, I invited an African colleague from Chad for a month. At the end of his stay, he said, "Your communication technologies are simply fantastic . . . but you don't communicate with each other anymore!" In the morning, mother listens to the news, dad reads the paper, and the kids are in front of television. You live in a communication world and nobody communicates.

Mr. Mitroff observed that we seem to set aside faith and religion when we go to work for fear of lacking respect for others or ourselves. If we want to try to integrate spiritual values at work, there may be preliminary fieldwork to be done at home. Often, we don't even express our values at home. We don't take time to talk about real things.

Participant: I am a law professor at the University of China. I am very happy that so many people here are involved in this research for integrating economic, ethical, and spiritual values. But it leaves me wondering how this can be implemented concretely. For example, who will be responsible for defining and controlling the application of deontology or ethical codes?

Recently, I participated in a conference held in Peking on the Asian financial crisis where we talked about the devastating effects of speculators. One of the representatives of the World Bank mostly talked about the internal financial weakness of those countries. During his talk, I was thinking of a bank robber coming in with a gun and asking for $1 million; he would be arrested, condemned, and sent to prison. And yet it didn't happen that way when speculators ruined thousands of people in Asia. Of course they didn't have guns, but the results were the same. Again, I ask, Who would decide of the content of ethical codes and control their application?

I am not very familiar with Christian religion, but according to what I understand, God established a certain number of rules in the Bible. Those rules have some weight based on our fear of ending up in hell. I really don't know if that is efficient, but it at least scares people. I also understand that in this religion, one has only to believe and he will be saved. So, after all his speculations, Mr. George Soros will be forgiven?[6] I don't understand that logic.

Participant: Both Mr. Mitroff and Mrs. Lefebvre insisted on the importance of words and language. Two years ago, we decided to change our association's name which contained the word Christian. That word scared many people in the health sector and was keeping them away from the activities that we were trying to organize to bring them together.

I work as a nurse in a hospital in which we are trying to reestablish some notion of human, spiritual, and ethical values to the health sector. You all know that the health sector is having major problems for a variety of reasons. Even though I was born in a religious environment, I don't talk in religious terms anymore, but rather in terms of spirituality or values, as emphasized by this forum's participants. This facilitates the dialogue.

Recently, I attended a meeting in the health sector in which Mr. Pauchant participated. He spoke about the present difficulties in the health sector and its swirling world. He suggested that we create different dialogue circles in order to slow down, sit down and reflect together to find a sense of meaning among us and then communicate it to the organization. I have tried to do this in my work environment, but that's very difficult. We are caught in reorganizations, crisis, needs; we are always hopping, too many fires to put out, too many very short-term goals, and so on. I am searching for ways to help me find some meaning, some wholeness. At this point, we are extremely fragmented.

Participant: I am a businesswoman. I left the business sector to go back to school and study in an MBA program at fifty-four years of age. I wanted to know what it is we teach managers that makes them so disrespectful of people. As Mr. Mitroff mentioned, I find this situation morally outrageous and I am angry. In my opinion, ethics and spirituality begins with respect for others, as underlined by Mrs. Lefebvre. God is within every human being. It will be only when I hear this new discourse that, maybe, I will feel less outraged.

Participant: I wonder what inspires people at work when we talk about management, work, and spirituality. We talked about motivation, about empowerment, about all sorts of things but we are not addressing fundamental issues of changing the way work is seen. Professor Mitroff wrote a book a number of years ago called *Frame Break*, where he spoke of the need to question very fundamental issues.[7] I, too, feel this is needed.

I worked in many large organizations and in the majority of them there is an enormous collusion not to speak the truth about some of these deeper issues and how we can reorganize work. I consider management to be a religion—or a dogma—held by managers. Nobody wants to put their neck on the line on these fundamental issues and go further. Yet, there is an incredible call for learning flexibility, to become a learning organization, to find some meaning at work, and so on. How do we change this when consultants can make $200,000 peddling things like competency profiles, job evaluations, and so forth. They are all good and useful tools but they do not address the fundamental issues.

Ian I. Mitroff: A number of the questions in the past few minutes seem to hint at the general theme: What can a traditional organization do to break out from the constraints imposed by the market?

I would like to mention Ben & Jerry's example because it is not perfect. In fact Ben Cohen is really considered more of a benevolent dictator than merely benevolent. To run a spiritual organization is hard; certainly not easier than a traditional one. The traditional ones have all the same dilemmas, but a spiritual organization tries to invent new ideas. They often need to use an integrative concept such as an "umbrella strategy" in management. For example, one notion discussed by Cohen is "caring capitalism." It is a contradiction in terms leading to all kinds of dilemmas: How do we do good, we have to make money. . . . We are in the stock market. . . . If we earned X amount of money and give a certain percentage away, a bigger profit would allow us to give more.

You see, they too can get trapped in the spiral of growth and greed. Another paradox would be, Do we hire people in tune with our spiritual mission or do we hire MBAs for their professional expertise?

The point I want to make here is that Ben & Jerry's understood the fundamental need for innovation and continual change. They made that a central issue in their strategy. They figured they had to be constantly clever not to make profits but to break out of the rules of the contemporary neoliberal market.

As I said before, Ben & Jerry's model is not perfect. Ben became so attuned to the outside world that he experienced what I call the "missionary paradox" where the missionaries are out saving the world but neglecting the children at home. The internal employees at Ben & Jerry's do not feel they are being fed. That is like wanting to paint the Golden Gate Bridge in San Francisco or the Eiffel Tower in Paris. When do you stop painting? Never! Because we don't have perfect antirust paints. But innovation and experimentation are not only left to chance. Fundamentally, it is necessary to develop a spiritual infrastructure in the organization. If only one part of the organization is spiritually engaged, if the approach is not systemic, it won't last.

PART II

FIVE CASE STUDIES FROM DIFFERENT INDUSTRIES ON THE INTEGRATION OF ETHICS AND SPIRITUALITY IN THE MANAGEMENT OF ORGANIZATIONS

In this second part, leaders in five organizations present their views on how ethics and spirituality are presently integrated. These businesses or organizations operate in different sectors: the banking industry in Chapter 5, by Claude Beland; the food industry in Chapter 6, by J-Robert Ouimet; a public organization in Chapter 7, by Vera Danyluk; healthcare in Chapter 8, by Yves Benoît; and a business school in Chapter 9, by Peter Sheldrake and James Hurley. Chapter 10 presents a collective dialogue on these various cases.

5

Ethics, Spirituality, and the Cooperative Movement in the Banking Industry

Claude Beland

EDITOR'S NOTE

In this chapter, Claude Beland, president of a very important financial institution, presents a philosophy and an organizational design that favors ethics and spirituality. President of the Desjardins movement that employs more than 43,000 people and manages assets of more than $70 billion, he describes the spirit of the cooperative movement as a societal project, retraces the history of the Desjardins movement through its founder Alphonse Desjardins, gives a brief summary of the recent changes that go against the cooperative movement's values, and presents specific examples of how his institution had to adapt to the reality of the economic market.[1] In conclusion, Mr. Beland identifies the reasons why he thinks the cooperative movement is the way of the future in a world "in search for meaning" and pleads for the development in society of a real education in democracy, responsibility, and solidarity so as to humanize society and the economy.

An example of an evolutionary organization, as described by Ian I. Mitroff (Chapter 2), the Desjardins movement succeeded in ensconcing Christian values in the cooperative movement and prospered in an industry governed by other values. These two victories have brought forth numerous critiques: Some say that it is not as capitalist as it should be and lacks efficiency and profitability. Others accuse it of selling its soul and interacting far too much with the capitalist world.[2] But, as Claude Beland explains in a recent book, the Desjardins movement preserved its cooperative spirit.[3] Still today, important decisions are made by 14,000 people following the age-old principle of one person, one vote. As a result, Desjardins was one of the rare financial institutions that opposed Canadian bank mergers. To be part of a dominant world while offering an alternative is the managerial paradox discussed by Claude Beland in this chapter.

Is there a particular ethic exclusive to cooperative businesses? If I refer to my personal experience of twelve years as president of a large financial cooperative, I would answer this question in the affirmative. There is, in fact, a particular ethic for cooperatives. It is inspired by the idea that everyone can find meaning in his or her life by direct participation in the supportive development of his or her surroundings. An ethic brought forth by the values of democracy, mutual help, and responsibility and by a vision of a society where everyone has a place and a role to play. The cooperative world believes in the slogan, "All for one and one for all." Yes, there is a cooperative spirituality and ethic.

However, given the major changes that have been upsetting the world in the last few years, I realize that, today, this ethic is put to the test. I don't have concrete examples of spiritual and ethical disintegration but I find it useful to stress that, regarding values, there are important challenges for the cooperative world.

To better understand my remarks, let me first present the Desjardins movement for those of you who don't know it. It is a vast network of local financial cooperatives called "Caisses Populaires." The first ones came into being at the beginning of the century. Since then they haven't stopped multiplying and developing. Today, there are more than 1,100 Caisses Populaires across Quebec. These are businesses that, by virtue of their cooperative status, belong to the members and where a volunteer board is elected each year at the annual general meeting of the members. As a group, they are called the Movement des Caisses Desjardins. This organization has become Quebec's most important financial institution. The Desjardins movement has more than 40,000 employees. It relies on the involvement of about 14,000 volunteer managers. It offers its services to 15 million members and its assets total more than $70 billion Canadian.

This cooperative model is not unique. As well as being president of the Caisses Desjardins movement, I am privileged to preside over the International Association of Cooperative Banks. Subsequently, I often have the opportunity to consort with financial cooperatives on all continents, especially in Europe where we find the world's largest cooperative banks. All those cooperatives purvey the same values.

From its origins, the cooperative movement presents itself as a true societal project. It began in the nineteenth century in reaction to the abuses of economic liberalism and proposed to resist this theory of laissez-faire dedicated to the fight for life. On the contrary, the pioneers of cooperation proposed a union for life approach. As well, the founders of the cooperative movement refused to accept a double standard of morality: one for social life, the other for the business world. They didn't appreciate the concept that a human being's conduct was determined by different rules depending on the nature of one's activities: a moral approach for commerce, another for family life, another for politics, one for spirituality, and so forth. What we find here is the rejection of fragmentation described by Ian I. Mitroff (Chapter 2). These founders wanted a system that would recognize human beings as a whole, a global being; not a father one moment, a businessman the next, a being with or without a soul, depending on the context.

From the start, the cooperative movement aimed to view workers and consumers as persons which is why the cooperative enterprise gives its power to its user-members. It invites them to take responsibility, actively contribute to the progress of their business, work with others and incorporate solidarity, this last element being the basic mortar of development of any society worthy of this name. In brief, we could say that by proclaiming that economic activity is not an end but a means to an end, the pioneers of cooperation were advocating what I would call an ethics of the common good and of responsibility in the hope of limiting the negative effects of profit ethics.

Alphonse Desjardins, founder of the Desjardins movement, was inspired by this cooperative ethics. As a Christian, he found in the cooperative movement values of solidarity, mutual help, fraternity, and charity that were taught in his religion. Hence, he used God as his main accomplice in his fight for the first cooperatives. In Alphonse Desjardins's documents we find this beautiful prayer written during the start-up of the first Caisse Populaire in a time when he doubted the feasibility of his project. In this prayer he says to God, "If you believe the adventure I am undertaking is prompted by pride, if you think it's a foolish idea which will not help my compatriots, rid my mind of this foolish idea. I am counting on You."

In order for Alphonse Desjardins to continue his work, one of Quebec's bishops, Monsignor Grondin, came to his aid by saying "No, this is truly God's will."

The founder of this great cooperative movement was very preoccupied by the poverty and vulnerability of too many of his compatriots. Many were exploited by factory owners or victims of poorly planned agriculture. Alphonse Desjardins, as stenographer for the Canadian Parliament in Ottawa, witnessed all the debates. To do his part, he looked for a concrete and efficient way to give a certain amount of dignity back to the citizens.

Throughout the course of his readings and research, Alphonse Desjardins discovered the European cooperative movement. After many months of study and correspondence with the leaders of various European of financial cooperatives, he founded the Caisses Populaires. His invitation read as follows:

Create in all your groups a center for savings and loans, a treasury where your strengths and energy will multiply and earn you the respect of all. Beside the church steeple, found a Caisse Populaire where your economic activities will flourish and where your civic virtues will find an admirable venue.

Understandably, many did not believe in Desjardins's project. They underestimated the solidarity and energy engendered by any humanely generous project inspired by a common action and by the desire to do good, not only for oneself but for others as well. Improving one's life and that of the community by pooling savings in a business where everyone is equal—one's contribution, as small as it may seem, thus becomes perceptibly valuable. This has proven to be an objective capable of mobilizing people and soliciting many decades of effort and strenuous work.

Soon, the Desjardins movement will celebrate its 100th anniversary. This is, for us, a great success. Its mission today is still the same: Through concrete action, contribute to the economic and social well being of people and communities while educating the public about democracy, economy, responsibility, and solidarity. But if the fundamental mission of the Desjardins movement hasn't changed and if the cooperative structure is still intact, we have to admit that the cooperative spirit and its management practices found more fertile ground in days past, as Mrs. Lefebvre explained in her historical review (see Chapter 3). During that period where an ethic of the common good was standard fare, mutual, fraternal, and community-oriented enterprises were flourishing because the daily practices of those organizations coincided with the values of the majority. Those values included solidarity and mutual help where the sense of community was strong and where people shared and practiced the same religion. It was a time when collective values were strong enough that people from different milieus were not influenced by more liberal or capitalist conceptions espoused by many economists and theorists. These people had a very different opinion. According to them, social preoccupation of business people would only hinder the economy. These defenders of profit ethics didn't hesitate to reproach entrepreneurs regarding their humanist preoccupations because, in their opinion, it had nothing to do with the primary objective of businesses: profit.

I would also like to add that it was easier to uphold the cooperative spirit when there was limited communication. Human isolation facilitated the emergence of a strong feeling of belonging to their surroundings, their businesses, and their institutions. As a result savings and loans cooperatives were closer to their members and allowed the former more leeway with normal management rules. It even permitted giving credit based only on the integrity of certain individuals. During the last few decades, however, the evolution of communication technology improved mobility, diluted the feeling of belonging, and opened new horizons to the point of shrinking the planet. Today, market globalization profits first and foremost those who have the capacity to conquer new markets that were up to now inaccessible. Only large corporations succeed in opening new markets. As a result, we see the creation of megaenterprises by acquisitions, mergers, or new partnerships. Globalization brought forth new competition on all markets and affected consumer behavior, including that of cooperative members, not only in Quebec but everywhere in the world.

Today, the consumer's individualism is constantly stimulated. It is even more apparent in financial services where choices are increasingly motivated by personal gain and are influenced by profit-minded financial consultants. Purchases, savings, or investments are chosen based solely on performance or individual gain without considering the effect on collective enrichment or local development. To that we add the increasing number of exchanges between nations creating certain normalization in the rules to which we must comply. The law of the market being dominant, the profit ethic has priority.

Given these changes and the evolution of the members' needs, financial cooperative practices have consequently evolved as well. Compared to megabanks, small financial organizations quickly realized that they didn't have the means to meet the needs of their clients or, in the case of cooperatives, their members. To face the competition, small financial cooperatives had to keep up with the latest in technology and hire specialists with greater skills (not necessarily people trained within the cooperative). To absorb these new costs, important financial resources had to be mobilized. Small cooperative enterprises couldn't do this alone and therefore were obliged to regroup, delegate responsibilities, create alliances, and sometimes even merge. This evolution was not without tension. Here are a few examples.

As you know, in a capitalist enterprise, capital is the measure of property that an investor holds in an enterprise. If you hold 50 percent of the shares of an enterprise, you are the owner at 50 percent. It is also the measure of your voting rights as a shareholder and of profit sharing. In addition, this capital acquires added value and has a speculative value that allows it to be registered on the stock exchange. This type of capital doesn't exist within cooperatives. It can't exist because the enterprise's control is practiced democratically. The "one person = one vote" rule confirms the democratic character of the cooperative. As for profit sharing, cooperatives will give profits according to the involvement of the member within the cooperative and not in proportion to invested capital.

If we look at the ownership and the control of the enterprise as well as profit sharing, cooperative rules differ from traditional businesses. In a protected market, cooperative rules were more easily integrated. But already, the normalization of rules that the dominant system (capitalism) imposes creates strong pressures on cooperative practices. For example, when cooperatives go on international markets to do financial transactions, they must adapt to the only recognized rule, that of capitalism. This often forces them to perform many legal contortions, which might lead to the belief that financial cooperatives look more and more like traditional banks.

For example, not too long ago, unable to find sufficient capital in cooperative ranks to reinforce its capitalization and development, (since the rules of capitalism for all financial institutions around the world are now decided in Bâle, Switzerland instead of locally) Desjardins was forced to create a stock corporation, Capital Desjardins Inc., a capitalist enterprise where all the shares are held by the cooperatives—which somewhat appeases our conscience. Cooperatives must act this way when they enter international financial markets unless they want to isolate themselves and limit their means. They have to play by the rules of the dominant system and to interact with institutions and capitalist instruments. Capitalism is so dominant that it is unthinkable that it adapt to the specifics of cooperative enterprises. As a consequence, many commercial practices with the Caisses have been modified in the last decades. And each new modification creates new ethical debates.

Here's another example. Not so long ago, members of the Caisses gladly accepted equivalent deposit interest rates for small and big investors. This was a concrete application of the equitable profit sharing rule. The thinking behind this was very simple. The $1,000 of the small investor had the same importance for him as the $50,000 or $100,000 of the big investor and we agreed that that was worth the same remuneration. But the competition of capitalist enterprises modified the perception of investors. Since competitors remunerated bigger investors more generously, they became less loyal to their Caisses. Major investors demanded remuneration comparable to that of the competitors, which forced financial cooperatives to modify their rules and install a remuneration system that favored bigger investors. Despite themselves, the cooperatives were obliged to soften their commitment to the equitable sharing of resources and thus contribute to the growing gap between the rich and the poor.

A similar change occurred for service charges. There was a time when there were no service charges in the Caisses as they were absorbed by the entire cooperative group. The number of transactions didn't matter. But, under pressure from members that did few transactions and refused to pay for others, cooperatives were obliged to change their rules.

I vividly remember that the word "marketing" wasn't part of the cooperative vocabulary. It was frowned upon. Instead we talked about "member education." But with the arrival of consumerism and confronted by the force of marketing and competition and its effects on our members, we had no choice but to modify our way of doing things.

At the end of the 1960s, there was a similar moral debate around consumer credit and at the end of the 1970s, regarding credit cards. The evolution of social demands and the needs of our members engendered new practices perceived by many as clashing with the ethical code and the basic mission of the Caisses. Up to now, this mission was to free its members of debt and get them in the habit of saving and foresight.

The same happened with our salary scales. In 1985 we operated with a cooperative salary scale. The gap between the lowest and highest salary was smaller compared to competitive capitalist enterprises. But it became necessary for cooperatives to conform their salary policies to what was being done elsewhere in the business environment so as to attract the necessary high-level managers.

These are a few examples that illustrate modifications that financial cooperatives were forced to incorporate into their practices under the constant pressure of their members and the external environment. That done, they distanced themselves from the cooperative spirit as it was conceived and lived in the past.

Does this mean that the cooperative ethos in management practice is a thing of the past? That there's no place in today's society for an ethic based on the common good that would distinguish itself from liberalism and individualism? I don't believe so. I think that it is a temporary or transitory phase but necessary to ensure the survival of financial cooperatives. To survive and develop, cooperatives have to reflect the majority of their members. These days, the members' values are influenced by new enticements that feed, for the most part, on the ethics of profit. But in my opinion, for many reasons, these tendencies are reversible.

First of all, it is important to know that, despite all the concessions they have to make, financial cooperatives still maintain their specificity and their structure (that being essential). They are still under democratic control. As well, the International Cooperative Alliance congress confirmed its cooperative rules in a charter known as the Cooperative Identity Charter. In this charter we find what might be called "the basic foundations of cooperative ethics."

Second, cooperatives remain, even today, instruments at the service of their community. Every Caisse has to reinvest its members' savings locally. At the year's end, surplus funds are returned to the community, which doesn't preclude the establishment of community reserves, which can be used for the development of communal projects.

Third, we have to be aware that the cooperative movement's top management is constantly fighting for its right to be different. The original inspiration that created the cooperative movement is still present. The flame is still burning. This vision of a society for everyone, within a spirit of continuity and eternity that gives meaning to life, still exists. It is the cooperative ethic that encourages all the questions and debates about changes, whether required by authorities or due to members' pressures.

Fourth, it has to be said that if cooperatives are influenced by the dominant system, they subtly modify it in return. There is a permanent tension, a dialectic that can become a humanization factor in today's world. We have never seen so many new cooperatives created and so many stock corporations adopt codes of ethics and even dare talk about spirituality. This forum is an example of this tendency.

Finally, because cooperatives allow populations to be more organized as big upheavals are shaking our planet, I think they are becoming more and more pertinent and that, in synchronicity with the development of a global economy, we are becoming citizens of the world. At the same time, people recognize the necessity to develop local or regional economies to continue to live where they want to live. To do this, people need common tools permitting them to be more responsible. Just like all cooperatives, people would greatly benefit from banding together and developing strong institutions and enterprises that they own and control.

The perverse effects of globalization and liberalism as we know them bring forth more and more worries and questions. The concentration of riches, the growing number of people without a political voice and increased poverty make many people stand up and say, "All of this makes no sense!" (we read and hear it more and more as Thierry Pauchant reminded us in the introduction of this book). When there's no more meaning there's no more life.

It is interesting to note that cooperators always had many allies in their fight to insert a bit more humanity in the economic world and in collective business. Today, a greater number of people and organizations in various parts of the world are fighting for a more humane society. They hope to bring the person back to the center of all preoccupations. They're working so that the economy is at the service of society and not the other way around. More and more organizations and businesses consider themselves part of what we call the social economy or the economy of solidarity. Moreover, at the last economic summit held in Quebec, as you know there was even the creation of a social economy stream and this stream continues to grow since it has become almost permanent. This research on the integration of ethics and spirituality in management and leadership in enterprises is at the heart of this forum and points out the importance of this need within the business environment, as mentioned by Mr. Jean-Marie Toulouse, the director of HEC Montreal (see Chapter 1).

One more wish needs to be expressed: Under the strong winds of globalization, we had to act quickly and trade teaching for the broader notion of education. Without losing any time, we had to rapidly acquire financial, economic, and technical knowledge to catch up with those who already have it. By doing so, I think that we have neglected society's education on democracy and solidarity. This education has to become a priority in order to humanize society and the economy. Here is, in my opinion, today's challenge, an ethical challenge. And if life is to remain appealing and meaningful for the majority, meeting this challenge is not an option but a necessity.

6

Reconciling Human Happiness and Profitability: Mission Possible Thanks to Sixteen New Management Tools

J.-Robert Ouimet

EDITOR'S NOTE

In this chapter, J.-Robert Ouimet, chairman of the board and chief executive officer of three medium-size food industry companies, describes how human and spiritual values have become institutionalized over the last twenty years within his businesses. Christian inspired, but open to other religions and spiritual traditions, this institutionalization is particularly sophisticated. It has been the subject of a great deal of research and experimentation during the last forty years; the subject of a doctoral thesis submitted recently by Mr. Ouimet; and it has integrated the personal observations of international person-alities such as Mother Teresa. This institutionalization is based on the defi-nition of the types of responsibilities and values to pursue. It has also given rise to the development of sixteen innovative management tools whose effi-ciency has been evaluated by nineteen systematic surveys at this point.

This case study is a concrete demonstration of the necessity to use sys-temic thinking in management (see Chapter 2), even if the experiment con-ducted by Mr. Ouimet is, for the time being, primarily focused within his organization (employees, managers, board of directors, and so on).[1] He is adamant about the difference between the need to humanize and spiritualize (see the introductory chapter). Mr. Ouimet, whose experiments have been covered in business magazines, concludes by affirming that the success of this institutionalization proves that it is possible to reconcile economic, ethical, and spiritual wealth in a market economy and in an industry where competition is governed by huge corporations.[2] He also suggests that this institutionalization is transferable to other companies and other cultures, if a minimum of four conditions are met.

From the outset, I want to particularly thank Jean-Marie Toulouse for his decision to hold the first Biannual International Forum on Management, Ethics, and Spirituality at HEC Montreal. This first FIMES marks the first step toward the achievement of an ideal and a dream that were born in my heart when I began my studies at HEC, and subsequently developed at Fribourg and Columbia Universities.

Allow me to share a unique experiment that has taken place over the last twenty years in the three companies I have had the privilege of directing. I have described this experience in a thesis for which I was granted a Ph.D. in economics and social sciences from the University of Fribourg in Switzerland.[3]

First, I will briefly describe the ongoing experiment that we have undertaken within our three companies, an experiment that we call *Our Project*. I will then introduce the main contributors, their responsibilities as well as the values embodied in *Our Project*. Afterward, I will enumerate the sixteen innovative management tools that we have discovered, experimented with, and tested in the last twenty years. Finally, after discussing certain quantitative and qualitative statistics derived from a number of surveys, I will outline the principal conclusions of this extraordinary experience.

WHAT IS *OUR PROJECT*?

Essentially, *Our Project* is the research and testing of innovative management tools that allow for the development of specific activities which promote the integration of humane and spiritual values within the company. This research was carried out in three food industry companies which I have the privilege of running. These three companies have employed, since the beginning of the surveys, up to 360 full-time and 199 part-time employees.

Since its beginnings *Our Project* has pursued one fundamental objective: to demonstrate that it is possible to reconcile the workers' happiness and profitability in a company that functions in a market economy, wherein one must make a profit, not only to survive but to develop.

Our Project, however, was not built in a day. It is the product of I don't know how many hours of reflection and analysis; be it the doctrine of social Christian thinking, or important texts like that of Arthur Rich.[4] It is also the result of a number of exchanges with many international figures such as Mother Teresa, who accepted to discuss and review *Our Project* with us. We based *Our Project* upon these many reflections, analyses, and discussions. Nonetheless it would not have been possible without having fulfilled the following two conditions which we established at the outset.

1. The full and total recognition of the collective and individual freedom of the participants in *Our Project*. This condition also implies that certain members of the top management and influential shareholders accept the innovative management tools that emanated from the project.

2. The complete understanding that *Our Project* could not come to be without the practice of certain types of spirituality like silence, meditation, and in certain cases, prayer, since spirituality is the irrefutable foundation of the project.

THE TYPES OF RESPONSIBILITIES IN THE DEVELOPMENT OF *OUR PROJECT*

Let us now look at the responsibilities of those that participated in *Our Project*. We identified six types of responsibility (the six circles in Figure 6.1) which form the basic structure of *Our Project*. The arrows on the illustration indicate the "value flow" between the six types of responsibility.

First Type: Responsibilities toward Those Who Work in the Enterprise and toward Their Families

These responsibilities are numerous and the two most important are the following:

1. The company must recognize that work exists for the individual and not the other way around; human dignity is primary and each person represents that which is most precious to the company because each person is created, inhabited, and loved by the Creator regardless of how we perceive him.

2. The company will encourage any activity that will encourage solidarity, fraternity, human dignity, and individual fulfillment, all within a climate of justice, equity, liberty, and discipline and with constant attention to efficiency and productivity.

This is quite the plan of action! But mission possible!

Second Type: Responsibilities toward the Consumer, Suppliers, and Clients for Our Products

Again the responsibilities are many. Here, there are two:

1. The company must listen to the consumer, their clients, and suppliers. In a market economy, if we consider that each consumer, supplier, and client is created, inhabited, and loved by God, then this market economy would be profoundly transformed. It would become humane and spiritualized without losing any of its productivity.

Figure 6.1
Our Project

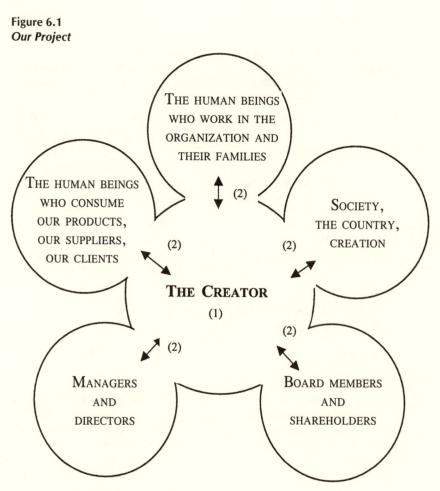

THE HUMAN BEINGS
WHO WORK IN THE
ORGANIZATION AND
THEIR FAMILIES

THE HUMAN BEINGS
WHO CONSUME
OUR PRODUCTS,
OUR SUPPLIERS,
OUR CLIENTS

(2)

SOCIETY,
THE COUNTRY,
CREATION

(2)

(2)

THE CREATOR
(1)

(2)

(2)

MANAGERS
AND
DIRECTORS

BOARD MEMBERS
AND
SHAREHOLDERS

2. In their attention to the consumer, the company must remain creative, disciplined, imaginative, determined, intelligent, use good judgment, show courage, and enjoy taking risks.

Third Type: Responsibilities of the
Directors, Executives, and Managers

What else is there to say but to repeat this sentence from *Our Project* with its deep content: "The directors must set an example and practice what they preach." Each of us can evaluate for ourselves the content of this quotation . . . I am absolutely convinced!

Fourth Type: Responsibilities of the
Board of Directors and the Shareholders

Contrary to what some might think, these responsibilities are quite diffi-cult to assume. Let me resume by saying simply that the board of directors and the shareholders have the enormous responsibility of managing the present and building the future while reconciling the happiness of each person working within the company with generating the necessary profit for its continua-tion. Quite the challenge, but again, mission possible; our research has proven it.

Fifth Type: Responsibilities toward Society,
the Nation, and All of Creation

What else is there to say here but that the company must be a good corporate citizen by participating in the quest for the common good as op-posed to only looking out for their own interests.

Sixth Type: Ultimate Responsibilities toward the
Creator, the Supreme Being, or the God of Love

Finally, the realization of *Our Project* is only ultimately possible if the people involved accept not only to work very hard, but also to call on their resources, to call on the help of their Creator or of any other transcendental value.

THE VALUES ASSOCIATED WITH THE SIX TYPES
OF RESPONSIBILITIES OF *OUR PROJECT*

I have briefly presented an overview of some of the principle responsi-bilities that are incumbent on those involved in pursuing our objective. We have come to realize that *Our Project* conveys at least twenty humane and Christian values. In Table 6.1, we have noted certain values that emerged from each of the six types of responsibilities inherent to the project. There are others, like listening to others, freedom, peace, serenity, authority, and appreciation. These values are interrelated and in continual movement in time. They vary according to the points of view, the changing needs, the culture, and the hierarchy of values of each person at work. As we will see later, we have been able to identify, and in some instances quantify, these values.

Unfortunately, in the time that I have, I will not be able to identify all the values that circulate within the company. Let me, then, identify those that can be found within two of the types of responsibilities that I have just described (see Figure 6.1 and Table 6.1). For example, in the values asso-ciated with our responsibilities as a board of directors or as shareholders, financial prudence is clearly identified as the third value, whereas justice is

Table 6.1
Principal Groups of Values Associated with Each Type of Responsibility of the Participants in *Our Project*

Types of responsibility	Values of the first order	Values of the second order	Values of the third order
Our responsibility toward those that work in the company and their families	Human dignity	Justice, truth	Productivity
Our responsibility toward the human beings who are the consumers of our products— our suppliers and our clients	Responsibility	Productivity	Solidarity
Our responsibility as directors, executives, and managers	Efficiency	Honesty, human dignity	Judgment, wisdom
Our responsibility as members of the board of directors or as shareholders	Humility	Justice	Financial caution
Our responsibility toward society, the nation, and creation	Working toward the common good	Solidarity	Justice
Our ultimate responsibility toward the creator, or supreme being, or god of love	Faith	Hope, mercy, forgiveness	Charity, love, fraternity

in the second order and humility is a value of the first order. Yes, I really did say humility was in the first order! This is only an example. But what we must remember is that these values are in continuous movement, in retroactive loops in time, as the arrows in the illustration suggest. And these values also vary according to the point of view, the needs, the culture, and the value scale of each person working within the company.

WHAT ARE THESE GREAT, NEW, NONCONVENTIONAL MANAGEMENT TOOLS?

The discovery and use of the many circulating values which we find in the six types of responsibilities identified in *Our Project* are neither a hallucination nor a static approach. On the contrary, the sum of these values has given rise to a large number of management tools which are equally innovative and nonconventional; to my knowledge, tools of this type have never been used over a long period of time in the same company elsewhere in the world.

I will briefly describe the entire series of sixteen innovative, nontraditional management tools, which were discovered and applied over the last twenty years. This, in fact, is the most novel contribution of our work.

The tools are grouped into three different classes according to the values which they advocate: seven of them relate to humanizing values, five relate to an equal mix of humanizing and spiritualizing values, and four relate primarily to spiritual values. I will attempt to succinctly describe each of these tools, fully aware that in a few words I can hardly render all their facets.

Seven Tools Proffering Humanizing Values

The first tool is benevolent action, whereby volunteers, often in groups of five to ten people, directly help people in need. A "Heart Prize" annually rewards a few people in the company who have demonstrated exceptional human and moral qualities and have carried out their job in an exemplary fashion.

The second management tool, one of the most sensitive, aims to help those who have been dismissed for whatever reason. Often, and it is easy to understand, these people have trouble dealing with the situation. This unconventional management tool used in a very original way, accompanies these individuals once they have left the company and brings them exceptional humanizing and spiritual values. In another instance, when an employee is being hired, their husband or wife is included at the end of the process, in order to shape, from the onset, the spirit of solidarity that must exist in the company as part of *Our Project*.

The third tool is a shared annual bonus that is paid to all the personnel in the company. The amount varies according to each of their responsibilities and based on the companies profits. A supplementary bonus, proportional to the number of children that each employee has, is paid out at the same time.

The fourth tool is the creation of an ombudsman who watches over the "open door" policy advocated by the shareholders and the directors. In some ways this position becomes the interface between the directors and the personnel and works to insure, in all situations, justice and equity in the enterprise.

The fifth tool is the establishment of an internal nonconventional communication network that is warm and based on absolute genuineness—yes I did say absolute—centered on openness, listening to each other, human warmth, and positive interaction. A network where one learns to say "hello," simply and honestly, a real "how are you?" that has nothing to do with manipulation or increasing productivity.

The sixth tool consist of two forms of essential internal surveys, carried out every twenty-four months. The first type of survey measures the movement of values in the organizational climate about well-being and human happiness. The second type of survey measures the benefits of the values in these innovative management tools for theirs users.

The seventh and last tool (but not the least) is the development of a biannual strategic plan for spreading the activities of the sixteen management tools. This strategic plan for human, moral, and spiritual management completes, in an absolutely essential way, the strategic economic plan. The latter, which most companies have, very rarely incorporates the humanistic and spiritual needs of their personnel.

The Five Tools That Proffer a Balanced Mix of Humanizing and Spiritualizing Values

The first tool consists of a brief period of silence, exchanges, reflection, and sometimes prayer at the beginning of certain meetings, like those of the board of directors for the last twenty years. In the long term, this management tool profoundly influences the culture and the management style of the company.

The second and third tools are used according to the wishes of the personnel. We plan monthly or semiannual testimonials of people from within but mostly from outside the company who present their personal development. These testimonials express, and often very emotionally, the joys and the suffering, the successes and the failures, which mark one's life. It is essential that these testimonials do not contain lessons or advice.

The fourth tool is a personal bilateral discussion between members of management. This personal discussion allows for an exchange on a number of subjects, be they interpersonal tensions, self-confidence issues, or misunderstandings, and they encourage the values of solidarity, fraternity, and in some instances, reconciliation and forgiveness.

The fifth tool is systematic study groups of *Our Project* which allow for a greater understanding and deepening of the values advocated by the project.

The Four Tools That Proffer Primarily Spiritualizing Values

The first tool is meetings of small spiritual support groups in the company. This is an essential management tool. These meetings allow a small group of interested people within the company to discretely affirm their Christian faith or any other conviction, in silence and internal prayer. Let us underline that this tool can be adapted to any enterprise, in any culture, anywhere in the world. Yes, mission possible! We will return to this subject.

The second tool is the availability of a quiet reflection room for members of the personnel who want to isolate themselves, in personal silence, relaxation, and if they wish, prayer. There is such a room in every different geographical location of the company. This management tool also encourages evocative wall murals that convey different, enriching values.

The third tool is gestures of reconciliation, of pardon and humility, made by the personnel in the course of the normal working environment when friction or tension occurs.

The fourth tool is accompaniment, which means having a specialist who is able to help executives and the personnel of the company in a personal, moral, or spiritual process, whether it is individual or collective.

SURVEYS ON THE RESULTS OF OUR PROCESS

Since 1990, we have carried out nineteen surveys in order to measure the results of *Our Project*. Seven surveys addressed the organizational climate and well-being, and twelve surveys were on the effects of management tools. The following are the twenty values identified and measured by these surveys.

Twelve circulating values:

Responsibility	Solidarity
Listening	Dignity
Discernment	Productivity
Justice	Caution
Efficiency	Liberty
Honesty	Fraternity

Eight fundamental values:

Peace	Faith and Hope
Serenity	Truth
Humility	Appreciation and Love

In a more general way, all these surveys have allowed us to identify a number of important tendencies and trends in values within the company. Here are three examples: (1) a greater feeling of belonging and loyalty among the personnel in the company, (2) a gradual increase in freedom of expression and participation in the innovative management activities, and (3) a considerable improvement, from all points of view, of communication within the company.

Even more broadly, all these surveys have allowed us to clearly establish that a direct correlation exists between sustainable growth of the psychic and physical well being of the personnel and the durable growth of the companies' profitability.

The surveys helped to establish the fact that due in a large part to *Our Project*, there has never been a work slowdown or stoppage in our companies, and that our rates of employee turnover, absenteeism, and work-related accidents compare favorably to industry standards. Consequently, our profit margins and growth are often superior to those of all comparable industries in Canada. Yes, mission possible!

THE CONCLUSION OF THE PH.D.

I have described the activities associated with our principle management tools. We discovered and have used them in our company for a quarter of a century. As we underlined, some of the activities associated with these tools are easier to carry out than others. But what has been encouraging and stimulating in our case is that the sum of the values proffered by the activities of our sixteen management tools have had very positive results. Indeed, the surveys have proven that over the years the sum of these values, which were offered to our personnel, has allowed us to do the following:

- Instill a sense of belonging to the company.
- Increase motivation, productivity, and creativity.
- Encourage more positive communication and an atmosphere of solidarity.
- Make shareholders and the board of directors, as well as management personnel, more aware of the primacy of the human dignity of each person working in the company and the importance of honest human relations.
- Create a climate of freedom, where everyone feels more and more comfortable expressing themselves, and criticizing constructively in order to improve things.
- Reduce absenteeism and the turnover rate without having a work stoppage or slowdown.
- Increase happiness and well-being of all personnel as well as justice and equity.
- And finally, insure the profitability and the growth of the company, which is absolutely necessary when one understands the highly competitive nature of the market.

Don't you think these results are encouraging for all of us?

With the track record we have just seen, proven by our research, we can all conclude that yes, our mission was possible, despite the fact that it embodied two seemingly contradictory notions:

1. running a business that is competitive, productive, and profitable
2. insuring that the people that work within it are increasingly happy

We know that many people outside the company thought, and probably even hoped, that this experiment would weaken us financially and in other areas. The opposite has occurred. In our company, founded sixty-six years ago, we are about to inject $16 million in various sorts of capital. We are looking to make important acquisitions and we have invested several million dollars in the past three years in direct marketing to consumers.

We are also convinced that *Our Project* can be universally applicable. Of course the choice of management tools would vary from one company to another and each must proceed according to their own rhythm and specific culture. But *Our Project* is universally applicable given these four irrevocable conditions.

1. It is essential that the attempt at any project similar to our own must take place in complete personal and collective freedom.

2. It is paramount to secure the approval beforehand of certain influential individuals. It is essential that upper management or an influential group of shareholders are committed to the idea that the goals of sustainable growth of human happiness and profitability in the same company are not contradictory objectives. Also, the initiators of the project must be ready to take the risks and assume the costs of this experiment, including the gradual institution of the innovative management tools.

3. It is necessary to create a small spiritual support group. There must be at least a few people working within the same company or organization who believe in the process and freely and systematically share their openness toward transcendence. This can, depending on the wishes of the group, take on many forms: silence, sharing, and if requested, prayer asking for the help of the Creator, God, to support the durable universalization and actualization of the project.

4. The integration of the activities associated with the management tools has to be very slow. One must be patient. The assimilation is beautiful, long, and often difficult.

If these four minimal conditions are not met, I am convinced that the project will be unrealizable and never have the chance to develop over a number of years, in a large number of companies and organizations in many countries and on five continents.

CONCLUSION

I am absolutely convinced that *Our Project* is universally applicable in other businesses and organizations—large and small—and on other continents, and that the durability of the project is insured if the four conditions are met. Thus the economic situation at this beginning of the third millennium will be a little more humane. It may also be a bit more spiritual, which does not impede the efficiency of the organization and the competitive profitability in a market economy. Quite the contrary! Thus the economic world will have a bit more heart and soul. Thus, work will exist for man, and not man for his work. The human dignity of each individual in the workplace will be progressively reinforced. And when a human being feels that his dignity is being honestly recognized and encouraged, his self-fulfillment and motivation increases.

This is a project that could exist in every business, and every organization—government or not—whatever their activities, their management philosophy, or their culture. Of course, it must be adapted to the culture of the enterprise or the organization and its environment, according to its rhythm, and most important, implanted in a climate of healthy personal, bilateral, and multilateral freedom. The establishment and assimilation must be slow to allow the people in the company or organization to adapt or, when necessary, become accustomed to the new reality.

This is also a project that can benefit everyone, regardless of religion or belief, on all continents. More than twenty humanizing and spiritualizing values, brought to the workplace through the activities associated with these innovative management tools, are part of all religions and most philosophies, clearly with particular emphases and different degrees of importance.

For those who are particularly interested in the Christian faith, I have studied the social doctrine of the Catholic Church for more than forty years. I am now convinced that this social doctrine can be realized in the real world over a long period of time. What has been missing until now was a structured and dynamic management system and the necessary know-how to make this new system work well. This would allow for the actualization of the social doctrine of the Catholic Church. My thesis demonstrated that this system exists, and that it works well, thanks to the activities associated with the sixteen innovative management tools.

It is possible to persistently live with humane and spiritual values within a company without fearing—like many wrongly do—that you will weaken its economic position and subsequently have to sell or go bankrupt. It is possible to live with these values in solidarity, in fraternity, in justice and equality, in constant respect of human dignity, and in a climate of freedom that encourages human happiness through the normal ups and downs of life. It is possible to give a heart and soul to a business and to any organization, without worrying about bankruptcy or having to sell the company. On the contrary, one can expect a sustainable increase in the competitive profitability by relying on the cumulative support of the values in the activities associated with the sixteen management tools derived from *Our Project*.

May this long reflection become a useful contribution to economic science, social science, and particularly to management science. May it also bring to light the theological, moral, and ethical dimensions of management within a company that plays by the rules of a market economy and in all human organizations.

Yes, it is possible to reconcile the growth of human happiness and well-being with the growth of the efficiency of the whole organization. Yes, mission possible!

7

Managing a Public Organization: A Projection of One's Ethical and Spiritual Values

Vera Danyluk

EDITOR'S NOTE

In this chapter, Mrs. Danyluk, reelected for a second mandate as president of the Executive Committee of the Montreal Urban Community, which includes more than 1.8 million citizens, shares a personal account of the role her spiritual life takes in the execution of her public leadership functions. She does not hide her discomfort at disclosing her intimate process and considers this sharing even more difficult than the carrying out of her political life. Taking a systemic point of view as well (see the previous chapter), Mrs. Danyluk describes her relations with the people's representatives, her employees, and citizens. Although she refuses to impose her religious views and practices on others, she points to the fact that she draws numerous qualities essential to her leadership role from her spiritual life: the energy, detachment, and serenity necessary to overcome difficult situations; the emphasis she puts on long-term goals rather than immediate brilliant feats; the implementation of rigorous ethics for the sound management of "the common good"; an increase in congruence between words and action; her enthusiasm for serving her fellow citizens and her awareness of the nobility of this task; the possibility of going beyond the mediocrity inherent in any democratic system; and the inner strength she needs in order to publicly reveal the failures of her administration.

Stating that she encounters the divine mainly through people, Mrs. Danyluk also emphasizes the fact that she draws her refusal of hatred, rancor, and resentment as well as her capacity to forgive from her spiritual life. In doing so, she meets the two conditions facing the complexity and irreversibility of human affairs proposed by the philosopher Anna Arendt: the power to promise, the promise binding what is uncertain in the future with contracts and laws, and the power to forgive, which releases what was bound in the past.[1] If Anna Arendt doubted that forgiveness could exist in politics, Vera Danyluk's leadership demonstrates the opposite.

When I was sworn in as president of the Executive Committee of the Montreal Urban Community (MUC), I brought along my mother, my sister, my husband and my . . . priest to the ceremony. Some people could have concluded that I would be reintroducing prayer at the beginning of the MUC meetings or that I would be managing the MUC on religious bases. No, I did not announce any such thing and, in fact, I did not want to offend any of the people attending the ceremony. My gesture was simply a testimony of my convictions, a reflection on my inner congruence. My personal path had naturally led me to act in harmony with my deep values. The common thread guiding my personal and professional agenda is what led me to this gesture. What is this common thread?

While reflecting upon what I would like to share with you today, I told myself that it was both a very simple and a very complex matter. It is simple, in that it regards what occurs to me naturally in the management of this major public company, the MUC, namely the expression of my deep convictions through my daily activities. It is also complex, in that I must attempt to express in words and clear ideas the complex and sometimes even mysterious symbiosis that exists between my inner growth and the effect it has on my personal and professional evolution. Such a process implies that I reveal my interiority, the ethics that are mine, as well as my spiritual path. Talking about all this unpretentiously presents a challenge that makes me somewhat anxious. Even more, I must admit that, during the last few weeks, I was stressed out by the thought of giving this presentation. I am not usually afraid of challenges, but the challenges involved in my political life seem rather easy compared to that of revealing myself to you today.

I am neither a philosopher nor a theologian, nor a university thinker. On the contrary, I spend most of my time dealing with extremely concrete problems, solving conflicts, and doing my best to ensure that our public services contribute to the greater well-being of the community. To do so, I have to rely on the help of the people's representatives and on the support of my employees, particularly the executives who extend the management values I advocate. I must constantly be connected to my ideal of high-quality service at the lowest possible cost for my fellow citizens. These issues have inspired the three parts of my presentation: my relations with elected officials, with my employees, and with my fellow citizens.

MY RELATIONS WITH ELECTED OFFICIALS

Let's first talk about the world of elected officials. Let's face it, I am part of it, I am in politics. It is not easy to do politics in a world of budget restrictions, of quarrels between the various levels of government and between elected officials. In a world of ferocious competition, the public arena is a place where attacks are the daily lot of people who owe their legitimacy to their election by citizens. The difficult moments I went through recently around the time of the renewal of my mandate as president of the Executive Committee of the MUC, painfully confronted me with former friends, a few mayors of suburban municipalities, the very ones who had elected me the first time, those with whom I have to go on working. Very recently, some of these people—those very people with whom I was in conflict—and I managed to unanimously choose a new director general and a new director for the MUC police department. How do I maintain the continuity between my inner conscience which advocates tolerance, faith in people, love of others, fruitful dialogue, and my daily political life, which put the values that carry me forward to the test? This is where I have to strive beyond these values to reach an attitude of detachment and serenity, which only my spiritual life can give me.

Unbelievable as it may seem, I still care for these people. You might think it is easy to say, especially in retrospect. Here, I am at a loss for words, I often stormed and cursed, at least inwardly, during the heavy battles that were waged against my public image, against my pride. At times, I felt torn apart by the clash between my painful feelings and my spiritual ideals. But I have always chosen to rise to a challenge, even when it appears to be almost impossible to face. The fierceness of the battles only revived my inner strength. My capacity to be one with God helped me put into perspective those situations which otherwise would have seemed insurmountable. This leads me to ask myself the following questions: Is communion with a living God necessary to achieve what I do in such a tough political universe? Aren't there people who succeed in the same way I do, without a spiritual dimension to their lives?

This question leads us back to the more global issue which brings us together here during this forum: Does the loss of ethics and spirituality in public management lead to one of two outcomes, either an increasing decline in public morality, or a dangerous and deadly return to religious fundamentalism in public administration, as seen in some countries where vicious murders are committed in the name of a religious ideal? This is why I would be tempted to talk about "suspended" success for those who believe only in short-term results. I myself devote the largest part of my energy to long-term planning, built on the basis of the highest possible integrity. As long as I am unassailable on this field, I believe I can face any political battle. And one of the very simple secrets to conserving my energy, which is boundless according to those around me, lies in my refusal of hatred. Rancor, hatred, and resentment are energy-eaters. I could not accept being devoured alive for very long, otherwise I would not even be here today with you talking about it.

MY RELATIONS WITH MY EMPLOYEES

This leads me to my employees, whom I love with all my heart and whom I want to be the happiest possible at work. When I first arrived at the MUC, I wanted to introduce foolproof management ethics. Management was already generally very honest, but even at the risk of offending some, beyond ordinary honesty, I advocated congruence between word and action. This constitutes a much greater challenge than one might initially believe. For example, since I have been president, expense accounts have not stopped shrinking significantly. This might appear of minor importance. But when one realizes one is spending taxpayers' money, ethics demands that they be respected, especially when one knows that the vast majority of them, although they earn a living, have seen their net revenues diminish over the last several years. How could it be justified if their money was spent on frivolous or luxury expenditures that did not result in services for them? If there are no ethics there, how can there be ethics anywhere? Maybe all this has earned me the affectionate title of "Mother Superior." But a Mother Superior who smokes. . . .

By the way, I do not mind the title if it refers to the Mother Superiors of some congregations, who will only accept investing their money in reputable companies. To me, this is an example of congruence between the spirituality of their daily lives and their business investments, as was clearly reported in a CBC public affairs program that was recently shown on TV. We cannot lead a double life: We cannot have religious commitments on the one hand, and on the other hand, act as though our daily management of public affairs were a separate compartment of our life, giving the impression that we can close one and simply open the other. One of the most tangible benefits of rising to the challenge of rigorous ethics, in a context where my employees feel loved, is their astonishing creativity that leads them, at the best of times, to surpass themselves both personally and professionally.

How many examples could I give you? I would like to give you two, which might be outside the professional sphere of my employees. Of course, I expect them to be professional and rigorous at work. But beyond this, my employees have created a charity fund of their own accord for the Montreal Urban Community and a group of these employees ask their colleagues for donations, which are used to help people who live in poverty or young people. I can also certify and I am witness to the fact that, at the MUC, many employees do volunteer work on their own time. They give freely of their time and sacrifice time with their families to work with young people who have trouble integrating themselves into society.

When we had to make substantial budget cuts at the MUC, I asked that it would be done without laying people off. It was a big challenge. In our society, with its high rate of unemployment, it was unacceptable, in my opinion, to have more people unemployed. I have an integrated vision of things and this is not always restful. How could we not lay off anyone while meeting the demands of local elected officials, whose citizens collectively express that they are fed up with seeing an increasing portion of their revenue go into various coffers of the state? And this not always for tangible services, at least not from their point of view.

MY RELATIONS WITH THE CITIZENS

The daily life of every MUC citizen is affected by the services we offer. From the moment he gets up until the time he goes to bed, and even in his sleep, the MUC citizen relies on a variety of public services that provide him with health, security, equity, quality of environment, and public transportation. I do not intend to sell our services to you. I am simply trying to convey to you how noble I think it is to serve one's fellow citizens. I believe that the MUC is the purveyor of civilization, and consequently the purveyor of ethics. Civilization and ethics are indistinguishable in my mind. How could a society be civilized without ethics? Our efforts to apportion the citizens' tax money to provide them with a healthy environment, to protect them from crime, to promote the development of companies that will generate lasting employment on our territory, are based on ethics. My leadership would not exist if it were not based essentially on ethics. The current reform of government bureaucracy in Great Britain is based on a return to fundamental ethics on the part of civil servants.

We all understand that the idea of ethics leads us back to the true notion of "the common good." Some Greek philosophers had a very pure notion of what the common good was, which led Plato to say that democracy was the worst possible form of government, because it imposes upon us the law of the smallest common denominator, that is to say, mediocrity.[2] But mediocrity is nothing other than questionable ethics manifested in a concrete form. Without rejecting the modern ideal of democratic life, I want to distance myself from the mediocrity inherent in all democratic systems. I seek a return to this notion of the common good which leads to the highest possible integrity on the part of public managers, be they elected officials or civil servants, because fundamentally, it is the citizen who entrusts the government with his money to receive better services in exchange. I suffer a lot when I find out that some of my employees may have been corrupt. It offends my ideals. I love my employees and I wish them well, but never to the detriment of rigorous ethics protecting those who have entrusted us with their personal good for the creation of the common good. Stealing from the common good means stealing from the community and stealing from one's fellow citizens. I will sympathize with corrupt employees regarding the sad reality of the sanctions they might incur, but I would be even sadder if they went unpunished. Thus, I agree with the quotation by Lord John Maynard Keynes, when he imagined a new future society.

The economic problem is not—if we look into the future—the permanent problem of the human race. . . . When the accumulation of wealth is no longer of high social importance, there will be great changes in the code of morals. We shall be able to rid ourselves of many of the pseudo-moral principles which have hag-ridden us for two hundred years. . . . I see us free, therefore, to return to some of the most sure and certain principles of religion and traditional virtue—that avarice is a vice, that the exaction of usury is a misdemeanor, and the love of money is detestable.[3]

For me, I repeat, public leadership is either based on ethics or it is not. I do not believe that leadership can be either amoral or immoral. It would not last. If the police did not put an end to it, the citizens would do so sooner or later, because public leadership that is not based on ethics is against nature, against society. It is the purveyor of decadence because it denies us the civilization that we wish to create collectively. Even though the ethical leadership of public managers is not always inspired by a relationship with God, at least it advocates values that resemble those held by avowed believers. Personally, I have the good fortune of being God's partner in the leadership I exercise, to the benefit of my fellow citizens. I have the humility to believe in Him and thus to believe that I would not be able to carry out the duties that are mine without His unfailing support.

Some people, no doubt outside this audience, already won over to the forum's theme, might see in me a precursor of a return to civil administration linked to religion. Do I need to deny it? I will confine myself to saying that this would be mistaking the values of one manager with those that a neutral public organization must promote in a context of cultural and religious plurality. Respect for a public manager who asserts her faith and who claims she is inspired by it is not different from the respect owed to any public manager who exposes his or her beliefs and convictions, whatever they may be.

CONCLUSION

I would not bring this presentation to an end without relating to you an event that confirms several of my proposals. Last June, during a meeting, I presented my directors with an assessment of my administration. I told them about the objectives and ideals that I had set for myself upon arriving at the MUC. I thoroughly exposed the failures and disappointments I had gone through. I made this speech with all my heart and was greatly moved. One could have heard a pin drop when I was presenting my assessment. My directors' attention was marked with astonishment and a certain degree of discomfort. Why was the president exposing her soul to such an extent? Why let some think that it was a sign of the president's weakness? It was so simple though. Supported by the trust I have in my directors, I wanted to share my innermost feelings with them. I told them I cared for them and that I expected them to go on backing me up, especially in dealing with the political reality surrounding me. I wanted to encourage them not to lose sight of the services given to our fellow citizens, especially when dealing with particularly difficult issues.

If I had not acquired serenity and detachment in my personal life, maybe I might have abstained from giving such a speech. It would not have hurt anyone. However, many expressed their loyalty and encouragement afterward. I could feel people's solidarity drawing closer around me. I communicated with the human beings behind the managers. Finally, the ultimate reality that inspires me are the people who surround me, be they citizens, elected officials, or employees. What counts is developing meaningful relationships, beyond issues, conflicts, and management decisions. It is through these people that I contact God. My entire personal path has led me to this simple reality. My personal growth hangs by this life thread: the human beings surrounding me and the public services we provide them with to enhance their quality of life. Concretely, as a public leader, my spirituality comes from this bridge toward others, this communion with society at hand and its fulfillment.

I am a believer: It is my choice, it is my faith. It is the key to my serenity and the source of my energy. I do not expect to work with people who have made the same choices I have. It is not necessary. What is necessary is that I live in harmony with my convictions and deep beliefs. My management of the MUC is, I hope, a reflection of my values.

8

The Quality and Performance of Pastoral Care: Clientele Satisfaction and Efficiency of the Hospital Stay

Yves Benoît

EDITOR'S NOTE

In this chapter, Yves Benoît, general director of a major hospital, draws a lesson from the integration of pastoral care in the health network. The recent reform that shook up the local healthcare system—and which is akin to other such reforms around the world—led the network itself to adopt a systemic approach, a key theme of this book. The various stakeholders of the system—doctors, nurses, directors, various governing bodies, professionals, union leaders, clients, representatives of the families of patients, and so forth—started a discussion on a key issue; that is, which values to favor. These values, namely respect, equity, immutability, transparency, responsibility, coherence, and partnership, are similar to the ones proposed by the cooperative system (see Chapter 5).

In the midst of all these changes, pastoral care was asked to decompartmentalize itself and to become part of multidisciplinary teams whose tasks are centered on the needs of clients. This had two major effects: first, a growing acknowledgment of the importance of pastoral care for health, while distinguishing between the spiritual and the religious needs of patients; second, the broadening of the very notion of care, from care of the body to care of the heart and of the mind. Finally, Mr. Benoît refers to numerous scientific studies which suggest that religious belief and spiritual practice has a posi-

tive effect on physical and mental health. This includes, for instance, a re-duction of cardio-vascular diseases, of depression, of states of anxiety, and a reduction of the length of convalescence. This has been confirmed by medical doctors from reputed research centers such as the Harvard Medical School, Duke University, and Yale University.[1] In conclusion, Mr. Benoît wishes to continue to encourage the ethical and spiritual contributions of pastoral care for administrators and workers in the health system.

Pastoral care in a short-term general and specialized healthcare center is often not well known in spite of the fact that it provides indispensable ser-vices for the health and well-being of the population. My purpose here is to present a recent experiment in one of these centers and by the same token to highlight the role of pastoral care in the healthcare process as well as its impact on the teams that provide general care.

If you had to be hospitalized at the Anna-Laberge Healthcare Center, or if you knew someone who stayed there for a while, here is what you would read about pastoral care in the hospital's guidebook:

Pastoral care at the Anna-Laberge Healthcare Center provides accompaniment. Its team listens to, and respects all people; their life experience, needs and their spiri-tual path. We also work closely with Pastors of various Churches. Therefore, it is not a question of religion. May your stay at the hospital be a time of healing and hope in your life.[2]

These are not mere words. In fact they describe a management philoso-phy which is on the rise in our healthcare centers. It is a philosophy of respect of the individual, of the sick person, of the "beneficiary," as we call them nowadays. My aim here is to describe a pastoral care unit as it has become; its role for our clients and its indirect contribution—which is be-coming increasingly direct—to the whole organization, namely the programs, the professionals, the physicians, and so forth.

Going beyond client satisfaction and efficiency of hospital stay, our pro-gram for quality and performance became a reflection about the whole or-ganization. Pastoral-care programs went from being rather hermetic, even isolated and unrecognized, to a multidisciplinary perspective oriented to-ward a client–program approach.

The healthcare system has gone through major transformations in recent years. Through the Reform bill and its objectives, I will try to explain the dynamics of this transformation that has been applied universally. After introducing the main contextual aspects, I will briefly describe the opera-tional strategy that was used to develop a quality and performance pro-gram.[3] Then I will focus on pastoral care. I will also lay out the various results of surveys and studies on the contribution of pastoral care, espe-cially to health, and on the contribution of spiritual practices in general. I will then share a personal reflection concerning the value of pastoral care when added to health management and I will end with two conclusions.

A FEW CONTEXTUAL ASPECTS

I will not try to explain the structure or the very complex workings of the healthcare system in Quebec. But a short review of the law will allow us to understand the legal framework with which we have to comply. Essentially, this bill states that health facilities must provide health or social care that is continuous, accessible, and respectful of human rights and spiritual needs. Their goal is to find solutions for problems of health and well-being and to satisfy the needs of the various groups in the population. Given this goal, the health system must manage its human, material, and financial resources efficiently and collaborate with the other organizations in the milieu.

Beyond the law, pastoral care has a particular status given our own beliefs and those of the religious communities that were often the founders of the first hospitals. Indeed, normally the health center's director general's office would be responsible for this unit but very often the latter could not control this unit very well. Religious authorities were in fact the ones running it from a distance.

But the reform placed the client at the center of the system. Then the healthcare system and the healthcare centers had to revise their delivery of care and services. We had to go beyond the standards of our professional corporations, our groups, and our manager associations. We had to change the mind-set of our managers and staff, which was based mainly on individualism and corporatism, to a multidisciplinary viewpoint centered on the client.

Without arguing whether the person is taken as an end or a means, the reform put the person back at the center of the system. This forced the adoption of a philosophy based on management values that most participants shared. In the midst of the great upheaval triggered by healthcare reform, hospitals were compelled to affirm themselves. One may recall the saga of mergers, closures, departures, integration, compartmentalization, restructuring, and so forth that shook us up as health institutions. This also destabilized us as individuals, professionals, and health managers. It thus became important and urgent to consult and determine together what we wanted to build as an organization. We had to agree on organizational objectives that would respect the basics of the reform, the notions of participation, integrity, affirmation, and equity. We also had to improve the conditions for the population's health and well-being and finally to enhance the performance of the system as a whole.

Obviously, these dynamics made us inquire very thoroughly about our benchmarks of quality and performance. Consequently, we decided to take up the Quality and Performance Challenge and to create a special program in response. The challenge was indeed considerable. On the one hand, we had to take into account the policies of the reform with its major financial objectives and, on the other hand, we had to begin using benchmarks to evaluate our quality and performance.

The values that we wanted to promote became the keystone of our change strategy. Values became the focus of our discussions. There were discussions over a period of six months. I remember once that we found ourselves in a workshop with 150 people. There were physicians, nurses, members of the board of governors, members of the board of directors, and representatives from almost all types of professionals, from workers to unions. We worked together on the notion of value and we distributed the synthesis of our discussions around the hospital in order to generate comments as well as to broaden a possible consensus.

The following values were retained:

- Respect—treating each other with consideration, at all levels, from top to bottom and from bottom to top of the hierarchy
- Equity—reducing gaps and improving the distribution of resources
- Accountability—being fully responsible for one's decisions
- Transparency—playing with one's "cards on the table"
- Responsibility—commitment to service for citizens
- Coherence—harmonizing words and action
- Partnership—working together in the same direction

In this approach, not only did individual values become organizational values, but the client approach became our critical perspective. Concurrently, we developed financial analyses with a variety of management information systems and we created quality benchmarks based on an approach that was recognized by the Canadian Council on Healthcare Services and by health professionals.[4]

We also developed our own ongoing program for quality improvement. We organized focus groups with patients and members of the patients' families in order to understand their expectations. Constituted on the basis of programs for patients, eighteen committees analyzed these results and found the gaps between expectations and evaluation of our services. For each of these services, multidisciplinary teams revised their mission, identified needs and expectations, and modified the approach or the process accordingly.

THE MISSION OF PASTORAL CARE

In the midst of these transformations, pastoral care also evaluated and reviewed its mission with the help of people working within the organization. For many outsiders, pastoral care was often associated with religious ceremonies and rites. Within a multidisciplinary approach centered on the needs of clients, this perception was inadequate. Pastoral care then proposed to promote the dignity of the person, the respect of their spiritual and religious values, their beliefs, and culture with the help of other healthcare professionals. To be more precise, pastoral care developed the following objectives:[5]

- to participate in the global approach to change with all the partners involved
- to satisfy the spiritual, moral, and religious needs of in- and outpatients
- to favor spiritual, moral, and religious growth
- to celebrate the faith of believers
- to improve the quality of life of in- and outpatients

Pastoral care answers two types of needs: spiritual needs and religious needs. Spiritual needs are related to the search for meaning: the meaning of life, of suffering, and of death. They correspond to the soul's thirst for happiness, peace, tranquility, and inner satisfaction. On the other hand, religious needs include needs of belonging, integration, coherence, actualization, and encounters with the sacred. They are satisfied by participation in sacred rites and by the use of symbols which establish a link between the faith of a community and its god or gods.

EVALUATION OF CURRENT PASTORAL CARE AND OF LINKS BETWEEN SPIRITUALITY AND HEALTH

Two types of assessment can be used to identify the contribution of pastoral care to health: surveys of internal perception of pastoral care in health centers and various scientific studies that have been conducted on the relationships between spiritual practice and physical and mental health.

Recently a survey was conducted involving 100 people in short-term health centers on the perception of pastoral care.[6] It revealed that the pastoral professional team—priests, group leaders, volunteers, and various associated staff members—is now recognized as a full-fledged member of the multidisciplinary team. This service, according to the survey, is known particularly for its attentiveness, its presence, and its support. Pastoral care is also seen as the official resource for sacraments. Beyond these tasks, it is furthermore recognized for its crucial contribution to decision making and its active participation in various committees. This perception is radically different from the one that prevailed in the recent past. Not so long ago, some institutions wondered if pastoral care really was indispensable and if its budget could not be redirected toward other activities.

We can also assess the contribution of pastoral care to health through the numerous scientific studies that have been conducted on the relationships existing between spiritual practice and physical and mental health. There are three types of studies: general studies on potential relationships between health and religion, specific studies on the relationships between health and limited religious activity, and systematic studies on the links between health and structured spiritual activities.[7]

Some of these studies suggest, for instance, that people who participate in a religious service are less likely to develop a cardiovascular disease or arteriosclerosis. Other studies propose that believers involved in spiritual practices are less depressive and more mobile after convalescence for a fracture, as they show a more positive attitude toward surgery or accept long and painful convalescence more easily than others.[8]

Other studies also found positive relationships between the practice of meditation or prayer and various types of discomfort and disease, such as heart diseases, dysfunction of the sympathetic nervous system or states of anxiety.[9] Finally, numerous studies demonstrate the positive contribution of pastoral services on the physical and moral health of patients in healthcare centers. They state that pastoral counseling has positive effects on patients to the point where patients may shorten their stay in the hospital by one or two days and reduce their intake of analgesics.[10]

Of course, one has to be very cautious about these results. In fact, other studies suggest that spirituality, meditation or a religious practice have no or even a negative effect on health.[11] We cannot speak of a rigorous causal link because the factors involved are numerous and complex. However, more and more scientists agree that spiritual practice and the contributions of pastoral care are positive for physical and psychological health, yet they ask for more studies on this subject. A professional medical journal recently published a detailed report on the relationship between spirituality and health entitled "Soul, Medicine and Spirituality."[12]

These studies also provide precious indications on the current integration of pastoral care in health institutions. These services are now available in extended care, in psychiatric care, in emergency, in intensive and palliative units, and in all hospital stays. Members of the pastoral team are also more and more integrated in multidisciplinary teams and their contributions are appreciated particularly in accompaniment, spiritual support, listening, and religious rituals.

CONCLUSION

I would like to formulate two conclusions. My first conclusion concerns the contribution of pastoral care in the healthcare system. The results of the aforementioned surveys demonstrate the positive contribution of these services. We have assessed these services ourselves and we see that they really answer a need, a fact that has been noticed by many of this forum's participants. The response to these needs can be quite easily integrated into the client–program approach now advocated in the whole of the healthcare system. But, to realize this, pastoral care must modify its mission, let go of its special status, and join the systemic approach of multidisciplinary teams whose task is centered on the client.

This integration of pastoral care to this global approach also has a major effect on other services. It modified the dynamics of the overall approach itself. It is almost like a contagious disease. The increasingly active participation of pastoral staff in multidisciplinary teams brought to light new dimensions. We no longer care just for the body, but the heart and the soul as well. This adds other dimensions to the so-called global approach. I noticed this myself within some multidisciplinary teams, and others have admitted witnessing this evolution. We also noticed it in our surveys. The dynamics of multidisciplinary teams is changing. As soon as there is a member of the pastoral care staff in a team, the discussion is different and values change. The notion of ethics and spirituality carry different values. And this integration is in full bloom. For instance, a project at St. Joseph Hospital, in Hamilton, has started in order to introduce spiritual language, process, and content in the training programs to help staff to cope with stress.

My second conclusion pertains more to the purpose of this forum. In the institution I represent, we have a long way to go in terms of a real integration of spirituality in management. I am convinced that we are on the right path and that we must pursue this effort. Managers have a role to play in ethics and spirituality. Whatever our function and responsibility, we must all have a plan that reflects our beliefs, a theme that other people also emphasized during the forum. In my view, the first priority is to respect oneself as an individual and to be an example for others. This is the profile that society should encourage in our employees and our managers. Our own fear of disease, suffering, and death often makes us shy away from personal discussions with colleagues and coworkers about the search for meaning and other spiritual themes. Specific workshops should be developed with respect to this as, I believe, it would give excellent results.

Four years ago, when I worked on designing the Quality and Performance Challenge, presenting its results in the context of an international forum on management, ethics, and spirituality was the furthest thing from my mind. At that time, my only objective was to listen to our staff. If I were to draw just one lesson from my experience to share with people working in organizations, I would say this: "Listen to your staff; they could lead you to principles of ethics and spirituality."

9

Business, Values, and Spirituality: A Case Study of a Business School in Australia

Peter Sheldrake and James Hurley

EDITOR'S NOTE

In this chapter Peter Sheldrake, the director of an important Australian business school, and James Hurley, the head of its new Doctorate in Business Administration (DBA) program, describe certain principles for the integration of ethics and spirituality in business education as well as its inherent difficulties. Like an echo of Ian I. Mitroff, who seeks a radically different thinking and structure in management education (see Chapter 2), the principles proposed by Sheldrake and Hurley include the necessity to conceive a program based on the true integration of personal growth and professional practice; the structure of the program must also be adapted to the values it professes and not the other way around; it should enhance a "learning community" that is developed by both participants and teachers alike as opposed to just accommodating individual students; and the program must change from one which is motivated by knowledge for the purpose of control to knowledge derived from compassion.

After describing the problems that arose from both students and professors, the administration, and the general culture, Peter Sheldrake and James Hurley propose different mechanisms and processes which they find essential to insure the success of such a program: the use of experiential learning, continued cross-fertilization between personal development, knowledge, and practice; the development of a secure learning space; the use of art and literature; the solid footing in the notion of "a calling," both personal and institutional; the ongoing training and supervision of instructors; promotion of a fundamental change in the university system; and the support of the program's legitimacy by businesses themselves. Finally, by way of a Quaker story, the authors remind us that ethical decision making originates in the depths of the soul and from a meaningful dialogue with oneself and others; a dominant theme in this book that will be taken up again in its concluding chapter.

This presentation is concerned with management education in the Australian context. As management educators, our interest is in management education as one way or one strategy for seeking the integration of ethics and spirituality into organizational life. We do not propose to offer solutions to the many and complex issues in this topic but to contribute to a conversation where mutual learning may take place.

We believe this conversation, this dialogue must be contained or have boundaries if it is to be fruitful. The boundaries must include a very concrete understanding of the context in which our conversation takes place. Central to the context is the notion of change and the uncertainty that change brings. Another boundary is the awareness of how we individually and collectively respond to the situations we experience: the hopes, the fears, and the deep existential movements of our soul. We make the assumption here that the processes of psychological growth and those of spiritual growth or faith are closely aligned and encompass moral and ethical reasoning.[1] Our conversation, too, must be bounded by the particularities of the situations affecting our decisions. For us, the particularity is the development of a management education program designed to nurture the values of the human spirit. Last, our conversations must be bounded by how we know the world.[2] Here we mean the processes by which we come to recognize and know the truth. For us, this is the question of how we move from decision-making processes based upon the need to control—whether it be of our human resources, our natural environment, or our markets—to a process of discernment welling from compassion. Thus, using these boundaries, our conversation is conducted in a space we have called a *containing space*.[3]

The notion of space must be central to any educational curriculum seeking to nurture psychological and spiritual development. In this presentation we focus specifically on our experiences in the design and implementation of a professional doctorate in business administration.

THE DBA PROGRAM

In May 1994, the university gave initial approval to a Doctorate of Business Administration. At that stage, the faculty of business offered only the traditional research path to a doctoral degree. The DBA program was conceived and designed in response to a number of contextual issues. These included the apparent inappropriateness and irrelevance of specialized and individualistic Ph.D. approaches for those working in the highly interpersonal and competitive worlds of business and government. There was too, the need to see a greater degree of integration between what managers learned about management compared to how they practiced management.

It seemed that conventional research and professional doctoral programs did not foster this integration. There was the need therefore to seek ways to integrate professional practice, professional knowledge, and personal development. The emphasis on practice was critical. The last contextual issue was the need to provide in an academic program a way to nurture the spiritual and ethical life of the participants, enabling them to foster these ways of being in their organizational life. The program was originally designed for people entering or in the consulting profession and for those in the area of human resources management.[4]

Figure 9.1 illustrates the main structural aspects of the program. What is critical is the aim of the program; that is, to help people to practice with professional and personal integrity. In setting this aim, the process embedded in the design is more concerned with the movement toward integrated personal development and professional practice rather than trying to measure some final state. Figure 9.1 indicates the reflective nature of the process. We believed that there should be a community of learning, with candidates in the program as equally responsible as the faculty for the processes guiding learning. That figure also shows that there were two principal dynamics designed to drive the program over the three years. The first dynamic was to facilitate movement from being an individual candidate to being a member of a learning community. Or if you like, a movement from self to self-in-relationship; the second was a dynamic for both candidates and faculty from knowledge conceived as the accumulation of content driven by the need to control, to knowledge derived from compassion and our relationship with others. This latter dynamic might be construed as a movement from decision making to discernment.

In method the program was designed to be experiential; that is, the actual experience of participants and faculty individually and collectively provided the means of making sense and meaning of theory as well as generating data on espoused theories and theories in action.[5] We believe the design provided for an integrated curriculum. Our assumption was that only an integrated experiential approach was capable of reaching the forces of inner reasoning essential to ethical behavior. Much care needed to be given in designing the structure so that it was congruent with the values of the program.

But structure alone does not guarantee that there will be learning space, a space for genuine conversation. The creation and protection of such space is the crucial role of faculty. Faculty must both understand the experiential process and have the skills to work through to the dynamics such an ap-

Figure 9.1
The DBA Program

Time : 3 yrs

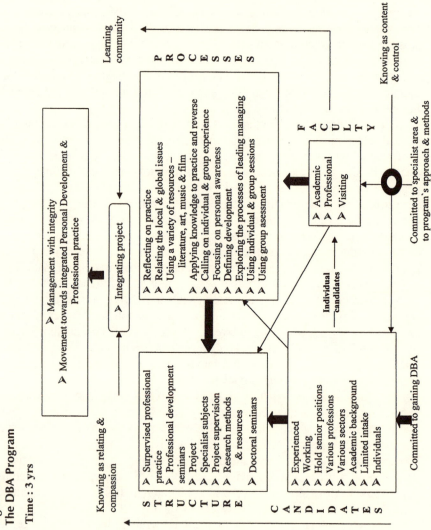

proach generates. Crucially, faculty needs to be able to foster an accepting and hospitable environment.

THE DIFFICULTIES

The design of DBA was in a sense utopian. This has proven to be especially so in the context of the emerging climate of higher education in Australia. The struggle to implement the program indicates some of the inherent difficulties to be overcome if management education is to be a viable strategy for integrating management, ethics, and spirituality. When viewed educationally as a holistic process, and when the difficulties of implementing such an approach are recognized, the question must be raised as to whether traditional management education can be a viable strategy for nurturing ethics and spirituality in managers faced with a competitive business environment.

The first area of difficulty arose around staffing. Critical to the success of the program, as we have indicated, is the role of faculty. First, faculty had themselves to work as a team, with each participant and during the entire program. Thus the faculty were to reflect the nature of a learning community. Essential too was the ability of faculty to be able to supervise the participants within the boundaries of the program and protect them from the pressures of the more traditional expectations for this type of program. In actuality, the program has had to deal with frequent faculty turnover, including a change in program director. Some faculty misunderstood the objectives of the program and had difficulty in adapting their discipline-based approach to a process-oriented approach. There have been insufficient resources available to compensate faculty for the time required over and above the administrative measure of direct contact hours. Furthermore, it has proved difficult at times for some faculty to deal with the complex group dynamics and the highly interpersonal learning situations generated by the program.

The second area of difficulty arose from participants. The program to date has proved challenging. The participants, most of whom are at senior levels of management, found such a program demanding of their time. More important, the design of the program did not provide the educational structure to which they have been accustomed, thus they were anxious and required more direction. Further, there has been resistance to the personal–professional development orientation, and questioning as to its relevance in the program. The issue of corporate confidentiality has been used as a reason for not sharing and helping each other, thus tending to minimize this aspect of the developmental process. Other difficulties have arisen around the behavior of particular members, such as the using of cell phones during seminar classes. The staff has had to resolve such matters without becoming too confrontational.

The third area of difficulty lay in university administration and the organizational culture of a university under tremendous pressures for change.

These problems surfaced in some of the administrative structures and procedures at both faculty and university levels, and with the organizational culture of a university in general. First, postgraduate education is facing tremendous external pressures in Australia. Universities are increasingly competitive, where postgraduate studies previously were managed by and large as government institutions. There is fierce competition for overseas students. This makes setting realistic fees difficult, putting smaller programs requiring a high staff–student ratio under financial stress; administratively it is more favorable to have large classes with fewer staff. Likewise, with high unemployment in Australia and especially with youth unemployment running at over 30 percent, there is pressure to encourage programs leading directly to professional employment. Such pressures shift the culture of the university. Traditional scientific disciplines are regarded as the "real" subjects while process-oriented subjects and courses are viewed as "soft."

Thus, this first professional doctorate program in administration in an Australian university was viewed with suspicion. The university's Graduate Studies Committee has been reluctant to recognize theses submitted by candidates from the program because part of their assessment was done by fellow candidates in the program. In summary, many of you will recognize the difficulties I have described as similar to those described by Argyris and Schön in moving from Model One to Model Two learning.[6] In this case, however, the movement was further aggravated by the particular social and organizational context and the program was shut down recently and replaced by a more traditional one.

LESSONS TO LEARN FROM THE EXPERIENCE

What might we learn from this attempt to develop a values-based program for managers? We note three important principles or guidelines emerging from our experience.

First, in a hostile and indifferent culture, faculty members that are connected with the program need a great deal of support if they are to create a space for learning. Such support may take a number of forms, but might include the provision for individual supervision and consultation about their activity in the program, team development sessions, and spiritual direction or companioning. Such support is particularly important in the formative stage of a program or when there is a change in personnel and the dynamics reflect a greater resistance to change. Support might also include actual training in experiential approaches and methods. It could include sessions to review the total program to insure its wholeness and completeness and prevent it from becoming the traditional, fragmented, discipline-based approach. Finally, faculty need contact with people, especially with people outside the university, who are professionally active in business, who support the values of the program and who are working on the integration of ethical and spiritual values within their organizations.

A second lesson is that there is a need to consider the program's administrative procedures; particularly the responsibilities of the program director in the selection of faculty. To have faculty appointed in their areas of expertise without the input of the director creates tremendous difficulties. This implies the need to develop a greater awareness among the university's senior administrators, despite the tremendous pressure they are under, to increase their awareness of the need of such a program and the educational and personal demands they make on faculty.

Third, and perhaps the most important, it seems that there is a need for some sort of transitional concept to assist participants and faculty in making the transition from knowing as the accumulation of content for purposes of control, to knowing based upon compassion; from decision making to a process of discernment. At the best of times, it is difficult for any of us to undertake what James Fowler terms, "the arduous and costly work" of making changes in oneself.[7] How well do any of us go about such change? A key element in change is the notion of transition. The provision of a "containing space" allows for the sometimes frightening and sometimes challenging task of disengaging from the known and secure.[8] Disengagement is the first step in making any transition. The experience of being contained in a safe space allows us to find the will and the courage to take that step into the unknown. In this space we can prepare ourselves for change. This process is also helped when we have our own way of expressing the nature of the journey in front of us, be it something tangible or a task, an idea, or an ideal. We avoid the word "vision" for obvious reasons. Choosing this expression is a creative act by each of us. It is not received from others without our consent, submission, or rebellion. Whatever its nature this "something" assists in the transition, enabling us to retain a sense of self even while we explore letting go of that which has up to that point been a source of how we define ourselves. What remains essential is that the space be held open for us, to both creatively and courageously explore an alternative mode of understanding the world and ourselves. Only if there is sufficient space to do this can we take the faltering and often stumbling steps toward the different ways of being.

We propose that to aid this transitional process we might need to return to an important concept in most spiritual traditions: the concept of *vocation* or *calling*.[9] However, we do not want to limit these terms to the individual, but to use them as relevant at the level of the organization in the society. We see it as relevant to talk of an organization's vocation as it is to talk of an individual's. Indeed, they are interconnected since the notion of vocation, calling, or following of a leader only makes sense within a social milieu. To reclaim such a term would, we propose, assist in the transition to a compassionate way of knowing the world and ourselves. It could provide mediation to assist in a major transition. Thus we could ask organizations as well as individuals within organizations, What is your vocation? and not, What is your share price? What is your market share? or What is your job?

Thus a person's work becomes how they integrate their various interrelated worlds as well as their responsibilities for the benefit of each, separately and together. Such a concept immediately changes what we mean by employed and unemployed, broadening the meaning to include the value of all of life's activities. It seems to us both paradoxical and a nonsense in our present situation of unemployment that someone working voluntarily or with enthusiasm and joy in a coastal management project or delivering pamphlets and newsletters for the local community historical society, are considered unemployed, while someone who is basically frustrated, bored and detached from their immediate experience but who receives a paycheck, is termed employed.

A STORY

We would like to finish with a story symbolizing a very important aspect of spirituality and the need to nurture whatever our particular spiritual tradition. We conclude our contribution to the conversation in this forum by recounting a brief anecdote from the writings of the Religious Society of Friends, more commonly known as Quakers.

When William Penn was convinced of the principles of Friends, and became a frequent attendee at their meetings, he did not immediately relinquish his gay apparel; it is even said that he wore a sword as was then customary among men of rank and fashion. Being one day in company with George Fox, he asked his advice concerning it, saying that he might, perhaps, appear singular among Friends, but his sword had once been the means of saving his life without injuring his antagonist, and moreover, that Christ had said, "he that hath no sword, let him sell his garment and buy one." George Fox answered, "I advise thee to wear it as long as thou canst." Not long after this they met again, when William had no sword, and George said to him, "William, where is they sword?" "Oh!" said he, "I have taken thy advice; I wore it as long as I could."[10]

Like William Penn, we feel uncomfortable with the dominant way of thinking and with values that seem to bring as much destruction as they bring promise and prosperity. Like Penn we would like to integrate our lives, to bring together our ways of knowing. Perhaps above all, we want that sense of union that our inevitable separateness denies us as already emphasized in their work. But we are aware that in this desire to live a more integrated life, we are out of step with our peers and the dominant culture. For us, like Penn, to be in such a position is uncomfortable, tapping into our deeper existential anxiety and uncertainty. The choice before us seems to be for one or the other, for the hard world of the bottom line or for relationships founded on compassion. In his confusion and uncertainty, Penn did what most of us at some stage do. We "split off" our deeper anxiety and disown our responsibility. He sought out an authority to give him the answer, to resolve his dilemma. For Penn, it was George Fox, founder of the Quaker movement. Of course, like Penn we might subtly bias our question, hoping for the answer we want. "This sword has saved my life; it's really foolish to think of not wearing it!" And how tempting to be in the position of George Fox. To have someone of eminence and social standing asking for advice, to be deferred to. Managers, leaders, key professionals, or even those much lower in the workforce but having a wealth of experience are often placed in this position, indeed sometimes seek it.

But George Fox does a remarkable thing. He gently places the decision with Penn. Ethical and spiritual decisions are not solely intellectual decisions, not decisions based on information alone, for Penn had all the information. Nor are ethical decisions arrived at by taking on what those in authority think, say, or require of us. For ethical decisions to be real, they must come from within the person, in full recognition of the relationships involved. Fox does not seek to control Penn, nor does he allow Penn to control him. Here we find a relationship of great integrity where Fox invites Penn to be responsible for his life decisions.

In our terms, Fox provides a containing space by encouraging Penn to listen to the truth within himself and to have the courage to follow it. But he does this without at the same time offering judgment. He provides space. Space contained by realities: the Quaker stance on pacifism, their simplicity of dress and lifestyle, the view of his peers, Penn's own experience of division and discomfort. Those are the boundaries. Fox, with his reply, provides the space for Penn to listen inwardly to his spirit. He further demonstrates his trust in both Penn and the inner working of truth.

The provision of such space is central to the conversation we hope emerges from working without our own boundaries. How do we provide such space within ourselves so that we can come to better understand the passions that drive us, can better face our deepest fears and the struggle between our destructive and creative selves? And how do we provide such space in our relationships with employees, customers, boards of directors, investors, our students, and those affected by our organizations' decisions? How do we avoid confusing the provision of structure with the provision of space? And how do we create such a space so it will endure time? For without such space, much of what is achieved will be superficial, lacking depth, lacking deep-rootedness.

The conversation in such a space will be with our ways of knowing the world and the passions driving us. It will be with the excitements and challenges of change but it will also be with the fears and uncertainties change evokes in us. It will recognize the many ways we and our organizations respond to change and uncertainty. It will also recognize with a sense of integrity the different ways people enter the conversation and listen to the contributions each can make. It will face the many practical challenges to be overcome if the space is to be held, encouraged, and grow. We recognize the difficulties faced by those creating such containing spaces. As Thorsen has observed,

Such a "holding environment" is difficult for most of us at the best of times. In times of stress, conflict, and confrontation, it becomes even more so. Such "holding" requires a willingness and capacity to expand and deepen our currently held views. It implies that certainties held "unthinkingly" and relied on as though they were universal and "obviously" right, may need to come to consciousness and even be let go. Such movement requires courage and trust. There can be no "sliding over," ignoring, or discounting differences. The "split-off," ignored, repressed and disowned, whether in our individual, group, or national psyches, needs to be encountered and accounted for.[11]

In light of the difficulty of the task, those in the conversation must be nurtured by the support of others and the literature and stories drawn from many spiritual traditions as well as the deep spiritual insights in poetry, literature, and the arts. It must be nurtured too, by entering into conversation with our physical world. Management literature and research that addresses issues of ethics and spirituality in the life of managers and organizations also nurtures and protects the conversation. For without this nurturing and protection, we deny the rich experience in which we are immersed and we face the danger of falling into naive subjectivism.

As Fromm remarks:

An extreme emphasis on individual responsibility can become an egocentric manipulation of others, a compulsion that defeats genuine morality and yields only a counterfeit sense of significance . . . a person cannot carry the burden of responsibility for his own moral salvation without a corresponding depth of culture to give him structure. Otherwise he will end up feeling isolated, lonely, and separated from others.[12]

Our story has another issue embedded in it. To enter into this type of conversation is costly. We do not always know the outcome of such a process and they may not be as we had at first anticipated or developed in our strategic plan. It may mean that we have to let go familiar ways of defining ourselves and defending ourselves from the inner sense of aloneness we all have. At one level, Penn paid a high price, isolating himself from his social class and letting go of those things he felt important and indeed useful. But because he was given the space, he addressed his anxiety, took responsibility, and replied, "I have taken thy advice; I wore it as long as I could."

How to let go is now a global issue and one, as human beings, we are reluctant to address. Yet we believe that unless the need to let go is addressed we will face social upheaval and environmental destruction that will make present concerns small in comparison. As managers and management educators we have a contribution to make. Such contributions may seem small and at times frustrating and irrelevant, yet we are reminded by John Milton of the following:

> *With good*
> *Still overcoming evil, and by small*
> *Accomplishing great things, by things deem'd weak*
> *Subverting worldly strong, and worldly wise*
> *By simply meek.*[13]

10

Dialogue on Part II

Claude Beland, Yves Benoît, Vera Danyluk,
James Hurley, and J.-Robert Ouimet

EDITOR'S NOTE

As said before, a dialogue is more than a series of questions and answers between speakers and the audience (see the introduction of Chapter 4). In order to go beyond the expert–novice pattern, the dialogue sessions during the forum allowed participants to ask questions and also offer testimonies to express their points of view and emotions. The diversity expressed in those dialogues on management, ethics, and spirituality, allows an initial evaluation of the themes preoccupying those working in businesses. Most fundamentally, a dialogue allows for the apprehension of the thought structure of a group and its basic assumptions, leading the group to a profound conversation contained in a holding space, as suggested by Peter Sheldrake and James Hurley in the previous chapter.

Participant: Certainly, talking about ethics or spirituality is in fact a question of intuition or grace for some. Thus, that experience is not measurable. My fear is that academics try to systematize that intuition which is faith.

We also talked about education. I just spent ten years at home raising my children. I realize that education doesn't begin at the university level, but during childhood, at elementary and high school. Every day, I watch over my children so they don't become a potential production unit. Teachers and professors should inculcate that critical sense at elementary and high school, even at university.

I would like to thank Professor I. Mitroff. Like him, I am often angry at systems that stop us from living in integrity with our faith. I also thank Mrs. Danyluk for her testimony that brought freshness to the subject. Thanks a lot.

Participant: Prior to becoming a professor, I worked in management for six years in two different industries. I've always tried to manage ethically. However, I had to face a certain number of contradictions, like here in this forum. First, I felt frustrated during our conversations on ethical decisions; for example, we didn't deal with the subject of investments in other countries that harm the environment. The definition that we seem to give to community in this forum seems only to refer to our immediate environment or our country. Second, I wonder if the employee–manager relationship is the most appropriate one to allow the expression of spirituality and divinity. Hierarchical authority is often damaging to people. If we are asked about our personal views on God within a hierarchic structure, the latter could be imposing its decisions according to another point of view. Third, I wonder if it is ethical for me to sell my services with regard to spirituality. Businesses will be tempted to use the precious resources of our spirit to increase productivity. And fourth, in relation to education management, I wonder if we should go from a sociology of control to a sociology of compassion or if we should rather encourage a sociology of democracy. Last, I want to ask this question to Mr. Beland: Is there room for a democratic government structure in our organizations?

Claude Beland: I will answer "yes" to the last question without hesitation. At this point, the cooperative movement's main problem is caused by the profound mutations in today's world. Everywhere around the world we question the pertinence of that movement, its values of democracy, solidarity values, mutual aid, and so forth, in business. Often, and not only in Quebec, but also around the world, we consult people—I call them ethics consultants—who have a certain distance from any particular business, to tell us if there is a future in staying focused on these values.

That takes me back to the question of education. Certainly, today's cooperative movement, even if it is internationally organized, cannot make the educational changes essential to the humanization of our financial and commercial relationships on its own. The dominant system is too strong. I make the distinction here between the Desjardins organization, the confederation, and the federations. We can, within the organization, respect and promote a certain ethical cooperation. But when we're looking for another kind of clientele, we become vulnerable and open to criticism. In response to that, we have created the ethical funds for regional development. I also founded a Quebec Fund, since people were saying, "It's terrible, Desjardins invests in other countries!" We didn't make that decision alone; our clients asked us to do so. And a cooperative system must listen to its members. We have $45 million in that Quebec Fund, but I'll tell you that there is much more in other funds. Let's not forget that the essence of cooperation is to gather together in a democratic manner.

Vera Danyluk: I would like to comment on the question of education of our youth. The personal growth I experienced in my profession came from being a teacher of moral and religion sciences and a pastoral worker for many years in the Archdiocese of Montreal.

Thirty or thirty-five years ago, here in Quebec, but also around the world, our children's education, including the transmission of values, went through important changes. We started with a very rigid system based on religion and then we transferred that responsibility to other groups. Personally, I am under the impression that at the end of the 1960s and beginning of the 1970s, with our new education law, we threw the baby out with the bath water. It is very sad. What we are trying to do today is recover our values. More specifically, I think it is true that our schools have neglected the moral and ethical characters of our children. That also confirms the importance of the parents' role in our children's lives in the first place. The issue is not only to transmit our values. We also have to raise them, and most of all, to set a good example. To me, setting a good example is primordial if we want to teach them our deepest values. It is not the media's responsibility to transmit values to our children. It is the parents' responsibility. We have to be vigilant and very present in our children's lives.

Unfortunately, one of the biggest social problem in our society is that too many children have been ignored too long. That is why, among other reasons, they are in the streets. That is a major problem in the Montreal Urban Community. Our young squeegees certainly didn't get the necessary support to orient them toward a healthy life.

James Hurley: Obviously education should start before university and college. I don't know if you are familiar with Ivan Illich's critical work. In the 1960s he wrote *De-schooling Society*.[1] His concerns were not so much whether we include ethics or values in the curriculum or what we teach, but was on the whole notion of the structure of schooling and of fragmenting lives, the idea of putting people in classes, setting them in rows, having competitive grades and encouraging the dynamics of the competitive capitalist society at a very young age. It is a fundamental critique of education. When children are sent to kindergarten because their parents work, it is "logistical management training." I think that Illich's whole critique on education should be reconsidered today. If we take the notion of vocation seriously, it should include family environment and parental supervision—which also can't be ignored at school. Any organization should consider the time that a father or a mother needs to spend with the child to be a good parent. I think these are the real issues; more important than questioning the importance of a few courses in ethics in a curriculum.

If I may comment on the question of consultants selling spirituality, our doctorate program was designed initially for consultants. It certainly was not designed to teach future consultants to sell spirituality. However, the type of knowledge I referred to concerns the origins of how to gather facts; is gathering information driven by curiosity and control or by compassion. It is very important that consultants become aware of the tacit values. It is not a question of democracy versus control. It is a question of being aware of the roots which motivate our willingness to know and to act.

Participant: I am the animator of the CIIT. In the word animator is the root animus or "soul." CIIT is a group of approximately forty large businesses that decided to work toward the integration or reintegration of handicapped people in the workplace. Not an integration based on charity, but based on economy, competence, and the added value of these people's experience. In this forum, a participant shared his experience of finding happiness after losing his sense of sight. That testimony is a message that should be heard by many disillusioned managers.

Our actions at CIIT answer, in part, the question, How are we going to turn spirituality into action? I will tell you that when somebody talks to me about a market's globalization, I am dizzy because I don't know what I can do concretely about that. However, if we could get the existing systems to cooperate to establish some solidarity, as we are doing now at CIIT, that would be a concrete application of spirituality.

It is a great privilege to participate in this forum, although my board of directors worried about the return on the investment of my participation. I told them, "It will be a human enrichment." And that's what it is. From the start, I feel enriched and I'm stunned by what I hear. Mrs. Danyluk expressed her convictions. I find that wonderful. Following her presentation, I had this thought: "Imagine a tribune of twenty top executives that came to share their convictions. What would be the results if, like Mrs. Danyluk, these people had the courage to share their convictions? I am surprised by the number of people in different businesses that share the same convictions, but stay silent. I'm also surprised that there are no links between these people and that we don't try to create these kinds of networks. If we allowed these people to express their deepest thoughts, I feel confident that we would create those bonds. Maybe this could be one of the tasks of this international forum on management, ethics, and spirituality.

I would like to share my vision of spirituality, which, to me, expresses itself in two movements. One movement is up, which is faith; my life is based on very high standards from which I can't fall. And the second movement is to go deep within myself. I'd like to share this phrase with you:

"The more I go within, the more I find others, because we are communication vessels." To me, spirituality is that. The highest inspiration and the possibility to establish communication between people, systems, and so on. If we were to develop that sort of spirituality, in a solid manner, whether it is outside businesses or between social organizations, I think we could build a more solid, just, and humane society.

Participant: I taught philosophy for twenty-seven years at a general and professional college. I've often been preoccupied by those ethical questions. Now that I'm retired, I spend more time in a not-for-profit organization. What struck me, among other comments, are Mr. Beland and Mrs. Danyluk's remarks; how difficult it is to act according to our beliefs. Goethe said, "To act is easy, to think is not easy, but to find an adequation between our action and our thought is the most difficult thing to do." Your testimonies on this subject are very impressive. I also think that each of us can live that on a daily basis.

Those serious and profound issues also raise many questions. Spirituality is a sketchy concept. Mrs. Lefebvre reminded us of the importance of words that are meaningful. I think ethics rest on the knowledge of human nature. If we could all agree on the same grand vision of human nature, we could make a giant step. But, knowledge of human nature is possible only if we observe and perceive a person's daily behavior, what he says and what he does.

For me, this is a base on which we can agree regardless of race or religion: not only the knowledge of human being itself, but the knowledge of the evolution of the life for a human being. A person of my age, for example, doesn't have the same concerns or needs of a younger or older person. It is very essential for me to understand the unfurling of phases of human life in order to talk about ethics in the enterprise.

Vera Danyluk: Is there a consensus on knowing of human nature? I have always been impressed by the expression "to feel good about one's self." Maybe there is no consensus; however, early in my life, I understood that if each individual felt good about him or herself, we could avoid many management problems and employee–employer relationships. Through spirituality or some inner balance in each individual, we could develop a sense of well-being. It would already be a great contribution.

Claude Beland: In my presentation, I was supposed to talk about a system's ethics and the means by which our cooperative system could survive within a larger banking system. But I would like you to understand that, personally and in relation with my own values, nothing better than being part of the cooperative movement could have happened to me. I feel very comfortable in that movement because I can express my own values. I often say that I haven't lost my identity. To me, identity is the harmony between my values and my actions within my workplace. I have this wish that one day I will be able to express my own values in society at large; the cooperative movement was also aiming at that. But to be able to live that harmony at work is already for me a gift of God.

James Hurley: I would like to comment on the possibility to define human beings. Quakers have no etymology or no written doctrine but have one statement that unites us. It is a very simple statement: God is in every person. The understanding of that statement has consequences on whatever we think or do, for example, being violent toward others. If we could just build on that statement, we would have a lot to work on.

Participant: I would appreciate if Mr. Beland could elaborate on this question: Can we say that there is an ethic within the larger banking system, other than that of the cooperative system?

Claude Beland: Certainly, the larger banking system has its own ethics. I prefer the ethical values of the cooperative system, of course. I think that the larger banking system doesn't encourage the equitable sharing of resources, nor does it give the power to users whereas the cooperative system encourages that. In the cooperative movement, we think a lot in terms of responsibility. Our aim is not to make happy consumers but rather happy citizens. And the only way to have happy citizens is to have them share control. Our message is "Group together, you are responsible for your enterprise." This is not completely visible, but I have experienced this for thirty years and I can say that it is very real. Our 150,000 volunteer board members know what they are doing. When they leave after twenty-five to thirty years, they come to me to thank the Mouvement Desjardins and say, "I've learned something. I enjoyed my experience because I was serving my community." I don't think that this state of mind exists in the larger banking system. I'm not criticizing it, I'm just comparing.

The cooperative movement aims to build a society where people not only survive but live fulfilling lives. In that sense, living means to satisfy all one's fundamental needs: physiological and affective needs, being appreciated and loved, working with people, and being able to say "we are doing something together." I'm not saying we succeed every time, but we are moving in that direction.

What are the essentials that we'll never abandon? We will never renounce democracy, the democratic running of the enterprise without which we would become something other than ourselves. Democracy brings solidarity and that's essential to us.

Participant: For about ten years, I've worked within the orientation committee of the *Echanges* newsletter. *Echanges* is a publication directed to managers in the civil service whose goals are sharing and exchanging our management values. Last year, we produced a series of issues on the search for meaning and we organized an event with Thierry Pauchant. It was greatly appreciated and we received numerous positive comments and thanks.

I would like to thank as well the organizers of this forum. As we discussed earlier, the word "spirituality" is taboo in our organizations. Certainly, my experience confirms it. I would particularly like to thank the organizers for daring to use that word. That seemed very significant to me. We will continue to address the themes of ethics and spirituality in our newsletter. In our organization, we often feel isolated in our desire to work at the promotion of certain values. Even if some of our colleagues share those values, there is no place to express them and the pressures of work stops us from taking the time to discuss them. This forum is a precious place and time which allows us to build networks—formal and informal—and to realize that, yes, there are people, elsewhere, with the same goals.

What I find particularly interesting in this forum is its diversity: There is an exchange between the academics and the public and private sectors. I think it is too easy to say "The private sector is concerned with profit, the public sector is concerned with public matters." More and more businesses talk about social responsibility, and more and more public managers are confronted with the need for financial self-sufficiency and even profitability. If we take the notion of the human bottom line seriously, each person, academic, or manager, in the private or public sector is responsible for this bottom line and that is within their organizations and in society at large. It is essential to have a space to exchange and communicate on these subjects, like this forum.

Participant: My question is for Mr. Benoît. If we take for granted that ethics and spirituality constitute the management norms, to what extent can an employer discipline an employee who derogates from these norms?

Yves Benoît: I would tend to answer your question using the principal of continuous improvement which has existed for many years in the healthcare sector. When a team has good will and a good team spirit, the group pressure encourages people to a self-discipline regarding the pursuit of certain values, and when they ignore those values, they are not comfortable. It's more about self-control than external or managerial control.

We try to help people in their search for meaning so we talk less about norms. That doesn't stop us, in an interview for example, to ask questions about human values, similar to what Mr. Ouimet proposed (see Chapter 6).

Participant: Beyond profit, my search for meaning has always been to create courses that explore other values, just like our cooperative management courses, which explore the duality between economic and social finality of a business, as Mr. Beland reminded us (see Chapter 5).

There is a possibility that the private sector is ahead of the public sector on these subjects. The private sector is today condemned to excellence due to globalization and increased competitiveness. Within private businesses, we have discovered that social values are profit earning. To become more competitive, the human being is reintegrated into the core of the business, human resources are mobilized and the consumer's voice becomes central. All that is missing in this evolution is the practical integration of spirituality. I thought Mr. Ouimet's presentation on the subject was simply extraordinary. In his remarks, I found all I needed: the absolute, values, ethics, behavior, tools, and methods. In my opinion that kind of experiment has a future since it demonstrates systematic methods.

Participant: Our school is situated in Saint-Jean-sur-Richelieu. We welcome everyone who wants to join the army; between 4,000 and 5,000 people a year, for a period of two or three months. Our goal is to socialize them and integrate them in the armed forces. Before asking a question I would like to share some experiences.

When I was involved with the peacekeeping missions, I had the opportunity to work within two different organizations. The first had integrated a certain form of spirituality and in the second, the notion of spirituality was more or less eliminated consciously for all sorts of reasons. I can actually testify that during times of great difficulties and intense stress, the more spiritual organization was more efficient than the other.

My second remark concerns the notion of values. In my work with the United Nations, I became responsible for negotiations in a certain sector, along with Croatians, Serbs, and Muslims. A few years ago in a course given here at HEC, we were taught to respect the particularities of different nationalities in order not to offend anyone's feelings. During my mandate, I tried to find the unifying values, what people had in common, instead of insisting on our differences. We ended up discussing our deepest values. That approach allowed us to go forward in our negotiations, instead of going in circles or backward.

My question is to Mr. Benoît and Mr. Ouimet. For many years, our organization has been sterilizing, consciously or unconsciously, religion. Everything was black and white back then: There were the English-speaking Protestants and the French-speaking Catholics. The social and religious customs were obvious and transmitted throughout the organization. Today, there is a greater diversity—that we encourage—and that diversity is also in religious and spiritual practices. How to manage that diversity? We always have this fear of political correctness and don't want to step on anyone's toes.

Yves Benoît: I will refer to my own experience at Charles LeMoyne Hospital, a large organization with 1,700 employees, 300 doctors, 4 unions, and so on. We tried to identify a common ground for spirituality. Whether you are Catholic, Protestant, Muslim, or something else, you will always be concerned with liking your patient, with communication, with accompanying him or her. Our Catholic clergymen have developed relationships with other religious communities. They are better at this kind of dialogue than us managers.

J.-Robert Ouimet: The main reason for the long-term success of *Our Project* is the existence, since the beginning, of a spiritual core of three to four people who, for thirty years, never gave up. I can tell you that we even signed spiritual contracts with Calcutta and Saint-Eustache. It is very difficult to maintain that kind of support and to bring new values into business, beyond our normal work. Whether it is an employee working on a production line for eight hours, or a top executive, or a budget manager, we all have had it at the end of the day. We have to go slowly, take the time it takes. This project has been spread out over ten to twenty years.

That support group can be very discrete. It is not necessary to talk about it within the enterprise. Later, some people are asked to read some documents produced by the group to present the project. At first, they are uncomfortable, and rightly so. Then, questions come up, and we talk. Slowly, we reach an understanding. It takes years.

Mother Teresa suggested another management tool that we tried. It can be developed from the beginning. It may appear very high-risk—Mother Teresa was high-risk herself. It consists of creating quiet rooms in each workplace. That may appear very strange at the end of the twentieth century. Many people were uneasy about it. They would ask, "Are they going to hold a mass six times a day? Are we going to have to kneel each time we pass the room?" It took four years for people to realize that it was not necessary to do that, that there was no mass and no one was watching them. But four years ago, in an anonymous survey, 82 percent of employees answered the question, "Do you want to get rid of those quiet rooms?" with "No, we want to keep them. They are a part of us."

Another useful management tool to establish such a project, which respects cultural and religious differences, would be acts of compassion. For example, first a few managers, and then some employees, go visit the Accueil Bonneau [a sleep and food shelter in Montreal] anonymously once or twice a year during their work hours. They serve meals for three to four hours. They say, "When we come back, we feel less overcome by our worries. It gives perspective to our problems."

Finally, that which matters the most is to delicately, slowly, and gradually establish those new management tools and to be respectful of everyone's freedom.

Participant: I am an internal counselor in the public service. I work in a big organization with more than 9,000 employees. I would like to thank the speakers and organizers of this forum with all my heart. It gives me hope. I work in a highly hierarchical organization and can see both the good and bad aspects of management. I also meet with many people who only learned to listen and unlearned how to think for themselves . . . unless we tell them to do so. These people express a human texture of individuals who feel diminished, who have lost their human dignity and their potential to create, to dare, and to think by themselves.

I counsel executives. After a few years of experimentation with the "total quality" concept, responsibility and mobilization training, and so on, I noticed that all this was useless; we were only reinforcing the primacy of business and not that of the human being. About four years ago, we integrated a training program on spiritual values without talking openly about it. That program was called Leadership and Ethics and about 100 managers participated. We were helping people in finding a new harmonious organizational model, independent from what the boss wanted, but where life was present. We never used the terms "Creator" or "God," but we talked about life, values, dignity, and justice; the same notions brought up by Mr. Ouimet.

Until now, we had many "horizontal" results; that is, among managers themselves, but not a lot of "vertical" results, since the organizational culture is still too powerful. But I saw men and women grow. I witnessed people make choices, people who said "no," who risked a lot. But we asked ourselves if, by doing so, we weren't creating a cleavage between the employees' values and those of the organization.

J.-Robert Ouimet: In my presentation, I talked about humility; not in a spiritual or religious sense, but in the sense of being unpretentious. I think that one of the key factors in your testimony is the ability to listen to the other. That quality demands humility to recognize that I don't have the answer to everything. Listening to others is a start. It is a profound element of human dignity and allows us to share our joy and suffering. It is also the starting point for management and that is why the support of a spiritual core is necessary. To me, the expression "human resource management" is simply not human. As human beings, we are not a resource. We are unique and creative individuals.

PART III

PERSPECTIVES FOR THE FUTURE INTEGRATION OF ETHICS AND SPIRITUALITY INTO THE ECONOMY, MANAGEMENT, AND WORK

In this final part, three future paths are proposed as a way to better integrate ethics and spirituality in economy, management, and work. In Chapter 11, I will propose the views of the philosopher and worker Simone Weil on the spiritualization of work. In Chapter 12, Roger Berthouzoz denounces the dangers of economism and proposes the application of a systematic perspective in management, a major theme developed throughout this book. In Chapter 13, Michel Dion examines the similarities and differences between the vision of Jews, Christians, and Muslims on economy and management. Chapter 14 offers a collective dialogue on the different views and on the themes covered during the two days of the forum.

In Chapter 15, the concluding chapter, I propose that each management thought and action is based on a certain conception of truth, goodness, and beauty. In that chapter, I present the reasons that motivate the urgency to develop a global and planetary ethic and to render spirituality more concrete and social, and I suggest some strategies to attain these goals. Finally, I introduce a systemic model derived from Ken Wilber's work to organize the key notions discussed in this book, with their positive and negative sides, and I propose priorities for the future.

11

For a Spiritual Ethic of Work: Some Inspiration from Simone Weil

Thierry C. Pauchant

EDITOR'S NOTE

In this chapter, I present some of the views of the philosopher Simone Weil (1909–1943) on the need to base our civilization on a spiritual ethic of work. First, I give an introduction to her life and work. Although having a significant influence in many milieus, Simone Weil is practically unknown in the field of administration—be it in business administration schools or in business itself. I will also suggest several reasons why the work of Simone Weil is fundamental when developing a spiritual ethic for work. I will then explain how she proposed a view of work that is both existentialist and spiritual, as for her the activity of work was the point of concordance between thought and action on the one side, and gravity and grace on the other.

Finally, I propose ten suggestions given by Simone Weil to develop this spiritual ethic of work. These suggestions include the following needs:

1. to limit the race for world domination

2. to rediscover the notion of limit

3. to see our business institutions as both instruments of production and destruction

4. to go beyond purely economic considerations

5. to secure and democratize work

6. *to favor concordance between thought and action*

7. *to root thought in the person*

8. *to reinvent politics*

9. *to develop a new adventure of the scientific spirit*

10. *to encourage the ability of subtle mindfulness*

In conclusion, I stress that the rediscovery of the works of Simone Weil—as well as those of authors such as Chester I. Barnard, Abraham Maslow, Marie Parker Follet, and E. F. Schumacher—is indispensable for developing a spiritual ethic of work in management, our organizations, and our societies. In my view, the profound meeting with a person who perceives the world and behaves in it from the transpersonal level of consciousness (see the introductory chapter) is one of the most powerful strategies for accomplishing these goals.

To define the paths and the practical tools that will spiritualize work, the current management and economic system will take time and will need the contribution of numerous people. In my opinion, Simone Weil's philosophy is one of the voices that must be heard concerning this or, better, one of the voices for which one must exert an effort of mindfulness, the notions of effort and of mindfulness being quite cherished by her.

SIMONE WEIL: A FABULOUS BUTTERFLY

I hope not to be disrespectful in presenting Simone Weil as a fabulous butterfly. This image suits her well. Like a butterfly, attracted by light, Simone Weil lived a brief life and burnt her wings in the shining flame. Although she died at the age of thirty-four, she accomplished the work of several human beings. She left a considerable work of 8,000 pages, currently reedited in fifteen volumes by the Editions Gallimard in France. But her writing did not prevent her from participating in all fights against injustice, misery, and the various forms of violence, whether physical, political, dogmatic, ecological, or spiritual, as she was always in search for truth.[1]

Simone Weil was born on February 3, 1909, in Paris. She spent a happy youth, in spite of a fragile health, in her well-to-do Jewish but nonpracticing family. Her father, a medical doctor, highly valued education. Simone Weil's brother, Andre, eventually became a world-renowned mathematician. From sixteen to nineteen, Simone Weil studied at the prestigious Henri IV school in Paris with the philosopher Alain (Emile Chartier). In 1929, at age twenty, she became a member of the "Ligue des droits de l'homme"—the Universal Declaration of the Human Rights was written only twenty years later, in 1948. She participated in union activities and started giving free courses to workers, an endeavor she pursued her whole life. She undertook all these activities while studying full time for her diploma in philosophy at the Ecole

Normale Superieure, one of the most prestigious schools in France, where she was nicknamed the "red virgin." In 1931, she started her career as a teacher, teaching philosophy, art history, Greek, Latin, and mathematics. At twenty-three, she visited pro-Nazi Germany. This trip prevented her from any aspiration to revolution. Although refusing to become a member of any political party or of a union, she became one of the thinkers of the French Communist Party after developing a friendship with Boris Souvarine, one of its cofounders. As early as 1933, she denounced in her papers the situation prevailing in the USSR while other renowned intellectuals remained attached to this dogmatism until the destruction of the Berlin Wall almost sixty years later; she also met with Trotsky in Paris and criticized him for not understanding the life experienced by workers.

At twenty-five, she worked in factories, namely at Renault, an experience that formed the content of her book *The Working Condition*, a work which is viewed as one of the first scientific studies on the life of workers and on production organization. In 1935, she started different dialogues on work with managers, managing directors, or CEOs such as Victor Bernard, Auguste Detoeuf, and Jacques Lafitte. At the same time, she was very much involved in the emergence of the *Front populaire* in France and in the Matignon agreements which, in 1936, for the first time in France and three years after the National Industrial Recovery Act in the United States, instituted paid holidays, the right to collective bargaining, the right to unions, and the forty-hour workweek. The same year, she enrolled as a soldier in Spain's civil war where she was wounded. After having lived through a spiritual experience in 1938, she brought together more and more in her research, writings, and actions the themes of work, management, politics, philosophy, science, and spirituality. While doing this, she studied philosophical, political, and mathematics works, as well as the Bhagavad-Gîtâ, the Upanishads, the Tao-Te-Ching, mystics such as Saint John of the Cross, and pursued profound dialogues with the Dominican Father Joseph-Marie Perrin, among others.[2] In 1940, she left Paris with her family, escaping German anti-Semitism. She rose up against the Vichy government and lived in southern France where she did various farm jobs while also writing manuscript after manuscript. Having moved to New York, she took sides with Harlem and revolted against racism. In 1942 she joined General de Gaulle in London, who asked her to write a study on the future of France after the war. Exhausted by her work, suffering from pleurisy, and discouraged from not being able to join active resistance in France, she died in 1943 and was buried in Kent, England.

A fabulous butterfly, Simone Weil may be said to embody, fifty years ahead of her time and with much more intensity, the current tendency voiced today by a majority of managers to maintain a distance with respect to religious institutions and dogmas in general, while desiring to open themselves to spirituality and to a personal quest for truth. (In the concluding chapter, I will come back on this search for truth, and will add the search for the good and for the beautiful.) All her life, Simone Weil stood up for the needy, tried to improve their fate, and lived in the same miserable conditions, at the expense of her personal comfort and health. At the same time, she kept a distance from organizations and collective movements. In these collective systems—including firms, political parties, unions, and religious institutions—she saw the large beast which according to Plato crushes the individual. The individual being crushed by the collective has already been discussed in this book.

While she resisted this crushing, and despite the fact that she had a left-wing heart and carried on union activities, Simone Weil refused to join any union or political party, and addressed a violent critique to the union ideology and to Leon Blum's socialist government. Instances of this paradoxical behavior are numerous: close to communism, she denounced the horrors in the USSR and Stalin; while hiding Trotsky in her home, she denounced his elitism and his lack of tacit knowledge of the worker's milieu; exchanging with chairmen and managing directors, she was suspicious of what they represented and she made friends with workers; born Jewish, she felt attracted to Catholicism, yet she refused to be officially part of the Church by choosing not to be baptized, and she studied Eastern and mystical spiritual traditions; as a last example, while working for General de Gaulle, she remained very critical of Gaullism and of the very notion of the nation–state.

The image of a butterfly that I used to depict Simone Weil also evokes the notion of metamorphosis in which a butterfly goes through the stages of a silkworm, a cocoon, and a chrysalis. Like many people who came to know her personally, I am convinced that Simone Weil had attained a high level of human development. To use the notion developed in the introduction of this book, she had attained the transpersonal level of consciousness. I am quite aware of an existence of idolatrous literature about Simone, and I don't adhere to it. Yet I am convinced that her philosophical work and, even more, her daily actions, suggest the sign of a great soul.

WHY MUST WE LISTEN TO SIMONE WEIL'S VOICE FOR THE FUTURE OF MANAGEMENT?

I will invoke here three reasons: the founding period in which she lived; her influence on contemporary thought; and her innovating views on work, management, and economy.

The Period in Which Simone Weil Lived Is the Foundation of Ours

Born at the beginning of this century, Simone Weil lived with the foundations of our own period. To study her work is to discover some of the historical roots of the most fundamental current tendencies. Her experience and her reflections, for instance on the two World Wars and the setbacks of communism and the infatuation for facism and nazism, are fundamental for a better understanding of the present high prevalence of armed violence, of the rise of neoliberalism after the fall of communism, or of the growth of cults and dogmatic ideologies in general. Moreover, her experience of the 1929 economic crash, the creation of the first social laws regulating work, the development of large business and of industrial technology, and the infatuation for the so-called scientific management methods such as Taylorism, allows us to have a deeper insight about our current situation characterized by the rise of unemployment, the loss of meaning, the growing influence of transnational firms and of infatuation for alleged magical methods and tools in management.

Simone Weil's Influence on Contemporary Thought

As Simone Weil published only a few papers during her lifetime, her influence was felt only following her death. It is only after the war that people who were touched by her in various milieus—this being quite revealing of the depth and diversity of her relationships—published her writings. These people were a philosopher, a Dominican Father, a union worker, and one of her students.[3] Albert Camus also helped to spread the works of Simone Weil on a large scale. As director of Gallimard's *Espoir Series*, he published twelve of her manuscripts, starting with *The Need for Roots* in 1949.

It will not be possible here to recount the influence of the works of Simone Weil on contemporary thought. I can only proceed with a few impressionistic strokes. Her work inspired people from all milieus and of all tendencies: believers, nonbelievers, right-wing and left-wing people, intellectuals and nonintellectuals, CEOs and workers. The ideas of Simone Weil are not bound by a particular school of thought, yet they borrow from some of these schools and make connections between them. Thus it has been a source of inspiration for many, and still is. Free, wandering, adventurous like a butterfly, yet stubborn in her quest and rigorous in the way she proceeded, Simone Weil escapes classifications.[4] The stature of the people she influenced is in itself evidence of her depth.

Albert Camus recognized the importance of her thought as early as the end of World War II. He even suggested that there were two keys to his own work: the myth of *Moby Dick* by Herman Melville, and the thought of Simone Weil.[5] Concerning her last book, *The Need for Roots*, he wrote the following comment which is still quite relevant: "It seems impossible to me . . . to imagine a renaissance for Europe that would not take into account the requirements defined by Simone Weil in *The Need for Roots*."[6] In France, many members of the Academy of Science have acknowledged the importance of Simone Weil. For instance, Maurice Schumann, one of the first Gaullists, immortalized by the tone of his voice when talking to the French population on BBC during World War II, was a personal friend of Simone

Weil and acknowledged the significance of her work.[7] Similarly, the philosopher Jean Guitton held Simone Weil "as one of the greatest masters of this century."[8] But Simone Weil also influenced people from quite different backgrounds, such as Thomas Merton, the well-known Trappist monk. After noting that she was often contradictory, being both "Gnostic and Catholic, Jewish and Albigensian, medieval and modern, Platonist and anarchist, rebellious and holy, rationalist and mystical," he proposed that "few authors have thought in such a significant way on the history of our time and have had a better understanding of our calamities."[9] An another example, Boris Souvarine, cofounder of the French Communist Party and author of an incendiary book on Saline's regime, was also influenced by her thought.[10] Similarly, George Steiner, the influential philosopher, while being critical of Simone Weil, declared, "In the whole of Western tradition there was only one renowned female philosopher: Simone Weil."[11] Finally, in spite of some virulent comments against the Catholic Church, the work of Simone Weil influenced two Popes as well as some debates held during the Second Council of the Vatican.[12] John XXIII, for instance, admired her books, and recommended them to people around him; also Paul VI declared that the three major sources of his intellectual development were Blaise Pascal, Georges Bernanos, and Simone Weil.

Simone Weil's influence is not a thing of the past. It is still significant today. Many associations were founded throughout the world to disseminate her ideas; in Germany, England, the United States, France, Italy, and Japan. These associations organize conferences and events on a regular basis. The French association publishes about twenty papers a year on the work and life of Simone Weil in the scientific journal *Les Cahiers de Simone Weil*. Each year, this review lists an average of more than fifty new publications, papers, books, theses, conference proceedings, shows, and radio and television programs on Simone Weil. For example, Huguette Bouchardeau, a French former minister of the environment, recently published a book on Simone Weil, and Michel Serres, from the French Academy of Science, mentioned that she was responsible for his spiritual instruction.[13] In the United States, Robert Coles, professor of psychiatry and medical humanities at Harvard University and recipient of the Pulitzer Award, recently wrote a biography on Simone Weil.[14] It is a shame that, in spite of this marked influence in many fields—arts, education, ethics, history, literature, philosophy, politics, sciences, theology, and so forth—the work of Simone Weil remains quite unknown in the business milieu, whether it be in schools of commerce, faculties of administration, or in organizations.

Dedication to the Field of Work and Innovative Conceptions

Simone Weil's innovative views about work come from various sources, namely her own personal development, her meeting with numerous people, her scientific studies, and the historical context in which she lived. But her innovations are also due to the power of her analysis and her intellectual rigor as well as to the fact that these ideas came from a young woman between twenty and thirty-four years old. Without idealizing femininity nor youth, Simone Weil's contribution in management and economic sciences stands out clearly in a field that is still strongly marked by thought formulated by older men.

Like the quote from Simone Weil heading this book, she proposed the spiritualization of work as a remedy to the rise of violence, to social oppression, and to the "uprootedness" of people. For her, this spiritualization stood in the way of the will to conquer the world, a will that is quite obvious today in many transnational organizations. As she stated,

Everybody is busy repeating, in slightly different terms, that what we suffer from is a lack of balance, due to a purely material development of technical science. This lack of balance can only be remedied by a spiritual development in the same sphere, that is, in the sphere of work.

A civilization based upon the spirituality of work would give to Man the very strongest possible roots in the wide universe, and would consequently be the opposite of that state in which we find ourselves now, characterized by an almost total uprootedness. Such a civilization is, therefore, by its very nature, the object to which we should aspire as the antidote to our sufferings.

The unhappy peoples . . . are in need of greatness even more than of bread, and there are only two sorts of greatness: true greatness, which is of a spiritual order, and the old, old lie of world conquest. Conquest is an *ersatz* for greatness. The contemporary form of true greatness lies in a civilization founded upon the *spirituality* of work. . . . The word spirituality doesn't imply any particular [religious] affiliation.[15]

Although Simone Weil wrote these lines in 1942, she nourished this idea for fifteen years. In her dissertation on Rene Descartes, written for her degree at the Ecole Normale Superieure, she concluded, as early as nineteen years of age, that work was the only appropriate path between thought and action. For her, a thought that was not confronted with the concrete reality of the world through action was meaningless. Conversely, action uninformed by conscious and rigorous thought was mere agitation. For Simone Weil, the distinct nature of work is the meeting of thought and action, their point of concordance where they can influence each other in an unending process.

She proposed the following:

If the world hinders me, it is because it is joined to thought and thought must conform to the world, following its nature. . . . I am always two, on the one hand a passive being subjected to the world, on the other, an active being which has a hold over it. . . . Can I not attain perfect wisdom, the wisdom of action, which reunites the two halves of myself? . . . I can reunite them through action. Not the supposed action where my wild imagination makes me blindly turn the world upside down with my unsettled desires, but real action, indirect action, action which is modeled on geometry, or, to call it by its real name, work. It is through work that reason captures the world and dominates wild imagination.[16]

Obviously, this conception of work is very different from the usual definitions. It is a long way from work seen simply as a physical necessity for biological survival. This definition also goes beyond the conception of work as synonymous with a job, a view that emphasizes salary and only takes into account the economical point of view. It is also quite far from the notion of work as a process of social integration, which looks at things only from a sociological point of view. Finally, it goes beyond the conception of work as a means of self-expression and self-realization, which emphasizes psychological contributions.

Although Simone Weil recognized these various contributions of work which correspond to the psychological aspirations discussed by Abraham Maslow (see the introductory chapter)—namely the levels of biology, security, belongingness, and self-esteem—she emphasized the existential nature of work, the need for actualization as defined by Abraham Maslow. For her, it is through work that an individual can assess his limits in a concrete fashion, that paradoxically he can both really understand his limits, which are imposed by the material world, and realize his freedom to act. It is also through work that an individual can get away from his fantasies while applying his thought to a concrete object and thus becoming more mature.

This conception of work allows one to better understand the wide gap that often separates the academic world and the business world, the first being perceived by some as too theoretical, the second as too materialistic. According to Simone Weil, an academic theoretical model, which is not applied to the concrete reality of the world, is not work, but rather an immature desire, a wild imagination. Similarly, for Simone Weil, an unconsidered action developed in a firm is not work either but an unsettled desire which is likely to be harmful for the world as a whole.

This concept of work allows one to realize the criminality of depriving an individual of work, by limiting him to a job that is cut off from the reality of the field, and conversely, by not allowing him to use his intelligence in his daily actions. Not only do we deprive this individual of making a living, a salary, of a social belonging and a sense of personal value, but also, we deprive him of the possibility of his very existence, of one of the most fundamental mechanisms at the basis of his maturity and of his authenticity as a human being. From this viewpoint, work is not only necessary for human dignity: it is its foundation.

Later in her life, Simone Weil finalized this perspective on work as a unique point of concordance between thought and action. She proposed that work was also the unique point of concordance between gravity and grace. While the first concordance is existential—as it corresponds to the need for actualization defined by Abraham Maslow—the second actualization is spiritual, as it corresponds to the need for transcendence as also defined by Maslow. By the notion of gravity, Simone Weil proposes that, without divine intervention, the soul follows the natural laws of gravity, that is, the "necessity"—as she called it—which is found in nature. For her, the laws which rule nature not only have an influence on our body, but also restrict full access to a higher level of consciousness and the development of the human soul. The force of gravity leads a soul to search for control, power, greed, self-interest, and so forth. As expressed by Simone Weil: "All the natural movements of the soul are controlled by laws analogous to those of gravity. Grace is the only exception."[17]

According to her, the soul can escape the law of gravity only by divine intervention—grace—which requires the individual to transcend his personal state, to empty himself from his existential content. We have already entered the theme of emptiness in this book by referring to the principles of Alcoholics Anonymous (see Chapter 2). In defining the steps for healing, Alcoholics Anonymous recognizes human helplessness with respect to addiction to alcohol and encourages alcoholics to turn themselves over to a higher power (God as I understand him) in order to regain reason.[18] This self-abandonment, or better, self-transcendence (which does not negate the person, but goes beyond it) is for Simone Weil the only process through which grace can manifest itself. This viewpoint is similar to that evoked in the introductory chapter of this book on the differences between the personal and the transpersonal level of consciousness, as well as the need to practice diligently a spiritual discipline.

In the following quote, Simone Weil suggests that what relates gravity, a necessary condition on earth, to grace and allows one to transcend gravity, is work. It is through work that we are confronted with the natural laws of matter and their limits, which restrict our actions and the development of the soul. In this book, Solange Lefebvre has proposed that one of the main purposes of religion and of spirituality is indeed the recognition of this limit (see Chapter 3). Simone Weil went so far as to suggest that this purpose of work is a divine law, in the same way as the necessity of death. Drawing from the book of Genesis, she proposed that work is not a curse, as it is usually thought, but redemption.

She wrote the following:

When a human being has, by committing a crime, placed himself outside the current of goodness, his true punishment consists in his reintegration into the plenitude of that current by means of suffering. . . . Man placed himself outside the current of obedience. God chose as his punishments labor and death. Consequently, labor and death, if Man undergoes them in a spirit of willingness, constitute a transference back into the current of supreme Good, which is obedience to God. . . . Whatever, in heaven, may be the mysterious significance of death, on earth it is transformation of a being composed of palpitating flesh and of mind, of a being who loves and hates, hopes and fears, wants and doesn't want, into a little pile of inert matter. Man's consent to such a transformation represents his supreme act of total obedience.

But consent to suffer death can only be fully real when death is actually at hand. . . . Physical labor is a daily death. To labor is to place one's own being, body and soul, in the circuit of inert matter. . . . The laborer turns his body and soul into an appendix of the tool that he handles. The movements of the body and the concentration of the mind are a function of the requirements of the tool, which itself is adapted to the matter being worked upon.

The human mind dominates time and ceaselessly and rapidly surveys the past and the future, leaping over any sort of interval; but he who labours is subject to time in the same way as inert matter that can only move slowly from one moment to the next. It is in this way, above all, that labour does violence to human nature. . . . Immediately next in order after consent to suffer death, consent to the law which makes work indispensable for conserving life represents the most perfect act to obedience which it is given to Man to accomplish.[19]

Of course, this quotation is not meant to be an idealization of suffering or a morbid desire to die. In this book, we already discussed the theme of a positive concept of suffering (see the first dialogue in Chapter 4). Nor should one see in this passage a denial of human personality, of its thoughts and actions. As we saw on many occasions in this book, to transcend the level of personality does not mean to deny it, but rather to integrate it and go beyond it. In accordance with this notion of transcendence, Simone Weil proposes

Figure 11.1
Simone Weil's Two Axes of Work

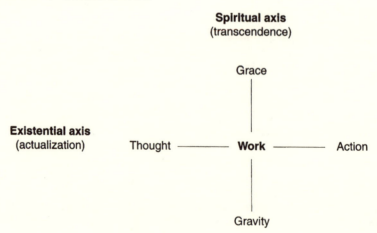

two axes for defining work as indicated in Figure 11.1.

The horizontal axis represents existential reality, which allows for actualization, work being the point of concordance or *ad-equation* between thought and action. The vertical axis represents the spiritual reality, which allows for depth, work being the point of concordance between gravity and grace. In the conclusion of this book I will return to these notions of horizontal and vertical axes.

Again, it seems obvious that the notion of work used by Simone Weil cannot be reduced to the common notion of employment that now guides the actions of government and business. For her, unpaid activity such as visiting a sick person in a hospital, helping children with their homework, helping a person in need, are forms of work under certain conditions: The person must try to develop mindfulness and direct his thoughts and actions on a task that transcends the person himself, while keeping in touch with the hardness and beauty of the material world. This is an example of the interrelation between the three worlds discussed by Ken Wilber (see the Introduction); that is, the material, the personal, and the transpersonal worlds. As stated by Simone Weil,

If on the one hand the whole spiritual life of the soul, and on the other hand all the scientific knowledge acquired concerning the material universe, are made to converge upon the act of work, work occupies its rightful place in a man's thoughts. Instead of being a kind of prison, it becomes a point of contact between this world and the world beyond. . . . The analogy which makes the mechanisms of this world a reflection of supernatural mechanisms . . . becomes luminously clear, and the fatigue induced by work, to use ordinary popular speech, enters into the body. The sorrow always more or less associated with the work effort becomes the pain which makes the beauty of the world penetrate right to the very core of the human being.

Thus only would the dignity of work be fully established. For, if we go to the heart of things, there is no true dignity without a spiritual root and consequently one of a supernatural order.[20]

Having defined the notion of work as proposed by Simone Weil, I will now briefly introduce ten suggestions she proposed to make work a point of concordance between thought and action and between gravity and grace.[21]

TEN SUGGESTIONS BY SIMONE WEIL
TO HUMANIZE AND SPIRITUALIZE WORK

Limiting the Race for World Domination

As already suggested, Simone Weil believed that there are two kinds of greatness: authentic greatness that is of a spiritual nature, and the lie of world domination. Having observed attempts at domination during the two

World Wars as well as the newly born business conglomerates which were becoming more and more competitive, she concluded that this desire for domination transformed everyone into slaves—the conquerors as well as the vanquished, the social world as well as the natural world. Far from adopting a Marxist position based on class domination, she observed that the race for power was harmful for both the working class and the managers as it was always unstable and demanding. Quite literally, she anticipated the suffering and the search for meaning expressed today by a majority of managers and described in this book. She declared,

There is never power, but only a race for power. . . . There is no term, no limit, no proportion set to this race, neither is there any limit or proportion set to the efforts that it exacts; those who give themselves up to it, compelled to do always better than their rivals, who in their turn strive to do better than they, must sacrifice not only the existence of the slaves, but their own also and that of their nearest and dearest. . . . The race for power enslaves everybody, strong and weak alike . . . the instruments of power—arms, gold, machines, magical or technical secrets—always exist independently of him who disposes of them, and can be taken up by others. Consequently all power is unstable.[22]

Recently, a number of people and groups proposed concrete mechanisms that could reduce this desire for "world domination."[23]

The Need to Rediscover the Notion of Limit

Developing the theme of giving up hubris that was quite alive in antiquity and to the *amor fati* developed especially during the Renaissance, Simone Weil suggests that like all natural things, human beings must unconditionally obey divine laws. For her, in a paradoxical fashion, obedience to these laws liberates the individual and gives him access to the transpersonal level. She wrote,

Brute force is not sovereign in this world. It is by nature blind and indeterminate. What is sovereign in this world is determinateness, limit. Eternal Wisdom imprisons this universe in a network, a Web of determinations. The universe accepts passively. The brute force of matter, which appears to us sovereign, is nothing else in reality but perfect obedience.[24]

If we are to apply this notion of limit to management and in the economic system, it calls into question the will to pursue unlimited growth, be it for productivity or profit. Although it seems quite normal—as suggested by developmental psychology—for an adolescent to want to test and go beyond limits with the illusion that the sky is the limit, a more mature human awareness realizes that the principle of exponential growth is not only impossible, but also dangerous for our social and natural world.[25] In the earlier quote,

Simone Weil not only suggests that the acceptance of certain limits is motivated by the most elementary logic or by the stages of development described in developmental psychology, but she suggests that this acceptance is also a divine commandment.

The Need to See Our Businesses as Instruments of Production and of Destruction

Simone Weil insists also on the need to view human and organizational activities as both productive and destructive, a notion that is quite close to the preceding one. For instance, she criticizes the administrative oppression of specialization, Taylorization, bureaucratization, while recalling that organized and cooperative activity allows us to achieve things which would be unattainable by individuals working in isolation. Similarly, she insists on the positive and negative aspects of technological progress, thereby expressing a nondualistic conception—a theme that was often referred to in this book. She wrote,

Besides, technical progress does not only serve to obtain at low cost what one used to obtain before with considerable effort; it also makes it possible to undertake what without it would have been almost unimaginable. It would be as well to examine the value of these new possibilities of construction, but also of destruction.[26]

The Need to Go Beyond Purely Economic Considerations

Long before economic sciences became the only social science honored by a Nobel Prize in 1969, Simone Weil already knew the dangers inherent in organizing the world according to a single discipline. She suggests that the economic imperative is only one of the numerous facets of life, equal to psychological, social, political, ecological, moral, and spiritual considerations. Quite ahead of her time, she predicted the exhaustion of natural resources such as coal or petrol and that their extraction would necessarily become "less fruitful and more costly."[27] Similarly, she insists on the fact that the race for economic domination creates waste, production of goods and services that are not really useful to society, the uncontrolled increase of the number of managers and other supervisory staff who become potential "parasites," oppression of mind and body, and lastly, on the fact that this race goes against the sense of work well done.[28] Today, numerous critiques point to dangers not of economic thought, but of economism.[29] Roger Berthouzoz will return to this theme in the next chapter.

The Need to Secure and Democratize Work

Given her experience as a worker in factories, or on trawlers and farms, and given the dangerous conditions her and her colleagues were exposed to, Simone Weil insisted on the need to make the activity of work healthier and safer. She also defended the need to democratize work in organizations. According to her, "the only mode of production that is completely free is the one where methodical thought is found in every step of the work."[30] It is important to note that this methodical thought is not limited to the specialized learning which is the basis of all professions. As suggested before in the two axes defining work, Simone Weil included in this thought the relationships between the concrete tasks and their spiritual meanings. In the following quote she noticed that the development of this kind of thought, which brings together material, personal, professional, social, and spiritual realities, would be quite difficult. In a similar fashion, we insisted in this book that the integration of ethics and spirituality at work and in management will require long and numerous efforts by a huge variety of people.

Suggested by Simone Weil is this beautiful image:

Naturally, a peasant who is sowing has to be careful to cast the seed properly, and not to be thinking about lessons learnt at school. But the object that engages our attention doesn't form the whole content of our thoughts. A happy young woman, expecting her first child, and busy sewing a layette, thinks about sewing it properly. But she never forgets for an instant the child she is carrying inside her. At precisely the same moment, somewhere in a prison workshop, a female convict is also sewing, thinking, too about sewing properly, for she is afraid of being punished. One might imagine both women to be doing the same work at the same time, and having their attention absorbed by the same technical difficulties. And yet a whole gulf of difference lies between one occupation and the other. The whole social problem consists in making the workers pass from one to the other of these two occupational extremes.

What is required is that this world and the world beyond, in their double beauty, should be present and associated in the act of work.

We are not, at present, either intellectually or spiritually capable of such transformation. . . . Naturally, schools alone would not be enough. All sections of the community in which something resembling thought still operates would have to take part: the Churches, trade-unions, literary and scientific circles. One hardly dare mention in this category political circles.[31]

The Need for Concordance between Thought and Action

As she did not endorse a class ideology that idealizes the proletariat and turns employers into devils, Simone Weil proposed to reestablish a concordance between thought and action for all people working in organizations, whether they be employees or managers. While she wished for employees to use thought and creativity in their daily tasks, she also wished that managers be more in contact with the field so that they might have the opportunity to really use their judgment. She thus anticipated the search for meaning now pursued by many managers:

Practical life takes on an increasingly collective character, and the individual as such an increasingly insignificant place in it. Technical progress and mass production reduce manual workers to an increasingly passive role; in increasing proportion and to an ever greater extent they arrive at a form of labor that enables them to carry out the necessary movements without understanding their connection with the final result. On the other hand, an industrial concern has become something too vast and too complex for any one man to be able to grasp fully; and furthermore, in all spheres, the men who occupy key posts in social life, are responsible for so much that it goes beyond the capacity of any single human mind. . . . Thus the social function most essentially connected with the individual, that which consists in coordinating, managing, deciding, is beyond any individual's capacity and becomes to a certain extent collective and, as it were, anonymous.[32]

The Need to Root Thought in the Person

Simone Weil also relentlessly defended the idea that the constant movement between thought and action must be rooted in the person rather than in the collective. She insisted on the fact that "The enlightened goodwill of men acting individually is the only possible principle of social progress"; that "several human minds cannot become united in one collective mind, and the expressions 'collective soul,' 'collective thought,' so commonly employed nowadays, are altogether devoid of meaning"; or that "thought only takes shape in a mind that is alone face to face with itself."[33]

This conception is in sharp contrast with a viewpoint often espoused today in all types of organization that a team spirit must be developed based on a consensus, on common values and on an organizational culture which is often directed by the vision of a leader, whether a chairman and managing director or a deputy minister. However, Simone Weil was not only against the hold of the collective—cultural, religious, or elitist—on the person, but against all situations where thought and action are beyond the person's control (the theme discussed earlier). Born well before the advent of computers and of the electronic highway which are often perceived as a means of freedom that will revolutionize the world, she denounces the impenetrable character of those technologies:

The mechanical nature of arithmetical operations is exemplified by the existence of calculating machines; but an accountant, too, is nothing else but an imperfect and unhappy calculating machine. Mathematics only progress by working in signs, by widening their significance, by creating signs of signs; . . . Like at each floor—if one may so express it—one inevitably loses sight of the relationship between the sign and the thing signified, the combination of signs, although they remain rigorously methodical, very soon becomes impenetrable to the mind . . . the more scientific progress accumulates ready-made combinations of signs, the more the mind is weighed down, made powerless to draw up an inventory of the ideas which it handles.[34]

The Need for Reinventing Politics

Confident that social change can occur only through liberalization of individual thought and action, Simone Weil proposed economical and political reforms that went beyond the organizational context. However she did not naively think that these reforms could be carried out by political parties, unions, or even the state under the guidance of a social utopia. She considered all these systems bureaucratic administrations in which, by and large, individual thought and action had disappeared as well. Moreover, she was convinced that these systems were concerned with the maintenance and growth of their own power, instead of serving the common good.

Given this observation, Simone Weil proposed to reinvent politics on the basis of freedom of individual thought and action, and to undertake major economic reforms. She suggested, for instance, a reform of the organization of work, reduction of the race for world domination, regulation of the function of money, and of speculation. These themes are quite topical today and are being discussed currently in various milieus.

Having gone through World War I and sensing the second, she suggested around 1935 that if these reforms couldn't be carried out, economic war would lead inevitably to military war:

The subordination of irresponsible slaves to leaders overwhelmed by the mass of things to attend to, and, incidentally, themselves to a large extent irresponsible, is the cause of faulty workmanship and countless acts of negligence. . . . The tremendous extension of credit prevents money from playing its regulating role in commercial exchange. . . . The parallel extension of speculation ends up by rendering the prosperity of industries independent, to a large extent, of their good functioning . . . the central bureaucratic organization, which is the State machine, must naturally be led sooner or later to take the upper hand in this co-ordination. The pivot around which revolves social life, thus transformed, is none other than preparation for war. Seeing that the struggle for power is carried out by conquest and destruction, in others words by a diffused economic war, it is not surprising that actual war should come to occupy the foreground.[35]

The Need for a New Scientific Adventure

Facing the difficulties of her times, Simone Weil suggested that only two attitudes were possible: capitulation or the rise of a new scientific adventure that would allow the human being to conquer anew his freedom of thought and action and his potential for grace. The scientific research program she proposed concerning work and science went beyond the notions of productivity, growth, and technological efficiency which are put forward today:

Those who have so far maintained that applications are the goal of science meant to say that truth is not worth seeking and that success alone counts; but it could be understood differently; one can conceive of a science whose ultimate aim would be the perfecting of technique not by rendering it more powerful, but simply more conscious and more methodical.

For this purpose, a serious study of the history of the sciences is probably indispensable. As for technique, it ought to be studied thoroughly—its history, present state, possibilities of development—and from an entirely new point of view, which would no longer be that of output, but that of the relation between the worker and his work. Lastly, the analogies between the steps of human thought, on the one hand in daily life and particularly in work, and on the other hand in the methodical development of science should be uncovered.[36]

The Need for Developing a Subtle Mindfulness

Finally, it is should be noted that Simone Weil's call for a "new adventure of the scientific mind" is equally spiritual.[37] All her life, she looked for processes, including scientific activities, that would allow the soul to grow. The generic term she used for these processes was *mindfulness*. At the existential level, given that work is a concordance point between thought and action, she proposed that this mindfulness be achieved by developing conscious thought during the act of work, an act directed toward a goal that concerns the person but transcends them at the same time. At the spiritual level, given that work is a point of concordance between gravity and grace, she proposed that this mindfulness be based on unconditional acceptance of the human condition as regulated by time and natural laws, and on the desire to go beyond the "I," inviting the divine to fill it up and thus transcending mindfulness itself.

Simone Weil proposed various processes for developing this mindfulness: contact with beauty, with people, with arts and nature; absolute concentration on the task to be done; acceptance of limits either imposed by a profound meeting with someone or by the immutable laws of nature; respect of the fundamental needs of the soul; prayer, not seen as an automatic recitation for obtaining a favor, but as a spiritual meditation which goes beyond thought; the patient desire for the divine; the concentrated study of scientific, literary, religious, and spiritual writings; sustained participation in sacred rituals; a personal commitment toward the most deprived and toward suffering in general, and so on. One thing is essential to realize here. Simone Weil always insisted that if man ought to desire communion with the divine, its source of this communion is in the supernatural, that is, in a reality that transcends the person and is beyond his will. She proposed

God is attention without distraction. . . . In time . . . we sense our ego. The acceptance of time . . . is the only frame of mind in which the soul is free. . . . It embraces infinity. God has given his finite creatures this power to transport themselves into infinity.

It is impossible to truly desire goodness and not obtain it. Or reciprocally, what it is possible to truly desire and not obtain is not really goodness. It is impossible to receive goodness when we have not desired it.

Goodness is something that we cannot procure ourselves, but we cannot desire it without obtaining it either. This is why our situation is very similar to that of small children who cry when they are hungry and are given bread . . . that is why all manner of supplicants are sacred.[38]

CONCLUDING REMARKS

I am convinced that fundamental scientific research should to be undertaken in order to rediscover the major works that have explored the relationships between ethics, spirituality, management, work, and the economic system. And this should be done through a profound exploration of various authors who were able to access the transpersonal levels of consciousness. While the works of Simone Weil are central in philosophy, the same applies to other authors in different fields that deal with the world of work and management. I think especially of the works of Chester I. Barnard in organizational theory; of Abraham Maslow in psychology; Marie Parker Follet in political science; Hermann Hesse in literature; E. F. Schumacher in economic sciences; and Hildegard von Bingen in theology, to give only a few examples.[39] Without leading to the idealization of their authors, the study of these works should help us to better imagine how a spiritual ethics of work could influence our organizations and our economic system during the third millennium.

To stress the importance of this fundamental research and of its general direction, I will let T. S. Eliot, a Nobel Prize winner in literature and the most influential English poet of the twentieth century according to some, have the last word. In his preface to the English version of *The Need for Roots*, while avoiding idolizing Simone Weil, T. S. Eliot saluted the grandeur of her soul and suggested that still today her work belongs to the future if we afford it an effort of mindfulness:

I cannot conceive of a person who would agree with all her ideas or who would not be violently opposed to some of them. But to agree or disagree (with Simone Weil) is secondary; what is important, is to connect with a great mind.

These kinds of books don't influence current business conduct; for men and women who are in these careers and have already adopted the market's jargon, these books are too late. This is one of those books which should be studied by the young before their spare time and their capacity to think is lost to electoral campaigns and the legislative assemblies; the effect of these books, we can only hope, will become apparent in the intellectual attitude of another generation.[40]

12

Economic Efficiency, Ethical Foundations, and Spiritual Values in the Management of Organizations

Roger Berthouzoz

EDITOR'S NOTE

In order to integrate ethical and spiritual values into management and the economy, the theologian, ethicist, and Dominican priest Roger Berthouzoz, an expert in economical and developmental ethics, draws from a precise source: the sociological and systemic theory of Niklas Luhmann.[1] Developing one of this book's recurrent themes, the necessity to accept a systemic perspective, he reminds us that the fall of Marxism should not lead to an idealization of neoliberalism. For Roger Berthouzoz, these two ideologies fragment the real, the first by the omnipresence of the state, and the second by the omnipresence of the market. By proposing that every system develops its own rationality and its own practices that give rise to its identity, he rejects both a corrective ethic imposed from without, and a utilitarian ethic appropriated by the system. He suggests an integrative ethic that must be discussed cooperatively, by all the partners within each system in order to genuinely improve decision making. As well, he postulates that ethics, like the Universal Declaration of Human Rights, should be inspired from above by noble values (human dignity, justice, solidarity, spiritual development), and from below by operating practices (charters of responsibility, codes of ethics, and management tools).

Certain of the theories introduced by Roger Berthouzoz in this erudite text are currently used in the most avant-garde scientific research in administration—the nature of complexity, systemic analysis, the theory of self-organization, the different forms of anthropological reality, and so forth. If this "adventure of the scientific spirit," as Simone Weil calls it (see Chapter 11), seems disconcerting at first, it is necessary if we truly wish to humanize and spiritualize our managerial practice and economic system, along with ourselves and the world in general.

As an ethicist and theologian, stimulating reflection in a forum—a place for dialogue and open exchange—organized in a business school, is for me, a challenge filled with meaning.

I would like to begin by a double interpolation: a saying by Jesus and one by Mahatma Gandhi. Jesus said "What good does it do a man to win the entire world if it is at the price of his life?"[2] This is precisely the issue of this entire process. It is not a judgment of the concept of "winning the world," but rather a call, in the form of a warning, and what is at stake is the meaning of life, the fulfillment of the existence of every man and woman. We have already insisted upon the search for meaning during this forum and Thierry Pauchant reminded us, through the work of Simone Weil, of the dangers inherent in the desire to conquer the world (see Chapter 11).

Mahatma Gandhi describes, according to his own spiritual reference, what he calls the seven capital sins of today's world: riches without work, enjoyment without conscience, competence without personality, business without morals, science without humanity, religion without charity, and politics without principles.[3] It is clear that the Mahatma does not condemn wealth nor enjoyment, competence nor business, science nor religion or politics. They all belong to the fabric of our lives. The sage marks out the issues and the orientations.

ETHICAL PRINCIPLES AND SPIRITUAL VALUES
IN ORGANIZATIONAL DECISION MAKING

Industrial, financial, or commercial businesses are the principal actors of the modern economic system. Their role is to see to the production and exchange of goods and services necessary for maintaining life. Like all human institutions, these businesses are inserted into a network of social relations. Because of this, they find themselves submitted to basic ethical values without which no durable social life would be possible. In this sense, the questions asked within this forum are not proposed as an alternative. In fact, once a societal relationship exists, values and convictions become involved. The issue would be to determine their breadth and their pertinence in the framework of economic activity.

Some of these values and convictions are well established. In business the principle of good faith, which makes one respect the contract or one's word in order to keep the system functioning properly, is generally accepted. The moral basis for human life in society was expressed in the document *The Universal Declaration of Human Rights* of 1948. It was then clarified in various pacts applied to different domains of personal and social life. Furthermore, in certain sectors of activity, we are forced to elaborate codes of conduct, which allow for the concrete application of fundamental values. These universal rights uphold the inviolable and inalienable dignity of each human being that must be respected and promoted. Recognizing these rights implies a series of demands in personal and collective relationships as well as certain responsibilities.

The reflection I propose concerns precisely the responsibility of business, within the conditions of its current existence and activity, in the context of the market economy. The company is perceived as an association of persons brought together to ensure production and profitable transactions, the latter being obviously decisive. One must establish responsibility with regards to profitability and decide if this means more than merely operating in a legal manner and providing the highest possible returns to the shareholders. The need for profitability can, in effect, be in conflict with the demands that morality imposes on the individual. In terms of solidarity for example, the restructuring or the merger of two companies could increase profits, but at the same time weigh heavily on those that lose their jobs. If there were no clear economic necessity, what would the criteria for the decision be? Within the company do we—and this is the fundamental question—acknowledge other aims besides that of profitable operations, particularly ones which may be complementary or eventually contradictory?

Philosophers and ethicists of our tradition and culture, like Paul Ricoeur, have noted that human activity is concerned with the conservation of life, but also with "living well."[4] How, to what extent, and can a company's activities take into consideration self-realization, personal fulfillment, or human happiness in just institutions? Which ethical values and spiritual resources can contribute to bringing such projects to fruition?

First, I will analyze the situation of the economic system in modern society. I will then study the existing relations between the economy and ethical and spiritual values. I will, in the end, propose methods for integrating these values into the managerial decision-making process.

THE ECONOMY AS A SYSTEM IN MODERN SOCIETY

In order to elaborate the problem, I will offer a sociological analysis of the situation of the economy in modern society, referring to the theories of Niklas Luhmann, a German sociologist, who after a lifetime of research, published a brilliant work entitled *The Society of Society*.[5] His thinking does not directly refer to a theological or spiritual tradition. It is a systemic sociological reflection whose spiritual and religious presuppositions are strictly sociological.

The strength of such a theory is derived from the fact that it confronts the complexity of social phenomenon, without trying to reduce them to simple schematics that would detach one functional element at a time in order to explain the relationships established between the other domains of social reality. This theory is founded on the hypothesis of the operational autonomy of each social system; an autonomy developed from a model in the life sciences centered around the notion of self-organization. This idea was proposed in the work of Humberto Maturana and Francisco Varela.[6]

A first corollary of Luhmann's theory, largely supported by experience, describes a strict reciprocity that presides over the interaction of the systems of social life. Not one of them—political systems, economic systems, education, art, and so on—has preponderance or an authority that absolutely subordinates the activities of the other social systems for its own ends. Subsequently this would mean that, for example, the Marxist theory of a state—that is, politically guided economy—is not pertinent. Clearly this is a relatively easy fact to confirm since the fall of centrally planned economies. However, and this is the most important lesson for us to consider: The pretension of the neoliberal model which would let society be run by the economic system, or by market forces, overestimates the capacities of that one system. The great economic crises in Asia and Russia prove this, particularly given the serious inequalities and the misery which now afflict more than one billion human beings. This fact alone should be enough to demonstrate that the optimism surrounding an exclusively state- or market-run society is unfounded. Nonetheless, the need for direction subsists, and it is a question of clarifying under which conditions, knowing that it is based on human decision making.

Sociologists and anthropologists consider that the major organizational characteristic of our societies is that of the differentiation of social functions brought on by the techno-scientific and industrial revolutions of modern times as well as the generalization of the democratic revolution. The latter is founded on the process of individualization that began in the Middle Ages and has developed decisively since the second half of the eighteenth century. Solange Lefebvre has already evoked this legacy (see Chapter 3). Individualization expresses the dignity of the human person as a distinctive and primary value for all societies and gives it form in the recognition of individual liberty and human rights.

In Luhmann's theory, the human person is characterized by the processes of the conscience and the production of meaning. This creates the individuality of the psychic system. People are always interacting and organize themselves by forming social systems which order the major spheres of human activity. Each of these spheres has its own rationality given its specific goals and procedures. I bring up this trait, which is discussed in systems theory, because often, when we question the integration of ethical and spiritual values in economic activity or management, we oppose it head-on by the possible consequences instead of taking its own rationality into consideration. In fact, the functional differentiation in a society is developed by means of the growing autonomy of social systems and their self-organization; not only does the functionality of a system carry its own rationality, but this system operates independently. Luhmann shows how the autonomous operation of each of these systems achieves their own unity, and consequently their identity as a system, by self-organizing themselves relative to their environment. The system then has a rationality to it as well as specific practices that only it can enact.

This conclusion is essential and we will see that it has important consequences for the interpretation of the relation between ethics, spiritual values, and the economy. Thus in modern civilization the economic system organizes the production of things, of all the goods and market services necessary for society, and it is the only system capable of doing so. The political system is the only one that can produce the required collective decisions for acting in the public interest which concerns all the members of society, and the only system that can carry out these decisions.

We can immediately see that the political system alone cannot directly influence the goals or processes of economics. Reciprocally, the economic system cannot be solely responsible for decisions that affect the collective. Furthermore, in the case where controls are necessary, the economic system cannot give itself its own legal framework. One is imposed on it. But by the same token, the law cannot impose itself on economics outside of the rationality of the economic procedures themselves.

The second point underlined by Niklas Luhmann is important. It explains how relations between the systems are established. Luhmann reminds us that the fundamental operation of the psychic system of the individual is the act of consciousness. However, the fundamental operation of social systems is communication, not only defined as speech, but also linked to practices and objects. In this sense, social systems constitute a series of operations, which include the creation of information, its transmission, and above all, its comprehension, which will result in either the acceptance of the message, indifference, or its refusal by the systemic partners.[7]

Indeed, this approach solicits a third observation: the affirmation of the autonomy of a system does not imply its total independence or autarchy. Each system is functional, and therefore, by definition, joined to an environment. However, the autonomy of the system means that it determines the relationship between its independence from, or dependence on, the environment which is made up of other systems. In other words, when we talk generally about the integration of ethical values into the economic system, we assume that it is only from this system that this type of integration is possible. My discussion will attempt to establish the place from which this coupling of the ethical and economical spheres could occur. Coupling is the term used by Luhmann to characterize relationships that form between social systems. The operation implies a process of coding and decoding. The crucial problem in a differentiated society such as ours will be the adaptation and the compatibility of the operations of coding and decoding.

It is in this context that ethics and the religious systems can and must assume their role. Ethics and religious systems provide a concrete understanding of human existence, the rights and obligations, destiny, the issues around personal lives and social relations. These systems set out the values and principles which aim to understand the human being and his desire for fulfillment. Founded on the conscience, they propose in an elementary fashion the first active principle: Do good and avoid evil. One must then follow it through, which would give us a whole new way of looking at our practices and at the reality of our actions. In fact, from the point of view of values, economical choices are not neutral, even if every managerial act does not automatically have a moral dimension.

But ethics and the religious systems are alone not able to make a concrete decision in the economic domain which calls for a managerial decision. For example, in the case of a merger between two companies, the fundamental principle, "do good and avoid evil," cannot become the basis on which to decide whether to go through with the merger. A complete analysis of the stakes and consequences of the two strategies must be undertaken.

The absolute, the universality of good and of values as well as the notion of the dignity of all human persons, must be promoted by the elaboration of ethical norms and practical directives. These norms and directives must consider the contingencies and diversity of individual histories, those of particular groups, organizations, and the society in question as well as the existing systemic interactions between the multiple domains of human activity. Therein lies a second moment of ethical reflection which cannot be accomplished in a vacuum for the systemic reasons cited earlier.

Let us use an example. In Christianity, we believe that God is the creator of the universe and that he created it, with all it contains, for the benefit of all humanity. Consequently, in social Christian teaching we set forth the principle of the universal destiny of all the goods of the earth. But this single affirmation is difficult to apply concretely. One must elaborate the ways in which these principles could be applied. In our culture, they are applied in the judicial norms of private property. However, this is not the only way to manage the appropriation or use of land. In other cultures, West Africa for example, a land chief is responsible for the application of the absolute principle. Their task is to distribute land according to the potential and the needs of the families.

To resume, the normative is practiced under the rule of an absolute principle and within the particularity of a practice situated in a singular cultural context. This should be the methodical process for all the major regulating values of ethics. It consists of maintaining, considering, and receiving the absolute and the universality of principles and putting them into practice according to norms which first will mirror them and second, establish the procedures. Finally, there is a third level, that of the establishing directives or rules that would bring this norm into effect in a given situation.

According to Luhmann's systems theory, it must be underlined that all problems and failures can be solved only within the functional system of their origin. This observation requires an effort to communicate in order to translate the requirements and demands of society into the language and the procedures of a given functional system. Two types of discourse on economical ethics become irrelevant as a result of this observation.

The first irrelevant discourse would be that expressed by a purely corrective ethics, which wants to be an antidote to the rational excesses inherent in the corporate system; a system whose goals are profitability and efficiency. However, we cannot intervene from outside a system, in the name of ethical values, in order to modify the objectives, decisions, and procedures within the system. For example, a general rule based on the principles of solidarity or fraternity cannot provide instant standards for economic decisions. Nonetheless, these principles will be decisive because they are a major structuring device for ethical decisions.

The second irrelevant discourse is the one that is narrowly functional; that is, in which morals are subservient to the interests of an organization. Ethics, as a strategy to increase the motivation and productivity of workers, becomes merely instrumental or is used as a marketing tool. That is a general criticism of certain ethical codes that have been adopted by large multinationals or certain treaties on business ethics.[8]

Systems theory leads us toward an integrative ethic. It establishes the activity of the economic system on a morally based foundation which consists of a plinth of values and orienting principles for an economic rationality; a rationality that could exclude the expected undesirable or perverse results. The difference will be visible in the goals established, the acceptable values, and the quality of decision-making procedures within the company.[9] This process presupposes the creation or strengthening of a relevant review structure within the economic system, both in companies and in the various industrial sectors. It can also benefit from establishing managerial practices and tools to operate a systemic relay with ethical and spiritual authority as proposed by Mr. Ouimet during this forum (see Chapter 6). The demands and criticisms of business activities and of the economic system can thus be heard and dealt with as well as the thoughts and values that emerge from the ethical system, spirituality, and religion.

THE CONDITIONS FOR THE INTEGRATION OF ETHICAL PRINCIPLES AND SPIRITUAL VALUES IN MANAGEMENT

A brief historical survey will help us to better understand the current conditions in which we attempt to integrate values into economic activity. The German sociologist and philosopher Max Weber undertook a very enlightening study on the birth of modern capitalist economy, in the context of the cities of the Middle Ages, particularly in Italian cities of the fifteenth century.[10]

These cities offered particularly the material conditions that allowed for dialogue and collective action by individuals who were freed from the traditional constraints of feudal power. Economic and mercantile interests developed and took the dominant form of the market in the sense that we understand it today. The contractual system became the objective basis for operations, without considering the quality of the individuals. Proceedings had to be established in order to authoritatively regulate operations and, in the case of a conflict, intervene efficiently to referee or judge. The intensity of modern exchange also requires legislation that works efficiently and securely. This judicial order does not initially consider the individual and their status but rather their activities. Its function is to regulate the exchange of goods and services. In this system, the moral dimension is insured by the strict requirement to respect one's freely given word: each participant in the organization or in the exchange, in the context of competition, expects his partners to keep their promises, particularly actualizing the norms of good faith and equality.

Max Weber points out another of the organization's problems in its relationship to personal ethics. In terms of responsibility, each action can be attributed to a concrete person, capable of being sanctioned. However, the institutional form of the modern enterprise is the corporation, especially the largest ones. In general, investors do not personally participate in the activities they finance and are not directly responsible for the operations, but they can nonetheless profit from them. The link between the person who makes their money available and the basic economic reality is even more tenuous when the investor is an institution, a pension fund for example, which works with the assets of a commonly held investment fund. In this case, the question of responsibility which underlies decision making must consequently become differentiated from and drawn from systemic theory in order to consider the positions of the various actors: namely the consumers or clients, colleagues within the company, public collectives, investors, suppliers, competitors, and so on. This must occur in the three major decision-making levels: the local establishment, the organization, and the holding.

A first condition necessary to the integration of ethical principles and spiritual values into management would be to clear up a major misunderstanding as to the nature of the marketplace, its role, and its actors. The general objective of the competitive market is to respond to the needs of human society and to satisfy consumers. Compared to other transaction models, the market proves to be the most effective mechanism. There is no ethical reason to question it globally, but one must remain conscious of its limits. For example, it is clear that everything is not merchandise, and that the market cannot satisfy all human needs.

On the other hand, the implicit or thematic anthropology which, from Adam Smith to the neoliberal economists of the Chicago school—that of *homo-economicus*—comes across as particularly simplistic from a realistic point of view. The presupposition is that the individual is eventually driven by self-interest, not by benevolence or altruism, and that he is always looking for the best possible advantage. The danger lies in reducing all understanding of the human being and his social relationships to this one model.

A second condition essential to the integration of ethical principles and spiritual values in management is anthropological in nature. It consists of reconstructing and repositioning ethical reflection in an anthropology that takes into account all the dimensions of the person's existence as well as his dignity. These persons are indeed engaged in economic activity, but an anthropological concept of the person must integrate at least three fundamental facets of their life, each of which have a decisive meaning for managerial decisions: the human being is wholly *nature, culture,* and *freedom.*[11] Wholly nature because the human being has material, biological, psychological, and social needs that must be satisfied; wholly culture because culture designates the fact that, and the way in which, each society manages the needs of its members and organizes their communal life according to the diversity of social systems which we have discussed; and finally, wholly freedom because the human being is a free being, founded in a radical—but not absolute—project of self-positioning with regard to his self and his existence. This being is also open to transcendence and the other, the you of interpersonal relationships and the everyone of life in the systems of society, while still being capable of self-actualization.[12] In his singularity, the human being exists according to his freedom, which is the most concrete expression of his dignity. The first ethical imperative would then be to be free, to be a free being and to create space for freedom, be it for the individual or for human societies. The creation of space for freedom means to create the potential for individual lives to seek out and find support for their fulfillment. This can be accomplished precisely by integrating ethical and spiritual values into the foundations and goals of the social and economic systems, as well as those of the organization itself.

CONCLUSION: METHODS FOR INTEGRATING VALUES IN THE ECONOMIC DECISION-MAKING PROCESS

The rationality of the market economy and the distinctive goals assigned to organizations, as cleanly and brutally expressed by Milton Friedmann, affirms that the social responsibility of business is to increase its profits.[13] This, however, is only a partially relevant judgment in this practical context. Increased profitability is not in any way the only goal of a company, but it is necessary in order to insure its ability to operate in the economic system. One must consider the interests and legitimate rights of all the actors concerned, as well as the values they embody. They cannot simply be subordinated to the objective of maximizing profits.

The first referential value that must be taken into consideration is the dignity of the human person and their inherent fundamental rights. These rights precede any study of social relationships, and are in no way instituted. Politics and all social systems are obliged to recognize and promote them, according to their ability and their responsibility.

The second tier of values that preside over all relations in society, particularly those of exchange, are those of justice. Their objective is to achieve equality between human beings. It is a question of a regulating principle valid strictly, in an arithmetical sense, when discussing goods exchanged or services offered, and to insure equality when people and differences in need or responsibilities must be taken into account. Another dimension of justice is involved in the rapport between each person, each business, and the society in general. All are required to contribute to the common good, so that it is possible to attain individual good and fundamental rights for all. This principle of contribution must always be taken into consideration when determining the goals of the organization.[14]

Where the values that qualify the person and their links to others are concerned, solidarity (love or brotherhood, in its Christian expression) is the most important. It is not a substitute for justice, nor an optional complement, like a surrogate. It is at the root of, or the motivation for justice and it is achieved as a goal of the just act.

Religious faith and the resources offered by spiritual values are, I would say, at the base of just and supportive actions. They are like the light that shows us the radical nature of issues, a strength and support in order to work toward the human fulfillment of all the actors and partners in the economic enterprise.

An ethically grounded reflection within the subsystem of an organization must imperatively specify the elements that would constitute an ethical basis for both economic activity and morally responsible aims and procedures. This dialogue with ethics must also be attentive to the spiritual roots of the project's supporters and to the accomplishment of the project itself. Those involved must have recourse to orientation tools to aid them in decision making and establishment of the project. There are essentially three types of tools that I can only describe succinctly here:

1. *Charters of economical ethics.* For example, *The Interdisciplinary Institute in Ethics and Human Rights* (IIEDH), of the University of Fribourg, has just proposed a Charter of Communal Responsibilities for Economic Activity.[15] The charter comes in the form of a reference for moral engagement, defining not just the values to be recognized, but the goals to be accomplished in the general spirit of partnership.[16]

2. *Codes of ethics*. These codes are found within different branches of the economy. The codes of ethics of organizations establish standards for applying major principles and standards adapted to specific challenges that may be encountered in business.[17] These go beyond professional codes of conduct, which are directly linked to government legislation.

3. *Management tools*. Finally there is the development of ethically and spiritually based management tools like those presented by Mr. Ouimet (see Chapter 6). These tools consist of methods and procedures that attempt to give concrete expression to the integration of ethical principles and spiritual values in all aspects of managerial activity and work in general. They can also facilitate the concrete application of human and spiritual values if they respect the deeply held attitude open to the respect and recognition of the human being, in all the dimensions of his existence.

13

Business Ethics and Spirituality among Jews, Christians, and Muslims

Michel Dion

EDITOR'S NOTE

In this chapter, Michel Dion, lawyer, theologian, and ethics professor, compares the principles of Judaism, Christianity, and Islam in relation to economics, management, and, more generally, work. To do so, he comments on the interreligious declaration initiated in 1984 by Prince Philip of Great Britain and Prince Hassan Bin Talal of Jordan, which has resulted in a code of ethics for international business signed in 1993. This declaration has been specifically designed to address the globalization of economic exchanges and to increase high moral standards in business practice.

Michel Dion comments on three fundamental themes: social justice and the search for common good; the management of Creation; and the principles of political economy including those related to competition, prosperity, the function of the state, human dignity, and the natural environment. He concludes by arguing that the development of a collective ethic from these three monotheistic religions is not incompatible with the affirmation of their specific differences, as a real interreligious dialogue can overcome this paradox.

This dialogue can be seen as a continuation of the work on existing relationships between religions and economy initiated by the great sociologist Max Weber at the beginning of this century.[1] Considering religion as the very foundations of our cultures and our societies, the work of Weber none-theless had a certain bias; the author was interpreting each religion alone, and his standpoint expressed only a sociological point of view. Michel Dion's commentary, based on the 1993 interfaith declaration, is more faithful to the three religions themselves; his commentary emanates from a dialogue of each group's own members and is applied to the business world. In the concluding chapter I will introduce another statement of interreligious ethics proposed by the Parliament of the World Religions, established in 1893. This work on interfaith dialogue is paramount if we wish to eradicate the world of events such as the World Trade Center tragedy.

I thank the organizers for having convened this unique meeting, as I believe this conference responds to current needs in societies.

In 1984, Prince Philip of Great Britain and Prince Hassan Bin Talal of Jordan initiated consultations aimed at a common interreligious declaration on ethics in international business. The aim of the discussions, which involved researchers from the three monotheist religions, was to reinforce the moral and spiritual values shared by Jews, Christians, and Muslims, in order to overcome prejudices that members of one or the other community may have toward the others. A code of ethics for international business was signed in October 1993 in Amman. Researchers and business people from the three religions had written it together.[2]

This 1993 declaration deals with the following issues:

- Globalization in business, as we know, has multiplied relationships with partners from various cultural origins. These partners have different approaches to business transactions and operations. Hence, sacred Jewish texts such as the Mishnah and Torah, the Christian Bible, and the Muslim Koran can help resolve conflicts that can arise from these differences.

- The aim was also to highlight the common values of these three religions in order to supply the ethical foundations for international business and to be used as guidelines by business people.

- The intention was also to respond to the current tendency of increased selfishness and dishonesty in various countries. The aim of this declaration was to recall what is considered as right and wrong relations in business in order to improve moral standards in international business.

- Last, another objective was to maintain high standards of behavior and to develop a better understanding of the social responsibility in business.

It was agreed upon that the application of the principles of the declaration could vary according to country, based on the degree of influence of the religion in each nation. I will focus in this chapter on some key themes emphasized by this declaration, referring to the main sacred texts of the three religions.

JUSTICE

In Judaism, justice is central to all human relationships including economic activities. This principle requires the constant control of prices and profits in order to prevent practices that would deviate too much from normal prices and profits; that is, those of a specific market in a given time and space. Demanding an excessive price for goods and services essential to life is contrary to the Judaic value of justice whereas higher profits are allowed for other goods and services. Those who take advantage of others by increasing prices beyond the normal standards violate their religious obligations according to which another's life should not be imperiled. They oppress others, which goes against God's will.[3]

In Christianity, social action is not only required by charity but by justice as well. No social class should impede another in their access to the advantages derived from labor and capital. Material goods should be distributed according to the requirements of the common good and social justice, so as to favor the development of each individual and of the community. For Christianity, free markets must be fair; that is, favor the human and moral development of societies while maintaining equal relationships. Christians who assume the responsibility of social justice inherent to the Gospel's message are ready to sacrifice themselves in order to overcome the structures of human alienation. God's love lives only in those who help the most helpless. Therefore, establishing trade unions and cooperatives—as explained by Mr. Beland in this book (see Chapter 5), granting adequate salaries to employees and respecting their health and their spiritual life, as suggested by Mr. Ouimet (see Chapter 6), is a matter of pure justice according to Christianity. All Christian tradition, particularly that of the Fathers of the Church, has highlighted the need to share and redistribute the surplus to the poorest.[4]

According to Islam, any improvement of material conditions must lead to greater social justice. This justice has meaning only in the fundamental interrelation between God, the universe, and human beings. Economic development then becomes a part of the moral development of Islam, since there is no contradiction between religion and the pursuit of earthly prosperity. According to Islam, the pursuit of prosperity is good in of itself and economic activities are an acceptable way to fulfill one's mission on Earth. Islam aims at reaching a balance between individual and social obligations, between material and spiritual needs, so that all activities are oriented toward the achievement of well-being in this world as well as in the afterlife. This suggests moderation in consumption habits, altruistic behavior, and the quest for personal peace. Thus, each economic decision has a spiritual and ethical dimension. Muslim business people who are fair and generous in their practice are more respected than those who are looking for maximum profits. In Islam, the best person is the most virtuous one and not the wealthiest or the most powerful. The individual, then, must be fair in his economic transactions with others. Justice also means a balancing of advantages, a harmony between the various interests and proportionality between needs and rewards. Each Muslim contributes to his well-being by contributing to the collective well-being. In this context, the production of goods necessary to life becomes central to Muslims. Finally, Islam emphasizes the social dimension of justice in all individual decisions and actions and gives concrete expression to the values that contribute to the growth of the common good.[5]

MANAGING GOD'S CREATION

According to Judaism, God is the only owner of Earth. This is why human beings must be more concerned by the poorest, who have rights limiting the power and authority of the wealthiest. All economic well-being comes directly from God and must be used according to His will. Consequently, Judaism tends toward an economic system that embodies justice and divine mercy.[6]

In Christianity, all wealth and forms of prosperity are also seen as coming from God. Therefore, property is not unconditional or absolute. All individual property rights exist in the context of the collective right to share the common inheritance of divine Creation. As God's creation, material goods have a universal purpose. Property, then, has an inherently social dimension. Ownership of the goods of Creation implies the mutual collaboration of individuals.[7]

In Islam, each follower is a manager of Allah's property which ultimately belongs to Him. The universe belongs to Allah and has been given collectively to human beings who have been granted the rights of ownership, use, and the transfer of private property. Prosperity must be managed as Allah would; in order to benefit the whole community. No owner can exploit his or her own goods in a way that could cause damage to others or to the community since Allah is the sole owner of the universe. Each Muslim is individually accountable for the management of Creation and therefore responsible to Allah for his management of natural resources and for the way he behaves in regard to the common interest of the community. In this way, Islam links the human being to Allah and makes him live according to His will. Each Muslim is His trustee of the natural resources that he needs to manage in a responsible fashion. The wealthier one is, the more one owes to Allah in terms of the management of material goods.[8]

PRINCIPLES OF POLITICAL ECONOMY

Competition

In Judaism, unfair competition is de facto forbidden. Unfair competition is prohibited when it aims to exclude an actor from the market. Healthy competition among traders, however, is a religious requirement in order to maintain the common good and public interest. Cartels are acceptable only to the extent that they produce greater benefits for society. They must be agreed upon by all parties in the relevant economic sector and be supervised by a rabbinical authority who insures that they serve the common good. Furthermore, these cartels must be managed with rectitude, mercy, and justice. Otherwise, monopolies are a profanation of God's name when they eliminate competitors from the market.[9]

In Christianity, liberalism that considers, among other things, competition as the supreme law of the economy, is criticized in the social texts of the Roman Catholic Church. In *Populorum progressio*, Paul VI defended free trade but made it subordinate to social justice (respect of common good, service of the collective interest by the state, the institution of fair wages and prices) and social charity (free and impartial acts for the achievement of the common good). His predecessors, Leo XIII and Pius XI, had already taken position on these issues. According to Paul VI, economic liberalism leads to the tyranny of money, excessive individualism, materialism, and social Darwinism (natural selection of the wealthiest who are the only ones to survive and grow). Unhindered competition only works well when there is no radical economic disparity between the parties. Under these ideal conditions, unhindered competition is an incentive toward social progress. Unhindered competition is acceptable only if it respects the demands of social justice. John-Paul II holds the same discourse in *Centesimus annus*, except that he adds that the requirement for truth must be considered in the satisfaction of basic human needs.[10]

According to Islam, the economy is based on cooperation rather than on unhindered competition. Monopolistic practices are prohibited because they constrain the circulation of prosperity. For Muslims, monopolies show a lack of harmony between private and social interests and impede on the moral and spiritual development of human beings. Monopolistic practices are allowed only to the extent that it is clear that they will create a greater collective good. Furthermore, brutal competition is not acceptable in Islam. Achieving material and spiritual well-being forbids the maximization of profit and blind consumption of goods and services. According to this religion, economic life is only a means for a spiritual end and prosperity is a means to live a virtual life. The goal of cooperation-based competition is to achieve the best interests of society as a whole.[11]

Prosperity for All

In Judaism, prosperity of the wealthy is seen as God given. The rich have to share their wealth with the poor, thus making charity a central notion. A great concern for the poor and a deep social conscience underlies the concept of charity. Social justice in this case means achieving just ends with just means. In Judaism, charity is not considered an act of mercy but an act of justice. Jews have a moral duty to protect the interests of the poorest. Compassion for the poorest is a divine commandment and charity has no limits. The first question every Jew will have to answer when they arrive in the next life will be the following: "Have you been honest in business?" Only afterward will they be tested on their knowledge of the Torah and on their respect for God's commandments. This shows the importance of honesty in Judaism.[12]

In Christianity, and more particularly in the social teaching of the Roman Catholic Church, there is sharp criticism of the superfluous prosperity of developed countries. In fact, this criticism stems back to the times of the Fathers of the Church (the first five centuries of the history of the Church), and more specifically to the words of St. John Chrysostom. Paul VI also calls for an equitable redistribution of prosperity to developing nations, since this would benefit developed countries as well. Why? Simply because otherwise, developed countries will be faced with the increasing anger of underdeveloped countries, with often unexpected political, economic, and social consequences. Prosperity should be held in the common interest. Thomas Aquinas also referred to the common use of material goods to help the least favored. It is a question of redistribution of the surplus. Whoever has received a larger share of earthly goods from God has received them to share the surplus with others. From Leo XIII to John-Paul II, the Catholic Church has always considered private property as a natural right derived from the reasonable nature of the human person. Since Pius XI, the popes insist on both the individual and the social dimension of property and labor rights and, therefore, on the rights of the human being himself. Property rights are subordinated to the universal purpose of the goods. The right to private property, according to John-Paul II, is fundamental to the development of the human person, but also has its limits in that it has to remain fair and equitable. For example, it must not lead to the illicit exploitation of human and natural resources, to abusive speculation, or to the disintegration of solidarity in the workplace.[13]

According to Islam, prosperity must not be monopolized by only a few people as that would lead to social imbalance. Islam actually attempts to abolish poverty, which is considered a negation of Allah. The wealthiest must assume certain social responsibilities. Each businessman has, for example, the moral duty to share his wealth with the poorest. Islam also condemns the accumulation of capital and proposes certain political and economic structures to insure its distribution since material wealth should be used in the public interest. Islam requires a balance in the use of property since greed is inherent to the human being and that one's thirst for prosperity must be controlled. The love of material prosperity is also considered as the source of all evil. Everyone must use his or her wealth according to Allah's will. Islam advocates moderation in consumption. Consumption of luxury goods and services is mostly considered morally reprehensible, similarly to Simone Weil, who was nonetheless influenced by a completely different context (see Chapter 12). According to Islam, prosperity and private property have distinctly social functions.[14]

The Functions of the State

In Judaism it is important that employers conform to the local customs established or accepted by the state. Local customs, legislated or not, may be used to establish salaries and working conditions and to prevent disputes between employers and employees. Therefore, employers cannot demand that their employees start working earlier or finish later than custom dictates. These, as well as local customs regarding pricing must be considered. Another example is holding down a second job (moonlighting) which can affect one's dedication to one's principle employer. If this custom is common and tolerated or supported by the state, then this practice can become legitimate.[15]

In Christianity, according to the social doctrine of the Catholic Church, the state has to support the common good without favoring the private interests of certain classes, unless it corresponds to the interest of the common good. State intervention must be used to stimulate the economy and not to limit individual freedom and economic initiative. The state is fully entitled to intervene and to enforce fundamental human rights, the individual being more important than civil society, which is in opposition to the Islamic view as we will see later. According to the Catholic conception, the state must insure that all goods are used in the collective interest. The state has the responsibility to improve the living conditions of the workers, via minimum wages, healthcare, unemployment benefits, and so on. The state must also establish the conditions necessary for the free exercise of economic activities and insure the respect of fundamental human rights. As well, it must intervene to protect citizens from violations of their rights, improve living conditions and stimulate the spiritual forces in society.[16]

The Islamic state is considered as the vehicle of the community of the faithful. The degree of intervention will depend on the wisdom and conscience of the leaders who must take into account the existing conditions in their society. The Islamic state must then convert natural instincts into moral qualities that can serve the common interests of the society. This state can suspend the property rights of a wealthy person who doesn't fulfill his social responsibilities. The state can also withdraw these rights from a person who has amassed undue wealth or who has acquired property illegally. Last, the state can intervene in order to prevent an excessive concentration of wealth to the detriment of the community, since Islamic law gives priority to collective as opposed to individual rights. In general, the Islamic state has to promote good and prevent evil, as well as to act according to Islamic law and Allah's will. The state must strive to be fair and equitable in its own transactions with its citizens and try to eradicate poverty and foster full employment. It must also intervene in order to secure the greatest wellbeing of the society and care for the poorest by guaranteeing them a minimum standard of life. Among its rights, the Islamic state can set a compulsory religious tax that will be redistributed to the poor. Furthermore, it has the right to mete out punishment for all dishonest activities, particularly speculation which is considered antisocial and any illicit means used to acquire a property, such as usury, alcohol, gambling, and so forth. Finally, the Islamic state may prohibit the establishment of monopolies and oligopolies and the practice of dumping.[17]

Employment and the Respect of Human Dignity

In Judaism, the employer must not deprive the worker of his wages or hold it more than twenty-four hours after the end of the work period, since the worker's family's lives may be endangered. The employer who delays in paying his employee's salary is considered to be taking his soul, his livelihood, and his life away. It is contrary to the Jewish law to have a contract of more than three years. Too long a contract is perceived as making the employer into a kind of God in the eyes of the employee and consequently as depriving the latter of a part of his dignity. Such a contract would implicitly indicate that the employee renounces his right to choose or change employers and therefore renounces his individual freedom. There is also a theological reason: The People of Israel may only serve God, therefore the sons of Israel must never be considered as the servants of their employers.[18]

Christianity emphasizes the transcendental dignity of work. It seeks to establish a social economy oriented toward the collective well-being while promoting fundamental rights. As a general rule, Christianity is opposed to all forms of totalitarianism which are considered as negating the freedom and dignity of the person, as despising God, and as the expression of an egocentricity that excludes social justice. The essence of Jesus's evangelical message implies the intense struggle against all forms of injustice or evil. According to Christianity, no social order, economic system, or political regime should threaten the worker's dignity, the loss of which would in turn threaten their legitimacy and morality. Each person is considered as having been created in God's image, implying a foundation of his or her inalienable rights. In the Christian conception, work both expresses and fosters the transcendental dignity of human beings. The dignity of work stems from the individual's sense of personal accomplishment acquired by fulfilling his tasks and functions. Through work, the person can be in harmony by working with and for others. He can better understand that Creation has provided everything that exists in the world for him.[19]

According to Islam, dignity at work is fundamental as well. To work in order to efficiently use the resources given by Allah is to praise Him. In this way, work is a religious duty. Equality is also a key Islamic value. All humans are equal before the law. Everyone must have the same chances in the working world even though differences do exist. However, as a whole, Islam emphasizes social equality that guarantees social harmony. The employer protects his employees and in return workers have to be honest, efficient, and diligent in their function.[20]

The Protection of the Natural Environment

The protection of the environment is a central concern in Judaism. Protecting God's creation is a divine injunction. Even in warfare, Jews have to protect the natural environment. The Torah underlines human beings' dependence on the natural environment and the need for every human being to respect that environment. This is so since the destruction of nature would have disastrous consequences for future generations. Judaism even goes as far as claiming that in mistreating nature, a human being ceases to be a human being since he imperils his own life as well as those of his descendants.[21]

According to Christianity, all Creation is at the disposal of man in order for him to complete it. The human being can therefore exploit natural resources to meet his needs and thus discover the action of his Creator in nature. In the Christian tradition, destroying the environment implies forgetting God; that is, negating the conception that this world is only possible through God's acts of creation. In Christianity, forgetting God is made possible by the omnipresence of technology that fills the human being with exaltation and makes him forget his own richness. The human being then substitutes himself for God and forgets his limitations. Solange Lefebvre (see Chapter 3) and Thierry Pauchant (see Chapter 11) have developed this theme in this book.[22]

According to Islam, every human being must insure that all creatures and the other elements of nature are not mistreated. To attain a harmonious relationship with the natural environment one must understand that, according to the tradition, all creatures are equal in the eyes of Allah and that they constantly try to please Him. Islam requires that all human, natural, and spiritual resources are used efficiently so as to reach an optimal rate of economic growth and improve the collective standard of living.[23]

CONCLUSION

I would like to conclude with three propositions. For me this interfaith declaration leads to three lessons:

1. It is clear how much the three monotheist religions share in terms of ethical principles and behavioral norms in the economic sphere.

2. The differences between them can become an opportunity for the faithful in each religion to understand the religious and cultural traditions of the others. This understanding should arise from a questioning provoked by the other, and not only from the person's own point of view within their personal religion. In this book we have repeatedly discussed the need for the respect of differences and for a real dialogue.

3. Finally, that the strategy of a community of ideas is not incompatible with a differentiation between the three religions to the extent that each partner in the interfaith dialogue respects his own tradition and at the same time is open to other perspectives.

14

Dialogue on Part III

Yves Benoît, Roger Berthouzoz, Michel Dion,
J.-Robert Ouimet, and Thierry C. Pauchant

EDITOR'S NOTE

This is the third and last dialogue presented in this book. In this dialogue, participants address questions previously discussed in the forum and explore the proposed themes within this section of the book. At this point, the reader should be familiar with the unstructured nature of a dialogue.

I will come back to the relevance of the dialogue discipline in the concluding chapter. I will then propose that such a discipline or practice is a process from which a "dialogical ethics" can emerge. I will also suggest that, under certain conditions, a dialogue can become a spiritual practice.

Participant: I have a question for Mr. Berthouzoz. I think I understood the essence of his presentation. However, I am disappointed with his conclusion on economical ethics charts, business ethical codes, and the creation of managerial tools. I said to myself: "Well, another system . . . another best way to do things in the world." I didn't really appreciate that part and was wondering whether it might possible for Mr. Berthouzoz to comment on it.

Roger Berthouzoz: I will explain what motivated this kind of conclusion. First, the underlying presumption of all my work is that each person has his or her own values. I addressed that question in order to introduce a problem, especially among people who tend to dispute the pertinence of a spiritual or ethical reference in business, or those who contest—which is even worse—that business goals are only about maximizing profit. According to those people, society's problems are not related to business activities. I agree with Ian I. Mitroff on that subject (see Chapter 2). We must rethink the profound meaning of an enterprise. An important inquiry must be carried out on the work in organization.

On the other hand, Solange Lefebvre (see Chapter 3) referred to the gap between private and public life. I am not sure that this vision of our existence, between private and public, is properly understood and analyzed. We actually have a private life in our workplace, which is also a human and social place. I think that we accepted this model of private–public life which embodies the problem of consciousness and freedom of consciousness, and we realized that there was a public way of living religion, values, or spirituality that could become lunatic or violent, and not just in the sixteenth or seventeenth century. Even today we suspect that faith, religion, and spirituality are sources of division and violence. Thus, to reconsider those aspects is a way to structure spiritual communication.

I must insist again on the usefulness of ethical charts. They allow people who have different convictions and goals, who have had different life experiences and yet who are sensitive enough to the most fundamental issues, to associate and converge so they can express, communicate and actualize themselves around these issues. We certainly could say: "These are nice ideas, but they are not realistic." The reality lies in the individual's decision and regular collective action—we know all that!

To finish, I would like to draw your attention to a subject I didn't really develop, but which is quite fundamental. Spiritual experience and faith can be a resource and provide the support necessary in order to actualize spiritual practices in business and the economic system.

Participant: There are many different religions and cultures as well as many theories on ethics. In this forum, we were asked to reflect on the nature of the problems that relate to those differences. I think that one possible answer could be that we have difficulty understanding and accepting each other. Moreover, how can we understand each other if we don't know what we are talking about? I think that the central problem is one of language and communication. It concerns our capacity to talk, to understand what ethics represents—that we can hold different meanings.

I really appreciated Mr. Dion's presentation. In future forums, it would be better that a presentation on the existing differences among the religions be made at the beginning: We would then have a better understanding from the outset of those differences.

Participant: My question is for Mr. Ouimet. It has been said that the integration of spiritual values in organizations allows, nevertheless, the business to be profitable. But we didn't really talk about this aspect of profitability, its nature and its efficiency. What is the connection between a business that promotes these values and profitability on a short-term as well as a long-term basis?

I also question the following: Is the excessive enrichment of business—to the detriment of the vast majority of citizens sometimes deprived of the essentials—ethical? Shouldn't ethics have consequences on an enterprise's wealth? Can we imagine an enterprise trying to establish a better long-term balance instead of aiming at short-term profits by integrating ethical values?

J.-Robert Ouimet: The answer to your question lies in Christian doctrine or in others I'm not familiar with. In practice, the starting point for enrichment or for the right to own property is really the parable of the talents: There must be justice and equity in employees' remuneration.[1] In our market economy, the only reference we have is in comparing two businesses of the same or similar size. From the moment human beings have equal remuneration and social security in similar businesses, similar countries, and similar activities, then there is a minimum of social justice.

In *Our Project* (see Chapter 6), it is clearly understood that managers have greater responsibilities than others. Why? Because they are privileged, their work is more secure, they are often better protected, and some have a better opportunity to save money. They are, in essence, less vulnerable if they lose their job. What is more, responsibilities are enormous for shareholders. The right to ownership implies serious obligations that, from the onset, go further than justice and equity. There is a necessity to slowly find the means to share growing values within the enterprise and to offer them to people working in that enterprise. Too often, we quickly conclude that we should give more money. As limited as it is, my personal experience allowed me to discover that what is needed, from the outset, is equity and justice and to treat people well. This is what is fundamentally missing: to be treated like real human beings, as people loved and inhabited by God, Allah, Jehovah, or whoever you choose. People really want to be treated well and with dignity.

I'm getting to the end of my answer to your question, which I probably couldn't answer very well. It is when one is confronted with bad financial results that one's values are tested. A bad situation can lead to layoffs or to factory closings. It is here that businesses that tried integrating spiritual values at work were unwise. We talk about Salomon's wisdom, not the wisdom of a thoughtful person confronting a difficult decision. Salomon's wisdom leads to the conclusion: "Okay, there is no way out: We must layoff some people and then we'll help them." In the past forty years, I went through three of four serious cut backs, having to lay people off, but I questioned each occasion very seriously. I didn't lose my job, my house, or my car. I asked myself how a manager should act "in God's way." For a lack of better tools, better understanding, and ability, we had to close the factory.

Participant: I really enjoyed Mr. Benoît's conclusion. However, I have a problem with Mr. Ouimet's four conditions. I would accept and integrate them more easily if they were desirable instead of necessary. Given the assumption that, within an enterprise, everyone has some spirituality to express, I wouldn't want these necessary or universal conditions to lead us from management by objective to management by objection.

J.-Robert Ouimet: I challenge anybody to work in an enterprise within the market economy for twenty-five years without using those four conditions (see the end of Chapter 6). Given the limits of my knowledge, I would be very happy if someone proved the opposite; that it would be possible to observe a growth in humanization and spiritualization values retroactively while the executives didn't care about them. I'd have to see it to believe it.

Yves Benoît: I mentioned in my conclusion that we were still at the first stage. I agree with the fact that we could find a core somewhere and work with resources. I agree with Mr. Ouimet when he says that if we want to go further, we'll need other people to join the project and that the entire organization should get more involved.

Participant: I would like to share with you an anecdote related to Mr. Ouimet's necessary conditions. His Ph.D. thesis has been a very laborious experience. I remember having imposed these conditions on him by saying, "Your experience is very beautiful, but it still should have a universal character to it. It should be replicable even if there are a lot conditions that could influence it." We wonder if, like any other scientific work, his thesis will be disproved. From this perspective, I accepted these conditions as universal ones.

Participant: I have a question for Mr. Ouimet. You said that businesses that applied those values do not exist anymore. I see a contradiction with what has just been said about the universality of the model. How is it that those enterprises that applied a similar model do not exist anymore?

J.-Robert Ouimet: I don't know any enterprise that succeeded in actualizing the Catholic social doctrine for twenty-five years without limiting itself to—and still, that is a lot—to the establishment of justice and material equity: salaries, total remuneration comparable to similar enterprises, and so forth. The difficulties appear—and I'm not familiar with all the enterprises so I could be mistaken—when executives, managers, and boards of directors must cut back during an economic downturn.

Those big enterprises, which don't exist anymore because they tried to "be good" to people, decided to cut salaries for six months. What could have been done in those cases is to look closely at the balance sheet, the profits, and to compare them with their competitors and, if necessary, to remove 18 percent of the human beings (which is more difficult than 18 percent of the employees). To be able to make this kind of decision without going crazy, if we really believe that each person is created, loved, and inhabited by God, we must either be part of a support group, or not make that decision and let the enterprise go. It was not God's will to let it go.

Participant: I had tears in my eyes when I heard Mr. Ouimet's presentation. I don't know if other people have had a similar experience, but I thought that if there were more philanthropic and happy employers like him, life at work would be much nicer. I would like to propose, if it does not already exist, that one of our goals be the definition of "ISO norms for human values." Those norms are gradually being applied now in the area of environmental issues. Maybe we could define some ethical, ecological, social, humanistic, and spiritual norms in management?

Michel Dion: In the United States, the Council for Economic Priorities in New York has created a series of ethical standards. They are not spiritual indicators. They identify enterprises that meet their ethical standards after verification. There are also ethical mutual funds for those who desire to invest ethically. If you want, you can invest in the portfolio that meets your ethical values. There are a lot of possibilities, but I think that an indicator based on spiritual values could be very innovative. To my knowledge, this doesn't exist yet.

Thierry C. Pauchant: We have started a project related to that subject. We call it the compass audit. It consists of evaluating an organization's efficiencies: economic, social, ecological, and spiritual. This approach is made possible because in a business economy and management we more often make use of a multicriteria approach, in which all kinds of data are involved. For example, the World Bank began recently to evaluate nations not only on their GDP (Gross Domestic Product)—the economic wealth produced by a nation—but also on the quality of life of populations, health conditions, education, and so on, and the quality of natural resources available.

In business, we are starting to use criteria beyond strict financial or accounting data. The Body Shop, for example, has an elaborate ecological audit; Ben & Jerry's evaluates its social contributions; social reviews are starting to appear with all the methodological problems they involve. The indicators mentioned by Mr. Ouimet are innovative. Medtronic, a Fortune 500 enterprise in the United States, has developed other indicators. In Canada, both Estelle Morin from HEC, who did a Ph.D. thesis on organizations' efficiency and Michel Guindon, an accounting professor, proposed another set of indicators. They include, for example, the number of dismissed employees in a year, the client's satisfaction, the number of law violations, the work environment, and so on. Those indicators are accepted today by "The Order of Certified General Accountants of Quebec."[2] Furthermore, a certified group of administrators proposed another set of indicators for establishing what they call "healthy management" (equity, transparency, and so on). These indicators are the basis for an accreditation system.[3]

The development of the multicriteria method allows new possibilities and, yes, we could imagine evaluating our organizations, not only on an ethical basis, but also on a spiritual basis. Abraham Maslow, for example, denounced working conditions that were "unhealthy for the soul." Simone Weil also defined certain "needs of the soul." With time, we'll inevitably end up with such indicators. Even accountants are interested in this type of approach since many of them consider their evaluations too one dimensional. They too are people like you and me, with ethical and spiritual aspirations. But to develop these kinds of indicators will require much time and a great deal of research.

J.-Robert Ouimet: In response to your question and comment and with all humility, allow me to suggest you to read the six chapters of *Our Project* (see Chapter 6). That work doesn't offer answers to all your questions, but you will find enough ethical moral and spiritual elements to discuss for a long time.

Allow me to comment on the following as well: I cannot prove it scientifically, but on the faith level, it seems that the first condition of universality is a spiritual support group. I personally went around the world many times, particularly India, and I'm convinced that a spiritual support group, either Buddhist, Muslim, Shintoist, Hindu, Christian, or Jewish—and I would add without hesitation an authentic atheistic group—is absolutely necessary. What we're talking about, and what we proved scientifically, is not only true in a Christian context. However, that has been our experience. We can say that the fruits are beautiful, but there are other ways to grow such beautiful fruits. I am convinced of that.

Participant: My work is related to ethics and management and I am very interested in this forum, but I feel a little frustrated by its Catholic ethnocentricity. However, Mr. Pauchant has commented on this. I was also reassured by Mr. Dion's presentation. I would have liked for this forum, an international event, to unite many perspectives and have been more open to other ethics, religions, or spiritualities. Here is what Saint-Exupéry said: "If we are different, my friend, far from harming me, you enrich me." It would be interesting that this forum be an occasion for sharing and opening and to consider the human being as an integrative entity, like nature, culture, and freedom, as suggested by Mr. Berthouzoz (see Chapter 12).

Participant: I find it also a bit unfortunate that when we talk about Christianity, we're only talking about Catholicism. Although I understand it, there is also Protestantism, whose first particularity is precisely that there are no intermediates between God and the individual.

I would like to mention also that there's an ecumenical document from the United Church which invites all religions, independent of their religious convictions, or atheists of good will, to take care of all of God's creation, which is in jeopardy today. I think that with this ecumenical call, the United Church expresses its wish for the unification of people of all religions.

Michel Dion: This remark is indeed relevant. Let's say that the Protestant religion, Lutheran or Calvinist, distinguishes itself from the Catholic religion. I didn't have time to make those distinctions in my presentation. But in my courses, I always differentiate Catholic, Lutheran, and Calvinist values and also Christian and orthodox values. But we have to admit that these worlds are not totally different. Those religions are relatively close to each other, but with important differences.

Thierry C. Pauchant: We are lucky to live at the beginning of a new millennium. With this new millennium, many historic events will take place. For example, a 1998 meeting involving scientists, politicians, and spiritual leaders, in connection with the United Nations, discussed the need to develop an "International Declaration of Human Responsibilities" to salute as well as to complement the "Universal Declaration of Human Rights" of 1948. Imagine! We would speak about rights, but also about responsibilities. Simone Weil had previously asked for that kind of international declaration in 1941. Her proposition can be read in her book, *The Need for Roots*, in which the first part is dedicated to the needs of the soul. Here again lies another source of inspiration for establishing spiritual indicators. For her, the notion of obligation surpassed the notion of rights since a person on a desert island wouldn't have rights but only obligations in order to survive. According to her, the obligation has a divine origin: Its conditions transcend the human's will and aim to nourish the body and the soul.

Participant: "It is always easier to practice chastity in a convent than in a brothel." Without comparing businesses to brothels, I would say that it is easier to express our spirituality in a forum like this than at work. Which brings me to this point: We heard a very moving testimony from a person working in the public sector. She was expressing what Mr. Pauchant calls the "crushing of the individual." I have often felt that, especially in large corporations. Someone who cannot use their free will is practically obliged to act against his or her conscience. What will we do in the next, in the following days or months, to expose executives to the content of this forum? It is only then that things will change.

J.-Robert Ouimet: I have a very practical answer to your question. To resolve that crushing of human beings, particularly those on the lowest rung of the ladder of the organization in a market economy, we should use what we call the "fifteenth management tool": surveys. These surveys respect anonymity and are designed by external experts. They contain twenty-five questions that we have been working on for eight years, so they are quite elaborated. They refer to about fifteen fundamental values and allow one to scientifically obtain a "well-being cardiogram" of an organization. Those surveys are not perfect nor are they complete. They are, however, better than nothing.

Often, the first two surveys say little. People are afraid, and with reason. After two or three years, they see that nobody has lost their job in the first six months after the first survey was conducted. They also notice that the company then tries to resolve, not the thirty-two problems mentioned in the survey, but about twelve or fourteen of those problems. A few months after the survey, executives evaluate which issues have been resolved. After four surveys, in a seven-year period, the crushing of individuals diminishes. It is scientifically proven. But there should be a little less pride on the executive level. I include myself here, nobody likes to be told the truth straight to their face. It is for that very reason that these external and anonymous surveys exist.

I hope I won't offend anybody, but, considering the quality and the beauty of what's been said in the past forty-eight hours, I propose that everyone here, wherever you are, take the time to express their gratitude to whomever you want—the Creator, the Higher Power, or God—for what we have experienced in the last two days.

Conclusion: All Managerial Thought or Action Is Based on a Certain Concept of Truth, Goodness, and Beauty

Thierry C. Pauchant

EDITOR'S NOTE

In this concluding chapter, I propose that management is first and foremost a manifestation of a particular notion of truth, goodness, and beauty. A conceptualization of this kind has epistemological, ethical, and aesthetic implications that are fundamental for the management of our organizations and their impact on the world.

Having commented on the current domination of our organizations on the structuring of our societies and of our lives, I will argue that our only choice is to collectively invent a global ethic and a spirituality that can transcend our differences. Returning to the notion of "levels of consciousness" presented in the opening chapter of this book, I will also present a systemic model drawn form Ken Wilber's work that suggests that complex relationships exist between these levels of consciousness and the health of our bodies, the values that are predominant in our societies, and the technologies and management practices that we use. This systemic model not only enables us to precisely define the potential dangers associated with integrating ethics and spirituality in management, but also allows us to propose some necessities in their development and application.

THE NECESSITY OF RENDERING ETHICS
MORE OBJECTIVE AND GLOBAL

In the introduction of this book, I proposed several reasons that motivate the development and use of certain ethical principals within organizations. As we have seen, several factors such as the employment crisis, the existential crisis of meaning, the ecological crisis, international terrorism, or the crisis of belief are leading different groups in society—employees, managers, consumers, investors, unions, governments, universities, religious institutions, and so on—to want to better define and integrate ethical values to guide management thinking and action. This systemic reality—that is, the fact that this demand stems from different interest groups or stakeholders— echoes the nature of an economy that is becoming more and more systemic, global, interconnected, and complex. In a systemic world, the differences between "us" and "them" disappear as ethical problems are affecting a collective "we."

Systemic thinking, since its inception at the very beginnings of philosophy and science in the seventh century B.C., has attempted to overcome the misdeeds of fragmentation.[1] On several occasions throughout this book, we have tackled the problem of fragmentation. For example, it has been suggested that there are important differences between deeply personal values that motivate individuals and those that are accepted at work.

When I speak of fragmentation, I do not wish to cast doubt on the benefits of specialization. However, we are more often than not forced to recognize that the effort put into specialization is not counterbalanced by a vision that is, at the same time, more integrative, more global, more systemic. Jean-Marie Toulouse, at the beginning of the book, insisted that what is needed in management education is a balance between technical and specialized training as well as an education that is both more general and more critical (see Chapter 1).

This problem of fragmentation, that is to say the lack of adequation between specialized skills and a more global vision that guides action, is by no means new. We can attribute the origin of this bias to Rene Descartes in science, to Adam Smith in economics, and to Frederick Taylor in management. However, as far back as the fifth century B.C., Hippocrates, the founding father of medicine, warned against the dangers of specialization and advocated instead for the need to embrace a more global and systemic vision of health.

Throughout this book, several people have insisted on using systemic thinking as a means of integrating ethics and spirituality in organizations. Ian I. Mitroff has suggested that a systemic approach is a *sine qua non* condition for any kind of sustainable change to take place (see Chapter 2); J.-Robert Ouimet based *Our Project* on the relationships between six groups of stakeholders and their different values and responsibilities (see Chapter

6); Vera Danyluk described the "adequation" that must necessarily exist between deeper personal values and the service toward employees, elected officials, and fellow citizens (see Chapter 7); Yves Benoît also stipulated that a better integration of spiritual values in the healthcare system was made possible through the creation of multidisciplinary teams (see Chapter 8); and Roger Berthouzoz warned of the dangers of using only one discipline—namely economism—as a basis for making decisions and taking action in business (see Chapter 12).

In a more general fashion, virtually all the contributors to the book, without having consulted each other initially, warned of the dangers of fragmentation and proposed that the desire to integrate ethics and spirituality in organizations stems from a will to live a more unified life that is less fragmented, in response to a need for rootedness, for belonging to a whole and for contributing to its betterment.

One of the most important contributions from systemic thinking into management has been to identify the issues that are important to its many stakeholders and how best to address them. The notion of stakeholders, larger than that of shareholders, includes all persons or groups that have a particular interest in an organization and/or who are affected by its activities.[2] One of the most notable difficulties in management, leadership, or strategy is to be able to deal both effectively and adequately with these groups whose issues and motivations differ so widely from one another. For example, the needs of consumers are often different than those of investors. The current emphasis placed on the needs of customers in both the business world and public administration can be seen as a counterbalancing of the past infatuation with the sole investor needs.

Most people do not realize that this problem of balance, when faced with divergent issues and needs, is in fact an ethical problem. Each group is in fact pursuing a different ethic, which influences its needs, its motivations, its desires, as well as its perception of true and false, good and bad, beautiful and ugly. The management problem, in ethical terms, is then not only a matter of choosing and applying one universal ethic, but responding adequately to different ethics, each of them able to defend, with legitimacy, their respective points of view.

If the first strategy stems from the fundamental belief that we live in a universe; that is, a world in which there is only one truth, one way of perceiving and of acting, the second strategy then posits that we live in a "pluriverse," a world in which there are many truths, many ways of perceiving and of acting.[3] The very fact that the notion "pluriverse," proposed by William James at the beginning of this century, is foreign for many people is indicative of the force that the universal ideal has in our societies and on our "habits of the heart," as Alexis de Tocqueville stated so eloquently.[4]

To give an example from this book, Claude Beland (see Chapter 5) described particularly well the different ethics that motivate the banking system in general, compared to the one that motivates the cooperative movement. To condemn or idealize one system over the other is exemplary of our habit to constantly fragment. Roger Berthouzoz (see Chapter 12) reminded us that every system generates its own rationality and set of practices, from which stems a specific sense of identity.

At the organizational level, an ethical imperative consists then of taking into account the interests of many stakeholders, be they internal or external to the organization and provided that their interests are perceived as moral and legal in the surrounding society, as well as to respond to the major issues that confront our world, as we will see later.

This systemic–ethical approach is founded on the notion of adequation, as formulated in modern science by Ross Ashby, and proposed throughout the centuries by such authors as Plato in philosophy, and Saint Thomas Aquinas in theology.[5] The principal of adequation, known also as the principle of requisite variety posits that a system, such as an organization, must contain the same level of complexity internally as that which is expressed in its external environment.

But the ethical problem does not only present itself on the collective level however. If systemic thinking enables a better understanding and ability to respond to the different concerns of disparate groups—such as financial, strategic, legal, logistical, but also social, ecological, moral, and spiritual—then these different ethics are also present on the personal level. They require a deep internal dialogue with oneself. If it is already difficult to study that which motivates entire groups, then to survey that which profoundly motivates us on an individual basis—our habits of the heart—is more difficult still. The first strategy requires a sociopolitical analysis, the second a personal introspection. Socrates's notion "know thyself" is not an easy task by any means, but is considered to be one of the essential abilities of all managers and leaders.[6]

The conflicts between different personal ethics are particularly evident in times of crisis. For example, several studies have suggested that after the Challenger explosion in 1986, a number of engineers at NASA were severely affected personally at the level of their subjectivity and their different ethics: These individuals were affected as managers, scientists, employees, engineers, citizens, parents, friends, human beings, and spiritual beings.[7] For instance, some questioned their very expertise as engineers, asking themselves "Am I a good engineer?" "Could I have done something to prevent the tragedy?" Others questioned the expertise of NASA and the collective dream of the conquest of space. Others asked far more personal questions of themselves: "Am I a good person who cares for my friends?"; "What else could I have done?" At home, some people had to confront their own children's question: "Mom and dad, is it true that you are responsible for the death of the astronauts?" The same anguish was felt after the World Trade Center tragedy.

As Chester Barnard suggested as early as 1958, the ethical question within organizations presents not only the problem of different interests as pursued by varying groups both within and outside of the organization, but also the problem of the multiple identities of each individual.[8] "From what point of view must I judge this situation?" "Which ethic must I adopt?" "That of my religious faith?" "That of my role as vice president of finance?" "That of my obligations as a member of the board?" "That of my responsibilities and rights as a consumer of the products of my company?" "My beliefs and values as a spiritual being?" More often than not, these different ethical roles, each valid from different points of view, will lead to very different thoughts and actions.

At the end of the 1950s, Barnard was one of the first people in the administrative sciences to propose that adequate training be offered to managers and leaders to enable them, as best as possible, to confront these complex issues and situations. Today we are still faced with a lack of preparation for complex ethical matters. To defend their own interests, many people in organizations even go so far as to impose a unique point of view formally and informally, in order to avoid ethical complexity and dilemmas of conscience. As we have seen, several managers suffer from this fragmentation and wish to act differently. It was suggested as well, in the introduction of the book, that different types of ethics are associated with different levels of consciousness. I will come back to this subject.

In Search of Truth, Goodness, and Beauty

In a certain way, this recognition for a more integrated ethic within organizations, and especially an ethic inspired by the spiritual, touches on a problem that has haunted humanity since the beginning of time: the search for truth, goodness, and beauty. This search has quite literally absorbed the lives of a multitude of people in the fields of philosophy, theology, spirituality, and mysticism such as Plato, Aristotle, Thomas Aquinas, Immanuel Kant, Wilhem Windelband, Kahlil Gibran, John Dewey, Hannah Arendt, Pierre Teilhard de Chardin, and Simone Weil, to name a few.[9] The search for meaning that preoccupies so many managers today can be seen, from a certain stand point, as an ethical quest: It stems from the realization that all managerial action and thought stems from a specific notion of what is true, good, and beautiful, concepts that affect, in very concrete ways, the practice of management as well as the natural, social, and spiritual worlds.

In an enterprise, a specific concept of truth, for instance, will affect the types of tools and approaches used in decision making: Will we focus on the use of statistical analysis or economic models? Will these take into consideration issues of power, the emotions of those concerned, the state of their soul, their intuition, their fundamental values?

A specific concept of goodness, on the other hand, will influence decisions of equity and justice, such as distribution of wealth: Should we favor shareholders, customers, employees, communities, or society at large? This concept will also influence the organization and structure of work itself, translated into policies in human resources as well as health and safety.

Finally, a specific concept of beauty will affect decisions made regarding product and service design, as well as environmental policies: Can we pollute a river in the name of efficiency and financial priorities? It will also influence the building of megaprojects—a freeway that runs along a beach may be practical, but is it aesthetic?

Of course, we must be cautious when making these types of generalizations. Without getting into over-technical philosophical considerations, reducing the search for goodness, truth, and beauty to ethics is a shortcut that carries with it all the faults of a shortcut. In philosophy and theology, this search corresponds to distinct, albeit interrelated, areas. The search for truth is an epistemological issue whose function it is to distinguish between true and false. The search for beauty is an issue of aesthetics, one of the most complex areas in philosophy which tries to establish the difference between the ugly and the beautiful. Last, the search for goodness is an ethical issue the goal of which is to distinguish between good and bad, moral and immoral.

Mentioning the different fields of epistemology, aesthetics and ethics is not a matter of splitting hairs. As we will see, it is essential that each maintain their specificity while being integrated into a larger whole. For example, Immanuel Kant distinguished between truth, goodness, and beauty in three different books that are considered a trilogy: *Critique of Pure Reason*, a book that deals essentially with epistemology; *Critique of Practical Reason*, a book on ethics; and *Critique of Judgment*, focusing on aesthetics. In the same vein in theology, Saint Bonaventure distinguished between three different realities: the "eye of the body," the "eye of reason," and the "eye of contemplation," proposing that each had different concepts of goodness, truth, and beauty.

It is dangerous, in general and for organizational life in particular, to regroup these different quests without differentiating them as well. We have witnessed this type of flattening of reality in the past, namely the dominance of one term over any other. Dogmatic religious systems have dictated behavior by imposing certain visions of truth and reality, from which were derived concepts of the good and the beautiful. Today, especially in economic milieus, we are in the throes not of religion but of reason, and instrumental reason in particular. This type of reason has its own concept of goodness and beauty determined by the concept of truth that it espouses, namely one that is concrete, tangible, observable, and quantifiable. The purpose here is not to condemn, once and for all, religion nor reason on the basis of their dominance during certain points in history. Rather, it is to be vigilant and recognize the differences that exist between the search for goodness, truth, and beauty and to not accept that any one can flatten the others.

The philosopher Charles Taylor is one of the voices to have spoken out the most against this flattening of reality by reason. To stress it once again, his point is not to condemn the development of this reason, but instead to find a balance between truth, goodness, and beauty; or, put differently, between epistemology, ethics, and aesthetics; or again, in yet another way, between the reality of the body, of reason, and of contemplation.[10] Taylor expressed it thus:

Modern freedom was won by our breaking loose from older moral horizons. People used to see themselves as part of a larger order. In some cases, this was a cosmic order, a "great chain of Being," in which humans figured in their proper place along with angels, heavenly bodies, and our fellow earthly creatures.

Once society no longer has a sacred structure, once social arrangements and modes of action are no longer grounded in the order of things or the will of God, they are in a sense up for grabs. They can be redesigned with their consequences for the happiness and well-being of individuals as our goals. The yardstick that henceforth applies is that of instrumental reason.

In one way this change has been liberating. But there is also a widespread unease that instrumental reason not only has enlarged its scope but also threatens to take over our lives. The fear is that things that ought to be determined by other criteria will be decided in terms of efficiency or "cost–benefit" analysis, that the independent ends that ought to be guiding our lives will be eclipsed by the demand to maximize output. There are lots of things one can point to that give substance to this worry: for instance, the ways the demands of economic growth are used to justify very unequal distributions of wealth and income, or the way these same demands make us insensitive to the needs of the environment, even to the point of potential disaster.[11]

The subtle differences that exist between the quests for truth, goodness, and beauty can be preserved by avoiding the previously mentioned flattening while also recognizing the integrated balance that exists between them. I would like to return to the notion of levels of consciousness, as presented through the work of Ken Wilber.[12] To be precise, the fusion that is to be avoided in the search for truth, goodness, and beauty is that of the prepersonal type, where the fusion to be strived for is of the transpersonal type. In the first instance, these different modes of searching, touching on the epistemological, the ethical, and the aesthetic, are not yet differentiated. A complete fusion of the three risks degeneration into a flattening of their differences by collapsing them into one theme. In the second instance, these different modes have been differentiated and have been allowed to mature, relatively speaking, having been personalized. A subtle fusion can then take place while preserving their differences and integrating them into a balanced whole.[13]

Discussing the philosophical and theological notions in a book destined for managers may seem somewhat out of place. Philosophy and theology, however, are not only the concern of philosophers and theologians. Today, more and more employees, managers, and executives are realizing that their professions are in fact applied philosophies and theologies. It is not an arm-chair philosophy or theology in which one deconstructs terms and ideas, safely tucked way from the day-to-day issues lived in the real world. By no means. More and more people that work within organizations and that are affected by them are realizing that management and leadership today are in fact a philosophy and a theology of action, the outcome of which has consequences on their own lives as well as that of the world, be it the natural, social, or spiritual.

In this book, Ian I. Mitroff is the person who has presented the problem most succinctly by saying that few people have the courage to address this directly. For him, management is, first and foremost, a "management of truth" and "management of spirit" (see Chapter 4). To state it differently, all managerial thought and action stems, be it consciously or not, from a particular ethic—taken in the generic sense—that is to say a certain concept of truth, goodness, and beauty. Each management thought and action therefore has important effects on the world at large, including the moral values and spiritual aspiration of individuals. In this light, the fundamental question is then not "Should we integrate ethics into management?" since a certain ethic is at the very foundation of managerial action and decision making. Rather, the essential question is "What type of ethics and spirituality do we want to integrate and promote at work?"

In other words, this book could have been titled *Managing the Ethics and Spirituality of Work*. This title would have suggested that, be it voluntarily or not, consciously or not, all managerial action rests on certain ethics and has important effects on the economic, social, ecological, moral, and spiritual wealth of the world. For example, a person who manages a mutual fund whose goal it is only to maximize returns, and the person who attempts to ensure a competitive return while respecting certain moral criteria that are decided upon collectively, are both living out certain ethical concepts. By the same token, general policies that deny the deeper values and spiritual aspirations of individuals, and others that encourage the fulfillment of these aspirations, are both managing the spirit, the first by crushing it, the second by encouraging it. It is very likely however, that the title *Managing the Ethics and Spirituality of Work*, or even *Managing Truth, Goodness, and Beauty* would have seemed bizarre.

This search for truth, goodness, and beauty and of their subtle balance is not simply an intellectual exercise mired in lofty words and concepts. It is one that is expressed in a very tangible way on a daily basis. For example, every day millions of people try and reach this balance by purchasing goods, services, and information in the marketplace. It is interesting to note that we are witnessing today a rejection of the false by a significant number of consumers, or more precisely, a rejection of the false, the bad, and the ugly.[14] It is estimated that a quarter of adults are expressing this rejection, a number which, when translated into market potential, accounts for 45 million consumers in the United States alone—not a negligible number by any means.[15] This rejection of the false, the bad, and the ugly is manifesting itself in very concrete ways: the purchasing of traditional houses that are set in more quiet neighborhoods or that need to be restored to their original state of beauty; a rejection of all that is plastic, of imitations, of disposable goods that are thrown away after use, of goods that are mass produced; a demand for craft and a return to more natural products such as cotton, oak, or granite; a will to consume products that are natural and avoiding those which are chemically treated, artificially colored, or genetically engineered; a will to not only throw away less but rather to recycle, to preserve, and to buy products that are more durable and reusable; resisting acts of impulsive purchasing or purchasing based a passing trend or a concern for status.

This search for truth, goodness, and beauty is also evident in the desire to know the history of products, their place of origin, by whom they were made, under which conditions, and the consequences of their making, be it positive or negative; the search for the authentic experience in tourism and travel, be it historical, cultural, spiritual, or religious; a will to invest in projects or enterprises that are not involved in immoral or even amoral activities, from which stems ethical mutual funds, green investment portfolios, and so forth; a desire for personal development through workshops, seminars, educational programs, software, videos, magazines, or books; a will to rediscover the great traditions and classics, hence the success of books such as *Sophie's Choice* by William Styron, or *Voltaire's Bastards* by John Saul.

In organizations and enterprises, this search for truth, goodness, and beauty is translated into choosing those organizations that are less aggressive with their marketing strategies, those that sell products and services or information that is deemed necessary and moral; in a management style that is more authentic, less bureaucratic and politicized, that respects the individual and encourages their creativity. It is expressed also in the rejection of manufacturing processes that are harmful to individuals in a social context, to nature, or to the soul; in the desire for congruence between the words and actions of management executives and of politicians; or in the will to know the real reasons that motivate decision making.

Three Reasons for Making Ethics More Objective and Global

Such comments on the search for truth, goodness, and beauty suggest that ethics is a very complex subject. Ethics stems simultaneously from disparate groups as well as from the complexity of the human character. It stems from more than just one subjective reality, while having at the same time very concrete effects. Despite this complexity and this diversity of sources and consequences—linking the collective, the personal, the subjective, and the material—we are nevertheless obliged to create more objective ethics. It is imperative that we make ethics both more objective and global. There are three fundamental reasons for this, and I will briefly outline them: first, the dominant position which organizations have taken in our lives; second, the global impact of modern technology; and third, the global effects of the dominant economic system, namely the market system.

The Dominant Position That Organizations Have Taken in Our Lives

Our world, quite literally, is becoming more and more organized. The most noticeable tendency, which is most often criticized, is the influence of international firms, or transnational organizations, as they are called.[16] Many of them have financial portfolios, technological capacities, and human resources larger than many nation–states. For the first time in history, in 1995 more than 50 percent of the 100 largest entities in the world—measured by their financial power—were private enterprises, as compared to nations. Between them, these enterprises control one-third of all the commercial transactions in the world, a number that continues to rise with their mergers, acquisitions, and strategic alliances. If the notion of the nation–state, emblem of democracy, still exists, then transnational enterprises become a force to reckon with today, gaining in autonomy through neoliberal policies. They are even wooed by the nation–states themselves.

Nevertheless, the growth of transnational enterprises is but one of the signs of a more significant trend. In 1938, Chester I. Barnard suggested that there were more organizations in the world than there were people.[17] Perhaps he was right. In our modern society, a person is involved with many organizations and is so to varying degrees, including, for example, private enterprises, political parties, universities and schools, municipal organizations, service-based enterprises, government bodies, volunteer organizations, clubs of all kinds, associations, churches, temples, synagogues, and so forth. Among them, it is worth noting the important increase of nongovernmental organizations.[18]

The increasing number of these organizations does not fully explain their influence. The internal logic and particular practices with which they are run (see Chapter 12), influenced by the surrounding culture of mounting utilitarianism and individualism, likewise influences our culture, our societies, and our personalities. In a wonderful book written by a group of sociologists, philosophers, and theologians, Robert N. Bellah and his associates describe the habits of the heart that these enterprises have helped forge. This book describes a certain modern concept of truth, goodness, and beauty present in the United States and many Western countries. It is suggested for example, that to to be right—the ancient quest for truth—is reduced today to simply having the right answer; that it is no longer about simply being good—the quest for ethics—but that we have to be good at something. Furthermore, the distinction between true and false rests with reference to money won or money lost. Touching on the theme of fragmentation, the authors themselves state the following:

The most distinctive aspect of twentieth-century American society is the division of life into a number of separate functional sectors: home and workplace, work and leisure, white collar and blue collar, public and private. This division suited the needs of the bureaucratic industrial corporations that provided the model for our preferred means of organizing society by the balancing and linking of sectors as "departments" in a functional whole, as in a great business enterprise.

In the mid-nineteenth-century small town, it was obvious that the work of each contributed to the good of all, that work is a moral relationship between people, not just a source of material or psychic rewards. But with the coming of large-scale industrial society, it became more difficult to see work as a contribution to the whole and easier to view it as a segmental, self-interested activity.[19]

Although the authors refer to the last century, their view is not that of the traditionalists mentioned in the introduction of this book, a group that favored a return to the past. Furthermore, it is likely in the future that this tendency toward personal interest and fragmentation will grow for many people, considering the level of unemployment, job instability, short-term contracts, or the mounting view that it is the role of the enterprise not to provide a job to an employee but rather only to make them employable.

The Global Impact of Modern Technology

If the impact of organizations on our planet is important, then the same is true for technology. It is clear that in many sectors we have overstepped, by far, the safety limits. Solange Lefebvre (see Chapter 3) as well as myself have commented on this absence of limits (see Chapter 11). To state it more directly however, we have witnessed recently a changing of the scale on which we are operating, quite without realizing it. Our mastery of and over nature requires that we accept a new level of responsibility. The impact of our advanced technologies has not only reached a global scale, but the systemic and manifold interrelated aspects are such that the effects can be counterproductive. For example, when a boat would sink last century, the damage, although tragic, was minimal. Today, a super-tanker accident can pollute about 500 miles of coastline.[20] It is also likely that the new technologies—biotechnology, robotics, supramolecular chemistry—will, in the future, have both positive and negative impacts on the world. In the following list I present many examples in which we have surpassed limits in different sectors. In some cases, we have overstepped what is considered the viable limit by 1,800 times![21]

Production of toxic products	In 1990, the American chemical industry celebrated the creation of its ten-millionth chemical product since 1957.
	After analyzing 66,000 medications, pesticides, and chemical products, a research group concluded that no toxicity data was available for at least 70 percent of them and that a full evaluation of their potential harmful effects was available for only 2 percent of these products.
	The international arms market has been evaluated at more than $2,000 billion, an amount equivalent to the total debt of Third World countries.
Energy	The level of energy used on a daily basis by an industrial society such as ours has been calculated at five to seven kilowatts per person. It is estimated that a viable level of energy consumption, on a global level, is not more than one kilowatt per day per person.
	Every five years, each North American produces an amount of waste equivalent in weight to the Statue of Liberty.
	One billion people, almost 20 percent of the total world population, consume 80 percent of the natural resources and disposable energy.
Water	It takes 1.1 million liters of water to produce one ton of corn, 4.5 million liters for one ton of rice, and 34 million liters for one ton of beef.
	The biological needs of one person are approximately one gallon of water per day. In the United States, the total consumption of water for personal, agricultural, and industrial use amounts to 1,800 gallons per person per day, namely 1,800 times more.
	One-quarter of the drinkable water available on the planet is polluted, of which the remainder represents only 0.009 percent of all water available.
	Every four years, a desert the size of Germany is created on the planet.

Work	In Japan, *karoshi*, which is death due to overintensity of work, is officially recognized as the second major cause of death in men, after cancer.
	In North America, between 50 and 75 percent of people at work demonstrate the characteristics of "Type A" personality—that is a chronic sense of urgency, an exaggerated sense of competition bordering on aggression, an aversion toward idleness, and irritability when confronted with obstacles.
Miscellaneous, by day and by hour	In 2000, unemployment affected 40 million people in OECD countries, compared to 10 million in 1973. It is estimated that more than 800 million adults are deprived of work today in the world.
	Every day, approximately 100 species of animals or plants disappear.
	On average, a person living in a Western country is exposed to 2,500 commercials every day.
	Every day, the equivalent of the financial value of the total yearly production in the world is traded on the international financial markets.
	Every day, approximately 10 square kilometers of tropical forest is destroyed.
	Every hour, 3,600 million barrels of oil are burned.
	Every hour, 1,500 people die of malnutrition.

The Global Effects of the Dominant Economic System: The Market System

Last, the weight of our organizations, the significance of instrumental reason, and the impact of technology are themselves propelled by the dominant economic system that itself is fuelled by these three components. Even though the market economy reveals itself as a system more stable than others and certainly more appealing to many, there is certainly room for improvement. This is one of the central themes of this book: Many contributors have warned against the dangers of economism, of a flattening of reality, which results in the predominant political discourse being an economic one, focused mainly on employment and material wealth.

Once again, we are in a situation in which certain notions of truth—the illusion that economic growth is the source of happiness—determines our notion of goodness and beauty. Basically, the search for ethics and spirituality in management and organizations stems from recognizing that, despite its many advantages, the fragmentation of reality as propelled by the ideology of the market system and neoliberalism is fragmented when compared to the complexity and the beauty of life in the world.

The evolution of the meaning of the word "world" or "globe" throughout history illustrates this fragmentation. Based on the Latin word *mundus*, which means "universe," this word was first fragmented when it no longer meant "universe" but instead "the world," the "earthly planet," or our "globe." A second fragmentation, or collapse of its meaning, came in the twelfth century, when the notion of society replaced the notion of the physical planet, from which stems the expression "being worldly." Finally, the most recent fragmentation appeared in the 1950s, with the introduction of globalization and globalizing, which reduced the notion still more, this time from the social to the economic, thus the expression "world-class organization." Therefore, from the vastness of the cosmos, replete with planets, gods and goddesses, we moved to our own planet, Earth, loaded with rocks, water, and humus. From there we moved more to our human societies, with politics, art, and emotion. And today, we have restricted the notion of world to one of economics: A world-class status is attributed to organizations that are high performers from an economic standpoint.

Some Strategies for Making Ethics More Objective and Global

The necessity for rendering the notion of ethics more objective and global is fuelled by the three reasons stated. The bet we made during the Enlightenment, of taming the Earth through reason, science, technology, and now the economy, has been won. As the French philosopher Michel Serres proposes, our scientific and economic prowess and the dangers they entail in surpassing viable limits literally push us toward morality and philosophy. He stated the following:

We have mastered the world and should therefore learn how to master our own mastery. Look at how quickly things turn around: the fact that we can do this or that, we must immediately control this ability. Do we dominate over the planet or reproduction? If so, then we must decide immediately and should I say, wisely, and under probable threat, what this domination consists of. Without realizing it, we have gone from power to duty, from science to morals and the iceberg has pivoted. For example: Could we choose the gender of our children? What would happen if future parents all chose girls or boys? . . . Yes, we are driven to morals and philosophy.[22]

In the global search for truth, goodness, and beauty, it is probable that we witness a revival of the good. Although traditional science attempts to establish that which is true or false in this material world—with all of its impact on the hearts and souls of people—forces us to not only to ask what is true but also what is good. Michel Serres expressed this need:

The question "are we telling the truth?" converges on the question "are we doing good?" To what extent do these newly created worlds expose our contemporaries and their successors—future generations, to violence, famine, pain, illness, or death. The epistemological problem of falsehood converges therefore on the ethical problem of evil. The law "tell the truth" converges on the commandment "Thou shalt not kill".[23]

Helping ethics to become more objective and global while respecting its subjectivity and rootedness in the personal will take time. In this book, many strategies have been suggested with which to begin this journey, positioning ethics on a spiritual plane. With the intention of highlighting the diversity of approaches proposed, I will mention a few of those strategies here:

- a journey inspired by a specific religious tradition, albeit open to others, disseminated by a small number of people within an organization
- the encouragement of a spontaneous integration, triggered, for example, by a reform touching the sector in its totality
- creating a safe space for dialogue and exchange, in which the levels of consciousness of individuals can develop
- using systemic thinking in the context of experimentation and continuous learning
- defining a management philosophy and developing a particular organization design, such as seen in the cooperative system
- calling on, be it consciously or unconsciously, the deep values and religious beliefs that drive people
- creating rituals and developing role models that inspire life
- using a code of values and ethics as well as specific management tools
- identifying and making use of those similarities which exist in different religions and spiritual traditions
- developing and integrating a new vision on the nature of work

All these strategies obviously have merit. Some strategies overlap with others and of course, more could be added to this already extensive list. This suggests that there are many possible ways to reach the same goal and that an important effort in scientific research needs to be done to evaluate the conditions under which these strategies can be implemented as well as to evaluate their performance in different organizational and social settings. I have included in the subsequent list certain strategies that have already been put into place:

- implementing professional oaths, as doctors do with the Hippocratic Oath
- using international law to establish minimum standards as was done, for example, with the ban on CFCs, chemical weapons, and antipersonnel mines
- mobilizing citizens of the world toward a change coming from the "bottom-up"[24]
- creating an *International Declaration of Human Responsibilities* to complement the *International Declaration of Human Rights* of 1948
- creating institutions to evaluate the ethical practices of organizations, such as the Council on Economic Priorities, based in New York City, which applies ten cri-

teria to evaluate the activities of 200 organizations and 2,500 products for its membership now totalizing over 1 million people[25]

- making use of the profound learning that takes place during a painful and major crisis, such as the ten principles created by the Coalition of Environmentally Responsible Economics after the ecological crisis created by the *Exxon Valdez* disaster, known as the Valdez Principles[26]

- proposing a new global contract, such as the one already proposed by the Group of Lisbon which proposes "to go beyond the mind-set of conquering"[27]

- creating training, education, and research-action programs to promote management tools that allow for the development of economic, ethical, and spiritual wealth

As Mr. Beland reminded us (see Chapter 5), it is less difficult—an expression which emphasizes that it is not necessarily easy—to put these ethical principles in place within an organization or an established profession, than it is within in a given society or at the international level. To emphasize once more, the development of more objective and global ethics will require high levels of participation from many different people, as well as the invention and adequate use of certain technology. It will likely also mean a certain level of suffering for both individuals and societies. Spirituality can not only serve as an inspiration to determine ethical foundations, but can also give the necessary internal drive needed to support the energy, faith, and hope of those people committed to this process.

THE IMPERATIVE OF MAKING SPIRITUALITY MORE TANGIBLE AND SOCIAL

Before addressing the subject of spirituality, it is crucial to first come back to the different perceptions between religion and spirituality, given their difference for managers. We have already seen, if 90 percent of managers in the United States are open to spirituality, close to 60 percent of them have a negative perception of religion (see Chapter 2). The following list, derived from the research conducted by Ian I. Mitroff and Elizabeth Denton, suggests that among those managers that reject religion but are open to spirituality, the difference between the two is very noticeable, even polarized.[28]

Religion	Spirituality
Organized	Personal
Formal	Informal
Structured	Nonstructured
Externally imposed	Internally driven
Directed	Chosen
Rigid	Flexible

Closed	Open minded
Imprisoning	Liberating
Dogmatic	Enriching
Brings division	Brings togetherness
Life after death	Life on Earth

This rejection of the religious, perceived falsely or not, as imposed, imprisoning, or dogmatic, is however paradoxical, as it is held by a majority of people who embrace the logic of the market economy.[29] The paradox lies in the fact that the ideology of this economic system has been deemed by some as the most recent and most secretive of . . . religions.

In a controversial essay, the theologian Harvey Cox recently proposed that our current economic system has all the qualities of an established religion.[30] He suggests that if religions have the existence of God as their founding notion, our economic system has a similar foundation with the existence of the market. What's more, he proposes that the three general characteristics of a traditional monotheist religion—omnipotence, omniscience, and omnipresence—are all present in the theology—as he calls it—of the market economy.

Omnipotence allows the definition of that which is real and that which is not. In the market economy, this translates into the affirmation that all things can be transformed into commodities that can be exchanged on a market and that the only truly important reality is the one determined by monetary exchange. The notion of land is a prime example of this phenomenon. Although it has been associated with many different meanings through the ages—be it the physical place where a people and a culture are rooted, the manifestation of Mother Nature, the aesthetic proof of the existence of the Divine, the land of ancestors, a place where one can reenergize, a place for relaxation, pleasure, and play or a place where a family meets every year, and so forth—today's meaning of "land" is often reduced to a real estate mind-set and to an economic market value. The same analysis could be carried out for work done by human beings, resources considered to be "natural," or trade of animals.

Omniscience, the idea that a deity possesses all knowledge, is also noticeable within the market economy. In this particular ideology, the market is supposed to determine the optimal price of all goods, services, and information as well as the remuneration deemed equitable in any given industry. This market is even personified, often referred to as feverish, jubilant, nervous, or optimistic. What is more, this market conforms to the results of multiple future consumption trend analyses, enabling it to anticipate demand and produce a counteroffer, furthering its omniscience. Last, this market consults the studies done by financial analysts that influence the observed phenomenon in the said market, coupled with the mediated interventions by the "high priests" of the economy and international finance, such as Alan Greenspan or George Soros.

Finally, omnipresence, the notion that the deity is present in all things, is also visible in the market economy. Econometric methods are used to determine the optimal threshold of the number of children a family should have, professional vocation, or even national health, education, and cultural policies that a government should institute. Furthermore, as seen in this book, the methodologies used in "marketing"—communication plans, sales and advertising strategies, promotional policies, and so forth—are used in the most intimate areas, such as love and spirituality.

The characteristics of the market economy are of course much more complex than those mentioned above and I do not have the space to fully develop all the subtleties introduced by Harvey Cox. I would like, however, to highlight two of his conclusions.

1. Although all media report on the violent outbursts that exist between religious groups, be it the Catholics and Protestants in Ireland, the Hindu and the Muslims in India and Pakistan, or the Taliban and the United States (which, for me, stops being religious as soon they preach hatred and violence), relatively few voices denounce the violence of the "religious groups of the market ideology," be it the economic misery of entire populations or the vast environmental destruction. The recent demonstrations against the various WTO meetings may be signs of change.

2. This new religion, perhaps the most secretive for it is not labeled as such, has become the most significant alternative when compared to the more traditional religions.[31]

If Harvey Cox is right, then the rejection of traditional religion by managers on the one hand and the acceptance of the dogmatic ideology of the market on the other, and this by the same people, is, indeed, very paradoxical.

Another paradox exists as well, involving the notion of spirituality. As we have seen in this book, managers open to spirituality are looking for a remedy to their sense of fragmentation, be it a remedy of reintegration, relationship, wholeness, rootedness, transcendence, and so on. The paradox comes from the fact that the very function of religion is, in principle, to enable this integration. In Latin, the word "religion" connotes this relational aspect. It comes from the Latin *religare*, from *re* meaning renewal, and *ligare*, to link, to attach, to bring together. Literally, a religion expresses a desire for liaison, for relationship, for connection, with oneself, others, nature, and the transcendant. To be religious in the sense of *religare* is to search for and honor this connection, to establish sustainable relationships, to connect emotionally and spiritually, to be close, which is, in effect, what managers are seeking through spirituality. We are far removed in this instance from dogma, imprisonment, or separation, all attributed to religious systems.

The function of connecting, of taking relations and relations of relations into consideration, of thinking and acting in terms of a greater totality, of wishing for and developing a harmonious whole, is also the premise upon which systemic thinking is based, something which we have referred to often throughout this book. Theoreticians have even described the links that exist between systems theory and religion (in the sense of *religare*) or spirituality. Such is the case, for example, in a wonderful book by Joanna Macy, in which she describes the similarities between systemic thought and Buddhism.[32] Similarly, the modern father of systems theory, Ludwig von Bertalanfy, recognized the influence of the philosophy and theology of Nicholas de Cues, a cardinal from the fifteenth century, who was in turn influenced by the pre-Socratic philosophers as well as the neo-Platonists, St. Bonaventure and Meister Eckhart. Ludwig von Bertalanfy even wrote a book on the thinking of Nicholas de Cues before publishing his ground-breaking book on systems theory.[33] Another paradox exists then, between the desire for unity, integration, mature fusion as expressed by managers in their search for spirituality and systems thinking, and a predominant denial of traditional religion, the aims of which were directed toward this *religare*.

My purpose in making these paradoxes more explicit is not to preach a return to traditional religions. It is, however, to make the reader more aware (if necessary) that these different perceptions of religion and spirituality are extremely polarized for many and that the rejection of religion is in itself paradoxical. Obviously, the second paradox can easily be explained by the fact that traditional religions no longer exemplify the *religare* as defined, or at least are not perceived as such. Although it is necessary to have more precise statistics on managers' perceptions on these matters, the work by Ian I. Mitroff and Elizabeth A. Denton suggests that what managers hold against religious institutions is their lack of congruence, their use of dogma, or their lack of pertinence when faced with the complex and concrete problems of the modern world. Research conducted in fourteen European countries, as well as the United States, the Philippines, and Israel, also suggested that a great majority of respondents, including managers, perceive that traditional religions cannot help resolve daily problems in today's world.[34]

It is not my purpose here to expose all the reasons that may motivate this situation. It is rather to suggest that an allergic reaction toward religion impoverishes life. The Protestant theologian Paul Tillich is one of the voices that best warned the business community of the danger of rejecting the religious spirit, which is quite different from the religious institutions. Speaking to an audience of close to 300 people, including a substantial number of CEOs from Fortune 500 companies, an event that was the feature article in *Time* magazine, Paul Tillich did not propose to return to the fold.[35] On the contrary, he warned against the inherent danger of atrophying the vertical dimension from one's work life or the depth dimension (see Chapter 11 in this book on Simone Weil). As stated by Tillich,

It is my conviction that the character of the human condition, like the character of all life, is "ambiguity": the inseparable mixture of good and evil, of true and false, of creative and destructive forces—both individual and social.

He who is not aware of the ambiguity of his perfection as a person and in his work is not yet mature.

While the ambiguity of perfection is true of the human condition under all circumstances, there is an ambiguity which is particularly true of our present condition. It is based on the fact that our culture is one-dimensional, determined by the drive toward expansion in the horizontal line: be it the push into outer space, be it the production of ever new and improved tools, be it the increase in means and materials of communication, be it the growing number of human beings to whom cultural "goods" are available—all this is one-dimensional horizontal expansion.

We must come to a rest; we must enter the creation and unite with its inner power. But it is hard to find such rest in one-dimensional culture. . . . The market of cultural goods requires always more production and more exchange; this is what ambiguity of expansion means.

You may think that these are words of a theologian who wants to sell the oldest cultural good, namely religion. He does not. Even if one calls the experience in the vertical dimension religious, it is not what this word usually connotes. . . . Religion as the experience of the vertical line is effective in every creative work, in artistic as well as scientific, in ethical as well as in economic creations.

Religion in this sense is the state in which we are grasped by the infinite seriousness of the question of the meaning of our life and our readiness to receive answers and to act according to them. . . . The vertical dimension, the dimension of depths, is present in the secular as well as in the religious realm.[36]

The phenomenon of the flattening of reality, discussed previously, is profoundly addressed by Tillich in the preceding quote. His comments on the unilateral development of a horizontal line, that continues to expand, that becomes more global, to the detriment of a vertical line—the source of depth—is the cry of the soul that we hear from managers themselves. Even if Tillich remarks that this vertical line does not stem only from religion, rejecting the religious spirit—which differs from the institutions that represent it—can lead to a significant impoverishment of our cultures and our personalities. Further, the blind rejection of religion can lead to cultural amnesia, forgetting the religious roots that are at the very base, even in today's flat world, of our civilizations and our habits of the heart. This theme has already been touched upon in this book. A specific example, that has direct implications on the practice of management and leadership, is the potential impoverishment of learning. It would be important, for instance, to learn from the thoughts and actions of great religious or spiritual leaders. I am referring here to, for example, l'Abbe Pierre, the Dalai Lama, Mahatma Gandhi, Vaclav Havel, Nelson Mandela, Martin Luther King, or Mother

Teresa.[37] It is obvious that these people—several of them having received a Nobel Peace Prize—not only integrated humanistic values, but also operated from the transpersonal level of consciousness. In other words, these individuals did not only operate as responsible human beings, committed to humanist and humanitarian causes. Their religious faith and spiritual depth inspired them and supported them, without which their actions would certainly have been different, limited, and perhaps even impossible. These men and women understood the need for and the joy that came from working for the *religare*. It seems to me that to cut oneself from these examples does in fact lead to impoverishment. I hope that in the future, managers will be able to go beyond their negative perceptions, not for the purpose of joining a traditional religion, but to benefit from the treasures that the religious spirit can offer.

The Need for Dialogue

To benefit from the religious spirit—which, to stress again, in no way obliges one to join a traditional religion—requires putting in place a process which is emphasized in this book: dialogue. In delving deeper into that which has already been said concerning ethics and the systemic approach, an ethical approach inspired by spirituality means including entities in the list of stakeholders that are seldom considered, such as downtrodden groups of society, future generations, nature, the Divine.[38] This systemic approach to ethics differs from the conventional one taken within organizations. It is not a matter here of applying one supposed universal principles. Rather, it is a matter of having a dialogue with oneself and every stakeholder or entity concerned, in search of uth, goodness, and beauty.[39]

This dialogical approach of ethics is based on a profound encounter between several people or entities, from the spoken word and from silence, reason and emotion, sensation and intuition, introspection and meditation. These entities include oneself and others, the different stakeholders—associated by choice or not with the activities of the organization—but also imaginary beings, such as the planet, God, the devil, or mythical characters.[40] Paul Tillich, in particular, insisted on this dialogical aspect of ethics, a position shared, for example, by Martin Buber, who comes from a different religious tradition.[41] As Tillich proposed,

A person becomes a person in the encounter with other persons, and in no other way. All functions of our spirit are based on what I call the moral self-realization of the centered self. This is what morality is—not the subjection to laws. The only way in which this can happen is the limiting encounter with another ego. Nature is open to man's controlling and transforming activity indefinitely, but man resists such control. The other person cannot be controlled like a natural object. Every human being is an absolute limit, an un-pierceable wall of resistance against any attempt to make him into an object.[42]

The recognition of the importance of dialogue, in particular the interreligious and interspiritual dialogues, as well as that between nonbelieving and believing individuals, is presently attracting many people. A few recent fascinating dialogues that took place include, for example, those between l'Abbe Pierre, the founder of the Emmaüs movement in France, and Albert Jacquart, a biologist and scientist; between the Dalai Lama, spiritual leader of the Tibetan Buddhist monks and Nobel Peace Prize winner and members of the World Community for Christian Meditation; between Umberto Eco, philosopher, semiologist, and fiction writer, and Carlo Maria Martini, a Jesuit Cardinal and university leader; the dialogue between Jay Krishnamurti, Indian philosopher and international figure in spirituality, and David Bohm, quantum physicist, seen by some as the heir to Albert Einstein; between Jean-François Revel, renowned philosopher and nonbelieving member of the French Science Academy and Matthieu Ricard, his son, a Tibetan monk and follower of the Dalai Lama; or the dialogue between Arnold J. Toynbee, the famous historian, and Daisaku Ikeda, a practicing Buddhist and president of several international organizations.[43] To me, these dialogues are concrete examples of a potential openness toward different people, an openness which is at the very base of developing a spiritual ethic. At this point, I would like to cite from a dialogue between Umberto Eco, an agnostic, and Carlo Maria Martini, a man of faith. This passage contains some of the conditions required for a dialogue to take place between a believer and nonbeliever, between people of different faiths or those practicing different spiritual disciplines.

Umberto Eco: Laymen do not have the right to criticize the way of life of the believer—except, as always, if it goes against the laws of the state (for example, the refusal to allow one's sick child to have a blood transfusion) or if it infringes on the rights of those that practice another religion. The religious point of view always consists of proposing an optimal way of life, whereas from a secular standpoint, all ways of life which allow for freedom of choice are optimal, as long as the choice does not exclude another's choice.

On principle, I consider that no one has the right to judge the obligations that a faith imposes on its followers. I have no reason to be opposed to the fact that the Muslim religion forbids the consumption of alcohol; if I don't agree, then I don't become a Muslim.

It is like a reception (there is nothing more common) where a tuxedo is required, and it is up to me to decide whether to conform to a custom which irritates me, because either I have a pressing reason to participate in the event or because I want to affirm my freedom by staying at home.

Carlo Maria Martini: Every time a religious principal or behavior is imposed from the outside without a person's consent, we violate their freedom of conscience. I would go even further: If these constraints existed in the past in contexts which differ from our own and for reasons that we can no longer share, is it necessary that the religion amends them.[44]

I hope that such basic conditions will be respected in the future, not only to establish a minimum level of tolerance between different points of view, but more so to enable the development of an ethic of dialogue and of spirituality in the workplace. It is important to stress that the fundamental goal of these dialogues should not be to establish a "synthesis of syntheses" of religions and spiritual movements in the world. If highlighting the similarities is necessary from a certain point of view in order to establish a common ground, this "synthesis of syntheses," as Michel Dion stated (see Chapter 13), threatens to impoverish the religious and/or spiritual systems by reducing them to their lowest common denominators. In order to search for truth, goodness, and beauty, a very delicate balance must exist between understanding and respecting the specifics while at the same time integrating difference into a larger whole—a fundamental paradox. In the past, many people have attempted to propose such a synthesis of syntheses or a *philosophica perennis*, an "eternal philosophy," introduced by Leibniz. Aldous Huxley has been the author who has perhaps most popularized this tendency in the twentieth century, with the dangers of flattening.[45]

As a resistance to the synthesis of syntheses, an interesting attempt at dialogue has been made by the Parliament of World Religions.[46] Although several of its most ardent defenders have themselves been criticized by the authorities of their own religions—as is the case with the theologian Hans Küng, who has been openly criticized by the Catholic Church—this movement signed a first declaration in October 1993 toward the establishment of a world ethic.[47] This declaration was signed by a group of dignitaries from varying backgrounds, including a Cardinal of Chicago, the spiritual leader of the Sikhs, an important Rabbi, a Muslim militant feminist, as well as representatives of different organizations such as the Ecumenical Council of Churches, the World Conference on Religions for Peace, the Lutheran World Council, and so on. Other nonreligious spiritual movements were also associated with this endeavor, such as the Dalai Lama, the Cambodian patriarch of Buddhism, Zen associations, Tai-chi centers, the theosophical and anthrosophic movements, various Aboriginal associations, yoga centers, the Joseph Campbell Foundation, as well as several other groups.

The goal of this parliament is not to create a religion of all religions nor a spirituality of all spiritualities, but rather to define a certain number of values, criteria, and concrete norms for human beings. Hans Küng and Karl Joseph Kuschel explain it using the notion of planetary ethic previously evoked:

In such a dramatic global situation humanity needs a vision of peoples living peacefully together, of ethnic and ethical groupings and of religions sharing responsibility for the care of Earth.

By a global ethic we do not mean a global ideology or a single unified religion beyond all existing religions, and certainly not the domination of one religion over all others. By a global ethic we mean a fundamental consensus on binding values, irrevocable standards, and personal attitudes.[48]

Even though this movement started in 1893 in Chicago, during a World Exposition, and produced a first document recently, many problems still remain. This is exemplary of the difficulties that arise when trying to get different people and different groups into dialogue. Of particular importance is the question of language, the notion of God not being recognized by Buddhism for instance. The culture of nonviolence, as advocated by the parliament, was also strongly debated. Many groups defended the right to self-defense, especially in extreme cases such as those who lived in Bosnia. The status of women and their rights for equality also posed problems, especially for the Muslim and Hindu communities and also for the Catholic Church with the issue, for example, of the ordinance of women priests. Finally, certain groups believed that the parliament was too representative of western societies and did not use sufficient spiritual notions offered from other continents and cultures.

Despite these initiatives, no one can predict the future of the religious and spiritual movements. However, it seems to me that there is a certain similarity between religion, spirituality, science, and the economy held within a perspective that is integrative and not fragmented. I once again give voice to Michel Serres on this matter, as I did previously regarding ethics. In this quote, he proposes that we are perhaps at a pivotal point in history where not only exact sciences are approaching the humanities, but also where a new balance, one that is less fragmented, between reason, ethics, and religion as in the notion of *religare*, is being sought. Serres stated,

We look after our separate enterprises, blind to their relations: We do not have a science or a technique of interaction. We conquered our efficiency with specialization, from whence comes our overall powerlessness; specialization is another reason for the unforeseen imbalances which can change an asset to a liability.

This integrative project seems insane whereas the age of computers makes it possible, whereas history and culture behind us has given it many names both long ago and of late. We say that the word religion, for example, originally encompassed the meaning of relation or relationship, which is our problem today.

If a visitor from another planet would watch what we call these days, ironically, the "news," he could not help but thinking that our universal culture, ravaged by wars and terror, is founded on human sacrifice.

Religion . . . spoke . . . of love; it approached the problem correctly, because the love relationship already deals with the local and the global, relatives, neighbors, fellow man, and the most infinite Whole.

Strange reunions that no one thought were this close. Attentive to these interactions, the new culture will reconcile not only the sciences and the humanities, but the most advanced rational thought with ethics [and religion] as well.[49]

I would like to add a second voice to Michel Serres's, that of a nonbeliever who is often quoted for his thoughts on the future of religion and spirituality, Andre Malraux. Even though the well known phrase "The twenty-first century will be religious or will not be" that is attributed to Malraux was not in fact said by him, he does express views similar to those cited.[50] Malraux suggests that it is very difficult to predict today which form this new integration will take, using a beautiful metaphor:

Basically, we live in a civilization which has given us powers that man has never known, and which has made science into a new supreme value. The drama is that we know this value is incapable of making a new human species. Meanwhile these are hallowed times, until something serious emerges; either a new human species, or a new religious fact, or perhaps . . . something totally unforeseeable.

If the next century will have a spiritual revolution, which I consider perfectly possible . . . I think that we will foretell this spirituality without knowing it, like the eighteenth century foretold electricity with the lightening rod.[51]

Spirituality: A Systemic Model

Even if it may be impossible to predict the form that spirituality will take in the twenty-first century and what effect this spirituality will have on the world, our lives, our cultures, the economy, and the actions of our organizations, we can nevertheless sketch some potential tendencies. Ken Wilber recently proposed a systemic model that is particularly interesting for linking different levels of consciousness and their diverse expressions. As I have already mentioned, ethics and spirituality are altogether subjective and objective, personal and collective. Wilber's model allows us to not only integrate these four different realities, a remarkable feat in and of itself, but also allows us to maintain their specificities, which is still more rare.

As proposed in the introductory chapter of this book, based on Wilber's work, different levels of consciousness, called very generally prepersonal, personal, and transpersonal, are associated with different realities, namely matter, mental and spiritual. We have seen as well, from the works of Maslow and Kohlberg, that these levels of consciousness are associated with some psychic aspirations and different levels of moral development. Further, we saw that these levels are not so distinctly separated from one another, but rather that each transcends the previous, that is to say it integrates it and surpasses it.

Although Ken Wilber worked mostly on levels of consciousness during the 1970s and 1980s, in the 1990s he proposed that each level operated in four distinct yet complementary realities, which include the subjective and the concrete, the personal and the collective. In a similar fashion, several authors in this book have proposed that spirituality cannot remain only subjective and personal. It must translate into the collective, be it in an organization or a society, as well as the concrete, through the use of management tools, for example.

In Figure 15.1, I present an abbreviated version of Wilber's four realities, synthesized into four interrelated quadrants.[52] Each type will be presented separately before relating them to the different levels of consciousness and discussing the relationship between these four modes of reality. Last, this model will allow me to highlight certain dangers inherent in each quadrant and certain conditions necessary for the development of their integration. Ken Wilber's model is extremely rich, indeed. It is at the basis of the recent founding by Ken Wilber and many associates of the Integral Institute, an institute whose mission is to promote the notion of integration in many sectors of activity, including business.[53]

In his model, Wilber proposes two pairs of reality modes: internal and external realities, as well as individual and collective realities. These two pairs form four quadrants as shown in Figure 15.1, namely quadrants A, B, C, and D.

Quadrant A refers to the internal reality lived by an individual. It is only slightly externally accessible through profound dialogue with that person. This internal reality is made up of the personal meaning individuals hold, their subjectivity, their dreams, their conversations with themselves, articulated by internal language or other form of intrapersonal conversation, be that through images, emotions, feelings, intuitions, and so forth. This is the reality of *I*; the world of images, thoughts, emotions lived by that person, internally, as modulated by the levels of consciousness, namely the prepersonal, personal, and transpersonal.

Quadrant B encompasses this personal reality but as perceived externally from the person, through the intermediary of the senses or technology, a tool that is an extension of the senses. This reality is the world of the individual *id*, of the organic matter that makes up an individual, their brain, synapses, muscles, senses, as well as their actions, and their behavior. This reality is observable externally by modern science, namely the positivist–logic sciences, using clinical or empirical observation, analysis, measurement, and advanced technologies (CAT scan, x-ray, and so on). It is not a matter of sensing a subjective meaning in some intrapsychic way, as in quadrant A. If the reality of quadrant B stems from the internal of the individual, as do the different neurophysiological processes in the brain, they are observable from the outside of the individual through the use of intermediary technologies.

Quadrant C also refers to the concrete world, that in which tangible, quantifiable, and measurable qualities can be apprehended from the outside. This is the world of the *collective id*. It is formed by institutions, enterprises, technologies, laws and rules, and management and leadership tools, such as accounting, finance, marketing, information and communication technologies, and so forth. This collective and concrete world can be lived at different levels, be it group, organizational, national, or global. It can be captured through the analysis of the economic system and the fluctuations

Figure 15.1
Ken Wilber's Systemic Model: A Representation of the Four Quadrants and Their
Interrelationship

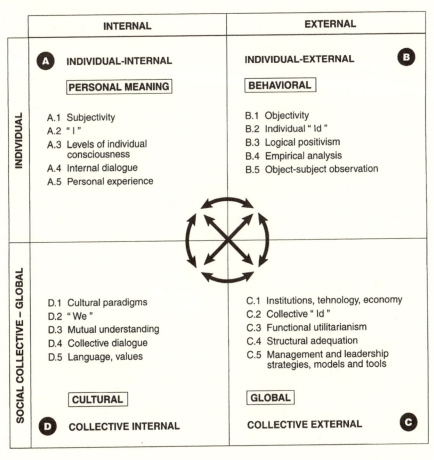

of goods, services, information, and capital. This world is governed by the complex relationships between the institutionalized and technological human world and the natural world, such as resources, geography, geology, and so forth.

Last, the world of quadrant D contains once again the subjective and the ineffable, as did quadrant A, expressed this time however in a collective fashion. This is the world of values, taboos, informal norms, and cultural paradigms. This is the world of the *we* expressed through a common language and common signs that are understood by others. This world allows for a collective dialogue that may potentially lead to a mutual understanding, even if this understanding is not derived from consensus. This world also represents the levels of consciousness that exist at the collective level, be it a group, an organization, a society or the entire world. It represents the central axis around which a culture is based, or, using the terminology of Abraham Maslow, the *biopsychosocial attraction* that is predominant at the collective level, the center of its cultural gravity.

The arrows at the center of the model (see Figure 15.1) suggest that the four quadrants are far from separated from one another but rather are in a dynamic and complex relationship. An example will help to understand this notion: Imagine that I desire—an internal and subjective reality of quadrant A—a glass of milk. This desire, associated with chemical and neural reactions in my body, will likely manifest itself in an action on my part, all of which are associated with quadrant B. I could decide to fetch a bottle of milk or even go and buy some in a store, both realities of quadrant C. However, even the possibility of being able to desire a glass of milk or being able to go to a store and buy milk, requires an interaction with the cultural world of quadrant D. This subjectivity at the collective level formed cultural habits such that in our civilization, human beings are used to drinking milk from cows that are, in a sense, always available in stores in exchange for a bank note that is recognized as valuable by everyone.

Ken Wilber's brilliance resides in the fact that he has integrated this four-quadrant model of reality—the personal *I*, the *behavioral id*, the worldly *id*, and the cultural *we*—which is both very simple and very complex, when one takes into account its actual and potential interrelations. In Figure 15.1, I present a simplified version of this integration. The twenty levels of consciousness, detailed in Figure 15.1, are represented in summary form in quadrant A of Figure 15.2. In it, only the levels of consciousness which mark the beginning of each level are represented; that is, the sensorial-physical state at the beginning of level I, the prepersonal level; the reptilian state, at the beginning of the second level of consciousness, the personal level; and the vision–logic state, at the beginning of the third level of consciousness, the transpersonal level.[54]

As the links between quadrant A (individual levels of consciousness) and quadrant C (concrete realities represented in the world) are likely those with which people interested in organizations and the economy are most familiar, I will begin with them. In an attempt to make this presentation more concrete, I have only indicated in quadrant C two manifestations relevant directly in management: the dominant social structure, starting with the first tribes of forty people, dating back 1 million years, to the recent phenomenon of globalization, which began to emerge after World War II; and second, the structure of the economy, beginning with the primitive prehistoric practices of hunting and gathering, to the very recent and still developing information-based economy.

It is essential to realize that the reptilian brain (quadrant B) and the level of consciousness associated with it (quadrant A), could only encompass a

Figure 15.2
Ken Wilber's Systemic Model Levels of Consciousness and Links to the Four Quadrants

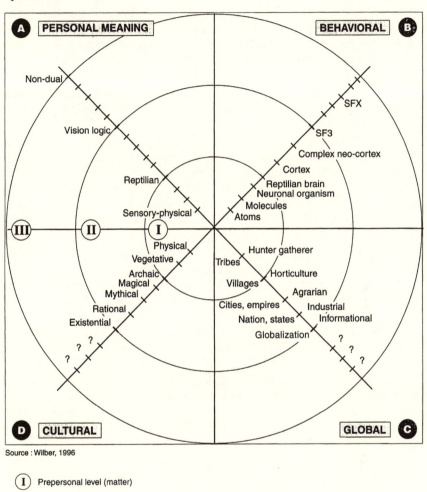

Source : Wilber, 1996

(I) Prepersonal level (matter)

(II) Personal level (mental)

(III) Transpersonal level (spiritual)

society which was culturally archaic (quadrant D), one based on clans, then tribes, living only on hunting and gathering activities (quadrant C). Realizing this allows for a better understanding of the determining effect that levels of consciousness have on the other quadrants. However, it is also important to realize that these difficult living conditions—based on survival in a hostile environment, life expectancy being only about twenty years—influenced in their own right the other modes of reality. For example, such harsh living conditions allow very little time for the development of consciousness, knowledge, arts, and so on. It is therefore important to understand that Wilber's model does not imply that one quadrant, for example quadrant A, causes the modes of reality expressed in the other quadrants. Instead of a strict cause-and-effect relationship, Wilber proposes a coevolution—a notion introduced to science through systems theory—which puts into relationship the four quadrants, without one dominating the others.[55] This fundamental difference between the notion of coevolution and that of cause and effect diverges radically from the traditional scientific concept which often uses the cause-and-effect principal, believing that certain variables are determining and others determined.

With time and the slow passage from the prepersonal level of consciousness to the "personal" level (quadrant A), man-powered horticulture practiced by agrarian cultures gave way to animal-powered agriculture. The structure of societies evolved at the same time, organizing themselves initially into villages, then cities, then first empires (quadrant C). Easier living conditions allowed for an increase in life expectancy to thirty to thirty-five years of age (quadrant B) and the development of a social culture that went from archaic to magical, and then to mythical (quadrant D). The archaic level represents one of the most primitive modes of thought; the magical level attributes to itself the power to magically influence things, such as making rain through the carrying out of a ritual; the mythical level attributes this power to a powerful being, a God or Goddess, and interprets a myth literally, such as the opening of the Red Sea and the drowning of Egyptian soldiers. In the same vein, this slow evolution gives rise to the arts and the sciences, reason and scientific inquiry, technological innovation and the initial mumblings of democracy. This period, between the sixth and fifth centuries B.C., also encompasses the first grand philosophies, religions, and spiritual movements introduced by Buddha, Confucius, Heraclitus of Ephesus, Lao Tsu, Mahariva, Patanjali, Plato, the sages of the Upanishads, Socrates, the Zaputecs of Mexico, and so on, as well as other religions that were introduced beforehand (for example, Judaism, the Zoroastrian tradition) and others that would follow (Christianity, Islam, and so on).

Following this development, the rise of the personal level of consciousness (quadrant A) with its implications on the cultural development of reason (quadrant D) and the advent of nation–states (quadrant C), is also related to the improvement in living conditions and life expectancy (quadrant B), giving way for a new world economic order: the industrial system. This system, which radically replaced human and animal power with that of the machine, also had major effects on the development of consciousness and the standard of living for millions of human beings. The industrial system was also associated with an unprecedented development of science and technology, as well as with radical social innovations such as the abolishing of slavery, the development of democracy, the birth of global government, nongovernment, and private organizations. As with all stages of development, the industrial era brought with it its share of calamities, such as extreme social inequalities, bloody wars, alienation, materialism, and the abrupt secularization of our societies. It also was instrumental in the destruction of the natural habitat, the effects of which are proportional to the force of the industrial system itself.

According to the integration of the levels of consciousness as established by Wilber and supported by many Western and Eastern traditions, it would seem that we are presently at the end of the personal level of consciousness, with its extreme individualism and utilitarianism discussed in this book. A portion of the population in our societies have, for example, developed an existentialist culture (quadrant D) in which, as we have seen, the refusal of the false, the bad, and the ugly is important. Furthermore, a growing portion of the population follows spiritual practices to improve their health (quadrant B). Our societies are also evolving more and more toward a global structure, called postmodern or informational, that both integrates and surpasses the industrial system (quadrant C). This movement is, however, limited to developed nations, accentuating their disparity from other countries (Africa, South America, the Middle East, and so on). This development of the personal level of consciousness and the slow entry of the transpersonal level, which is not only experienced by a minority of people (quadrant A) but is also slowly transforming the culture of the planet (quadrant D), may well explain, at least in part, the present emergence of a spiritual searching in society as well as within organizations.

It is interesting to note that the model proposed by Ken Wilber does not attribute the emergence of the transpersonal to a particular alignment of the planets as some propose nor to the alienation created by the industrial system. Wilber proposes something more fundamental, namely that this evolution is the result of a slower historical evolution and coevolution of the four modes of reality, from matter to mental and from mental to spiritual. What is more, he suggests that this slow evolution is a transcended emergence of the Divine, the Spirit, the Tao, and God. This notion of transcended emergence expresses the fact that if each level is distinct—matter, mental, spiritual—they are also related in a complex fashion. For Wilber, the Divine manifests itself through this coevolution, revealing itself in more complex ways, initially through matter, then through the mental and finally through the spiritual realm itself.

If the historical explanation that Wilber provides is seductive—and necessarily simplified as all theories are—it remains nevertheless impossible today to predict what the future in a transpersonal world will be, hence the question marks inserted in Figure 15.3. There is one fundamental reason for this impossibility: Never before has such a level of development, one that touches simultaneously our levels of consciousness and our bodies, our culture and our institutions, our science and our organizations, been experienced by a civilization such as ours. Andre Malraux, previously cited, was perhaps correct when he said that we can not anticipate what a transpersonal future world would be like, just as we could not predict electricity in the eighteenth century.

However, Wilber's model does warn us against certain dangers in this transpersonal world as well as suggest the requirements for its development. They are summarized in Figure 15.3, based on the fundamental as-

Figure 15.3
Dangers and Needs

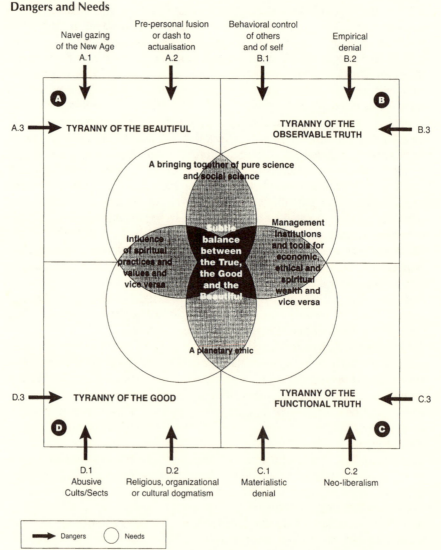

sumption that if one of the quadrants should once again dominate the others, our world would experience another flattening of reality. Using Wilber's model allows for a synthesis of the dangers and the requirements as expressed in this book, as well as a relation between them.

Beginning with quadrant A, the first danger is to fall into New Age navel gazing (see the black arrow A.1 in Figure 15.3). This navel gazing starts when the spiritual quest is exclusively contained in quadrant A with the intention of exciting the personal and subjective senses. Spirituality is not just individual and subjective. Although it is that as well, it must also be translated into the other quadrants, namely the concrete and the collective, lest it serve to enslave the world and our culture in the journey of only a few. A traditional Zen story states this particularly well. After many long years of silent meditation and having witnessed an illumination, a young disciple runs to his master. For three days, he explains what he has discovered and asks him, at the end, what he thinks. The master, having remained silent throughout, answers "You should wash your dirty sandals and go back to your village to work."

A second danger would be to succumb to the prepersonal fusion or the actualization race through work (see arrow A.2). I have already described the dangers inherent in confusing the spiritual quest and a desire for prepersonal fusion in the introduction of this book, which is associated with a trapping in quadrant A. The actualization race through work is also restrained to this quadrant through the desire of attaining a heightened sense of existence through personal realizations, thereby flattening the other modes of reality. In this chapter, we have already spoken of the dangers of individualist utilitarianism and Abraham Maslow proposed certain metapathologies that could emerge if a person cannot transcend the attraction of self-actualization.[56]

Using ethics and spirituality to exercise behavioral control over another person is a third danger that stems from demagogical manipulation (see arrow B.1). In the same vein, the use of spiritual practices to obtain behavioral control over one's own body or even to favor physical health is also dangerous, reducing spirituality to only a method. This tendency, of using spirituality to better one's physical and mental health is very popular nowadays.[57] This risk disappears when this use of spiritual practices is transmitted to other quadrants over time, provided that "one returns to one's village to work." Likewise, remaining constrained in quadrant B, wanting only to measure objective facts (see arrow B.2) can led to the denial of the reality of other quadrants. Empirical denial of the subjective realities (quadrants A and D), which cannot be measured but only discovered through sincere dialogue, leads once more to a flattening of reality.

Denial of the material (arrow C.1) although likened to the denial of the empirical is motivated by other factors. It is not just a matter of considering that which can be measured objectively—a strong tendency in science in general as well as in management practices—but to consider as valid only that which brings financial gain. The opportunistic attitude of certain people toward spirituality for such financial objectives comes from this denial and flattening of reality. The neoliberal danger (see arrow C.2) rises from this muddle of materialism and utilitarianism, while denying all the while the personal dimensions of individuals (quadrant A), their physical health (quadrant B), as well as considering as important only that which can be exchanged in the market system (quadrant D).

Last, the danger of abusive cults (see D.1) and that of religious, cultural, or organizational dogmatism (see D.2) both stem from the demagogical manipulation of cultural elements. This eliminates the need for collective dialogue that is at the base of all rich and evolving cultures, and replaces it instead with an agile and self-interested monologue that uses a pseudoethic or pseudospirituality. This type of paternalism within organizations, which sometimes makes use of humanist and spiritual notions, is part of this dogmatism.

More generally, one can apprehend these dangers by examining the definitions attributed to truth, goodness, and beauty, which is the general theme in this chapter. Ken Wilber's model allows a better understanding of the phenomenon of flattening. It also allows us to locate the epistemological, ethical, and aesthetic searches within each quadrant.[58]

In most of today's sciences and practices in management, the truth is often associated with the external reality of objects and issues. It is based on that which can be observed, analyzed, and measured objectively. Within this tendency, triggered during the Enlightenment period, the truth belongs to quadrants B and C. Of course, to attempt to measure objectively a phenomenon is not a problem as such. In fact, this ability is a considerable advantage in science and in management practice. There are, however, two risks that one must heed: attempting to measure something which cannot be measured, such as that contained within quadrants A and D which are subjective by nature, and reducing the search for truth, goodness, and beauty to merely a search for the measurable truth. These dangers are identified in Figure 15.3 by the arrows B.3 and C.3, labeled "the dictates of the observable truth" and "the dictates of the functional truth." In both cases the realities from other quadrants are denied. It could be that that which is considered beautiful might be the black smoke coming from the chimneys of factories, showing their functional use. This flattening of reality could also lead to defining the good as far as a company is concerned as guaranteeing the highest return to its shareholders, excluding all other responsibilities that may not be included within existing legislation.[59]

In the same vein, the good that belongs to the collective sphere of the *we* (quadrant D), can easily be distorted when that which is considered to be good by one group is that which defines truth and beauty (arrow D.3). In this case, for instance, profits may be maximized to the detriment of working conditions of employees in foreign countries or health and safety problems may be denied in wanting to protect the company's image. The tendencies unfortunately occur in many organizations.[60]

Finally, beauty, domain of the interior reality of the *I* (quadrant A), can be distorted when this definition of beauty flattens the notions of truth and goodness (arrow A.3). For example, the beauty of a computer program, as defined by a programmer as being the most complicated program ever, working at the edge, creating a captivating suspense for its designer, may not be the program that an organization would want to use.[61]

Having thus mapped some of the potential dangers in each quadrant, I suggest five conditions that seem necessary for the integration of ethics and spirituality at work. The first, situated at the center of the four quadrants, is the development of a subtle balance between truth, goodness, and beauty, respecting the specifics of each, but refusing to separate them from one another. The other conditions, all interrelated, summarize some of the themes discussed in this chapter: a bringing together—and not a separation—of the pure and social sciences which include the humanities, philosophy, and religion; the creation of new management tools and institutions; the defining of a global ethic; and the influence of spiritual practices on values and culture.

I would like to emphasize one conclusion from Ken Wilber's work. If indeed he is correct, despite all the reservations one may give about a theory, we are only at the initial rumblings of an even more complex emergence of the spirit. Throughout the history of the planet and of human beings, Wilber helps us to understand the gigantic step that has already been taken, despite long periods of recession and many catastrophes, crises, and breakdowns that we certainly experience today. The evolution from the prepersonal and the personal level as well as the development of this second level, help us to imagine the scope of the changes that could occur in the future now that we are at the portals of the transpersonal level. Essentially, Ken Wilber's message is one of hope based not only on the support from historical documentation, but also on his faith in the ever more complex emergence of the spirit.[62] This hope must be counterbalanced, however, by the many potential pitfalls that this evolution may encounter. It must be stressed as well that this evolution, as described by Wilber, does in no way mean that human beings must be passive when faced with this evolution and simply await the slow manifestation of spirit in the world. History suggests quite the opposite: the necessity of human activity, which itself stems from the natural and spiritual realities.

A FEW OBSERVATIONS ABOUT THE GROUND COVERED IN THIS BOOK

To conclude, I would like to propose twelve general observations about the journey that we have taken in this book. They are very humble in comparison to those mentioned previously from Ken Wilber's work, which extended from prehistory to the present. This is by no means an exhaustive list, but rather a first attempt to summarize what can be learned, in my opinion, from this book.

The first observation brings a sign of hope. Within organizations there seems to exist a large number of managers and employees that wish to better integrate ethics and spirituality into their work. This transcends the differences expressed by those groups called modern, traditionalist, and transmodern (see the Introduction). This desire is motivated by a desire to overcome a feeling of fragmentation, of wanting to be able to express one's deeper values at work as well as to be able to feel and establish a sense of relationship with others, the natural world, the universe, and the transcendent. As our world is becoming more and more organized, it is necessary that the men and women working within organizations participate actively in the slow process of evolution that Ken Wilber described.

A second observation is that there exist numerous cases, six of which are presented in this book, in addition to many others such as Ben & Jerry's, The Body Shop, Medtronic, Tom's of Maine, and the YMCA, that show that it is possible to integrate ethics and spirituality without compromising the efficiency of an organization. This efficiency can be defined in many different ways depending on the organization, such as by financial profitability, operational efficiency, product or service quality, balanced budgets, customer satisfaction, or any other measure deemed appropriate.

In private enterprise, the question of whether the integration of ethics and spirituality leads to a higher level of profitability seems to be a trick question which is always posed to for-profit organizations in comparison to those that are not-for-profit. It is imperative to realize that often the introduction into business of values other than financial ones is made through the back door, under the premise that it will bring greater financial gain! This convention of stating that "more happiness brings more profits" is not only a dangerous fragmentation of reality, but stems from a poor knowledge of scientific research done on the subject. Literally hundreds of studies have attempted to establish a cause–effect relationship between a more humanistic approach to management and an increase in productivity and profitability, dating back to the 1930s with the Hawthorne studies. The conclusion of these studies is unanimous: The cause–effect relation is present in 50 percent of the cases at most, which means that the supposed increased efficiency is a matter of chance at best.

Frederick I. Herzberg, the founding father of motivation theory at work, concluded after a critical analysis of these studies that managers should not look for gratitude from their employees after showing them affection.[63] As far as he is concerned, treating employees with decency, ensuring them a fair wage, and respecting their dignity is normal human behavior of one human being toward another and that it is an illusion to expect that such normal and decent behavior should have an impact on profit or productivity. He said,

Should managers expect workers to be grateful for a good job environment? No! Caring for the animal needs of workers does not make managers better human beings. It simply makes them more compassionate animals. Paternalism was hated precisely because of this inversion of expectations. An animal does not expect or deserve a reward for its compassion. Caring is a natural animal reaction; even chimpanzees care for wounded members of their tribe.[64]

Likewise, Jim O'Toole, who spent years working on issues of humanism and democratization in the workplace, stated that managers that engage in a more humanist approach of managing do so by personal choice and not for reasons of financial gain, which are by no means guaranteed anyway.[65] Obviously, more research must be done on this specific issue since the previously mentioned studies were focusing not on spiritual values but rather on humanist ones.

Another observation stems from these studies. Even though we cannot establish a relation between the humanization of work and productivity, it has been shown that this process does lead to changes to the work itself as well as to how it is perceived. Abraham Maslow, one of the leading experts on this matter, proposed that one could not satisfy people at work, but only—and much more profoundly—increase their level of discontent.[66] Expressed in the language we have used in this book, this means encouraging the development of their levels of consciousness, helping them to move from one pole of aspiration to another.

The fact that I expand on this matter of profitability or productivity is not fortuitous. Since the famous Hawthorne studies conducted at Harvard in the 1930s, the humanist movement within organization studies has often been distorted and reduced to paternalism. I sincerely hope that the spiritual movement will not suffer the same fate. This fear has been widely expressed throughout this book by managers themselves and contributes to the slowing down of the spiritualization process within organizations. From what I can see, a general observation that can be made from this book—and which appears to be much less dangerous—is that it may be possible to encourage an ethical and spiritual development within organizations undergoing strong competition, all the while maintaining acceptable profit levels. To state it somewhat differently, it is possible to establish a new balance between economic, ethical, and spiritual wealth while remaining competitive and ensuring the survival of the organization. How to achieve this balance requires a tremendous effort in experimentation and scientific research.

The third observation is equally as important: Even if ethics and spirituality are wished for within organizations—taking into consideration the reservations just mentioned—certain notions seem more difficult to accept by a large majority of managers. The notion of religion, for example, is perceived very negatively as is that of the New Age, which is widely rejected. These different perceptions imply the need for developing a language that is specifically adapted to each organization as well as to each of its stakeholders in order not to alienate nor offend them. It seems that words such as "prayer," "sacrament," "universal," "dogma," or even "God" make certain people uncomfortable because they are too closely related to religion. In the same vein, words such as "aura," "cosmic waves," "astrological maps," or "extrasensory perceptions" are to be avoided because they are too closely associated with the New Age movement. Scientific research on such matters is severely lacking.

Another observation is that there exist different strategies for the introduction of ethics and spirituality in organizations. These strategies include both a conscious desire of a few influential people as well as an external force of change which allows ethical and spiritual values to emerge along with other considerations. These different strategies seem to cover the whole gamut of strategies as described, for example, by Henry Mintzberg and colleagues, extending from the planned to the emergent strategies.[67] Even though different strategies can be used, it would appear that the painful experience of a major crisis is necessary in many instances to really set the journey in motion. Furthermore, if a guarantee, no matter how minimal, is needed to legitimize this spiritualization process, it is not only one leader who can assume this responsibility. Warren Bennis, internationally renown for his expertise on leadership, claims that creative collaboration within an organization is less the feat of great leaders than it is of great teams.[68]

If different introductory strategies are possible, the need to integrate ethics and spirituality into an organization in a systemic manner is another fundamental observation. To ensure the crystallization, development, and survival of this introduction, ethics and spirituality must be present in all traditional administrative functions of an organization, as well as globally in its culture, its management and leadership style, and in its strategies toward its stakeholders. If ethics and spirituality are only partially included in the human resource policies, for instance, the integration will likely not only be superficial but may be an indication of manipulation of ethics and spirituality for the purpose of increasing profitability and productivity. As we saw in Wilber's systemic model, spirit is present in different realms, be it the subjective *I*, the behavioral *id*, the global *id*, and the cultural *we*. Any attempt to confine it is a flattening of reality and a crushing of the soul.

Another observation is the need to be open to continuous change and to be ready to change radically, if need be, one's strategies, methods, and tools in response to the inevitable appearance of different paradoxes. In other words, when it comes to ethics and spirituality, universal, systematic, and planned models are inappropriate for the complex nature of the realities that these models attempt to promote. From this point of view, the notion of universal cannot be interpreted as a solution that is unique and thereby applicable to everything—which could lead to another flattening of reality—but rather as a celebration of the diversity which exists in the universe, respecting all the while their specificities in the global and complex universe.

This need to be opened to change and experimentation, while following certain codes of conduct, requires patience, perseverance, and the establishment of processes that help to deal with the discouragement that may come with the introduction of ethics and spirituality. Although it may be desired, this introduction and integration is nevertheless delicate, controversial, slow, and potentially dangerous. It would appear that there is an important need, for those who are committed to this process, to practice a spiritual discipline, be it individually or collectively. This will not only help these individuals to develop a more subtle mindfulness and inspire them spiritually, but nourish their hope as well.

One of the conditions that seems paramount to developing spiritual ethics in organizations is to demonstrate that spirituality brings new dimensions that are otherwise inaccessible by an approach that is only humanistic. This is not meant to contradict the intentions and aims of humanism. As it has been suggested on several occasions in this book, spirituality transcends humanism, that is, it contains it and goes beyond it. This book has proposed preliminary lists and personal accounts of the contribution of spirituality. However, more rigorous demonstrations of the differences triggered by introducing spirituality into organizations are needed to convince the management community to go beyond humanistic efforts. As we have seen, the actions of leaders that are spiritually motivated, such as Mother Theresa, are often seen in the public eye as only humanitarian aid going beyond the normal call of duty, while they also differ in nature. In particular, the existing links between the levels of transpersonal consciousness, as defined by Ken Wilber, with all the other modes of reality—subjective sense, physical health effects, the influence on ambient values and culture, and the development of new institutions, technologies, and management tools—need to be scientifically documented.

Despite all the good intentions, the introduction of ethics and spirituality in organizations can bring about counterproductive and even harmful consequences for individuals, organizations, society, and the world in general. In this book, some of the more obvious dangers have been identified. Action-research dedicated to ethics and spirituality within organizations should not only be dedicated to their positive effects but also their potentially dangerous effects. This idea of shadow encompasses several notions introduced by different traditions, such as greed, the devil, Hecate, Kali, the false, the bad, the ugly, Satan, sin, rakshasa, Thanatos, the *via negativa*, and so forth.[69] It is noteworthy that the New Age movement rarely, if ever, (with the exception of, for example, the Jungian approach) mentions this darker side, even though, quite literally, all religious traditions address it in a very serious manner. The need to recognize this dark side requires that people working on introducing ethics and spirituality into organizations are particularly attentive to these processes. They need to have undergone adequate training, to follow a spiritual practice themselves, and to have access to competent people that can assist them with their development. Research is also needed to be able to better understand the conditions that lead to these negative effects, including psychopathologies, dogmatism, paternalism, and the formation of dangerous sects.

Another important observation is that it is not only paramount that we stop crushing the spirit through management training and education, but we must encourage its blossoming by creating space and time specifically for that purpose. Just as a caterpillar needs a cocoon to become a butterfly, human beings need an asylum, as Erwing Goffman called it, to be able to nourish the ethical and spiritual development in connection with the practice of management.[70] In management and leadership, many specialists have insisted that personal development or the development of the self is essential.[71] Faculties of management and business schools, with some exceptions, are lagging terribly in this area when compared to other professional schools such as medicine and psychology. In these areas hundreds of programs, which integrate mental health, physical health, and spirituality, are currently offered by several renowned institutions such as Boston College, Harvard University, Loyola University in Chicago, the University of California at San Francisco, and the University of St. Thomas.[72] As well, a major research effort should be undertaken in order to scientifically test both the positive and negative contributions of various self-help and spiritual techniques to the practice of management; for example different types of meditation, art therapy, spiritual retreats, certain martial arts, contemplation, and so forth.

From a scientific standpoint, the effort thus far has been put on testing the existing relationship between spirituality and mental and physical health (quadrants A and B in Wilber's model). However, from a systemic perspective, it is equally necessary to develop an expertise in the other quadrants, namely the cultural and institutional dimensions, as well as the technological and material dimensions (quadrants C and D). Important action–research needs to be done to discover, test, and disseminate the experiments recently conducted in different organizations both in different countries and in different time periods, looking at that which has been done throughout history by different religious orders and communities. The Trappist beer of Orval, produced in Belgium for centuries, is but one example among many others.

An important lesson to retain from this book is the need to institute dialogues in organizations. From the Greek, *dia*, "through" and *logos*, translated by Martin Heidegger as "the pattern that connects" and by Simone Weil as "love," dialogue is a discipline that allows for the exploration "through the pattern that connects." This exploration of binding love is an echo of the notion of *religare* introduced previously. In this book, the need for dialogue was proposed with the aim of exploring the similarities and the differences between different traditions, to develop respect, tolerance, and mutual learning as well as to rediscover our cultural heritage. Furthermore, it was suggested that dialogue is one of the most fundamental strategies through which spiritual ethics can be developed in organizations, as the practice of dialogue is similar to practices currently used in business, and yet different enough. Essentially, a dialogue with oneself and with others is the process that allows one to explore quadrants A and D in Ken Wilber's model (the personal and collective subjective domains) whereas the other two quadrants, B and C (the external realities of the individual in the world) can be explored through traditional sciences, which are less dialogical but monological.

The ancient tradition of dialogue was rediscovered in organizational studies in 1990 by Peter Senge of the Sloan School of Management at MIT, following the research of the quantum physicist David Bohm.[73] Other studies have suggested as well that under certain conditions, dialogue could also become a spiritual discipline.[74] Without making it a panacea, it would appear that using dialogue circles within organizations as well as between different organizations would allow for important advances in the introduction of ethics and spirituality within organizations and within management practices. It would also allow for the development of what we could call dialogical ethics which would associate all the people and groups with an interest in an organization with regard to the process of decision making and discernment.

A final observation that we can derive from this book is that many questions still remained unanswered. Those listed have been compiled from the three dialogues that were held during the forum, transcribed in Chapters 4, 10, and 14 in this book. These questions, which stem from an audience of 200 people from the organizational world, should be relatively representative of the ones that managers today are asking themselves regarding the introduction of ethics and spirituality in management.

The list is structured along general themes. For each question or affirmation proposed by a participant, a counteraffirmation proposed by another participant is given, in order to put into context some of the emerging paradoxes. Direct quotes from participants are in quotation marks.[75]

Themes	Questions and Affirmations	Counteraffirmations
Emotional component that animates the will to integrate ethics and spirituality at work	"Many people are stifled at work."	Suffering can also be positive and from it can come action.
	"I feel anger toward managers." "I live a moral outrage."	Life at work is already good but could be made better.
	People must again find their dignity and their ability to be authentic.	Helping individuals to grow can make their lives in an organization even more difficult.

	I find in this forum the respect for diversity and different points of view, which is essential for any integration of ethics and spirituality at work.	I find it a pity that this forum is dominated by Catholicism and that nonreligious spiritual practices are not more present.
Structure and power within organizations	The integration of ethics and spirituality within organizations is inevitable since it is requested by a large majority of managers.	"Is the organizational milieu appropriate for developing spirituality?" What are the dangers of this? Can they be avoided?
Introduction strategy	A crisis or an epiphany often brings about change.	The process can be introduced by a small support group.
	A systemic approach is necessary from the start.	A slow and incremental approach is essential.
	This integration of ethics and spirituality at work is happening naturally nowadays.	How can we slow down in a world of constant acceleration? "How can we change when it is possible to make $200,000 for professional activities that are shallow?"
Implementation	Spirituality resides in the subjective and personal domains.	Spirituality is also concretely expressed at the organizational and social levels for the good or the bad of people.
	Spirituality is first and foremost contemplative.	Spirituality cannot be separated from action.
	There exists a universal model that is adaptable to different contexts.	There exist many radically different paths; we have to work not only with cultural diversity but also spiritual diversity in the world.
	We need an ISO for spirituality.	"Faith cannot be measured."
	Basic needs of innovation and continuous change must be respected.	This integration must originate from a founding text or doctrine.

	Establishing charters and codes is indispensable.	"Who will define and control ethical codes?" "Is this a return to the one best way?"
	It is absolutely necessary to respect the freedom of the "other" and to be democratic.	The democracy that we encourage imposes discordant actions.
	An organization can establish norms.	Group pressure is preferable.
	Spirituality begins before anything with respect for the other.	The need for humanization and spiritualization are complementary but different.
Ethics, spirituality, and profits	The integration of ethics and of spirituality at work allows for higher profits.	Their integration comprises a paradox between for-profit goals and not-for profit goals.
		Ethics should lead not only to a more just distribution of wealth, but to a questioning of the very goal of profit maximization and the promotion of other values.
	We need to develop tools and approaches for this integration.	"Is it ethical for me to offer my services in spiritual matters?"
Education and training	"Most programs are structured to stifle the spirit" which requires a radically different design.	Can such a transformation occur in the current politico-economic and scientific context?
	"The first job that needs to be done is in the home."	Most families can no longer fulfill their educational roles.
	The dichotomy between private life and work life needs to be mended.	Work provides several occasions for intimate relationships.
	Control has to be replaced by compassion.	Control has to be replaced by democracy.
	Moral and religious education needs to be reintroduced.	The ideology of control in education has to be fundamentally revisited.

	The basic problem is a communication problem.	"It is mostly by example that values are influenced."
Research–Action	"We cannot talk about this subject because it is too subjective."	Despite its subjectivity, this can be studied.
	Very few tools exist, they need to be developed.	Tools exist; they need to be gathered and tested.
	Research in ethics can only be conducted within a collective system.	Research in ethics has to be carried out based on the phases of human life.
	Spirituality is too personal to be studied.	"The needs of the soul" need to be more clearly defined.
	All research on this issue must start from an agreed-upon definition of the human being.	The view that spirit, Tao, or God animates every individual is enough.
	The use of ethics and spirituality for the sake of profitability is inevitable.	Research efforts must also focus on potentially dangerous aspects and must propose strategies through which to avoid them.

It seems obvious that these themes, developed by the participants of the forum themselves, offer yet another synthesis of the voyage started in this book. Even though, in many cases, the counteraffirmation can be seen as complementary to the affirmations, it remains that the ambiguity of the themes requires an important effort of research.

CONCLUDING REMARKS

A book such as this one does not end. The work to be done is huge and passionate, and it requires a lot of courage, faith, and enthusiasm. I would like to close with a final word from Chester I. Barnard, whom we quoted at the beginning of this book. Turning to this CEO and scholar will allow me to appeal to my fellow Ph.D. colleagues, who work in schools and faculties of management around the world, in an attempt to bring together the scientific, humanistic, and spiritual traditions.

Barnard was a recognized CEO in the AT&T group between 1930 and 1960 and is known today as one of the great theoreticians in administrative sciences. He was concerned with the advent of morality within organizations and was also a very spiritual individual. He proposed, for example, that the possibility for a real cooperation in organizations was dependent on the quality of human development, one influencing the other, as we saw in this book. Moreover, he believed that the terms of this interdependence could not be understood by science, but rather by philosophy and religion.

It is interesting to note that a CEO, with all his responsibilities, was the first to suggest theoretically, in 1938, that there existed a relationship between organizational efficiency, cooperation, and the development of human consciousness, morality, ethics, and spirituality. Often such people, with notable exceptions, do not have the time or the training to contribute to the advancement of scientific knowledge.[76] This responsibility falls principally to scientists. We have suggested in this book, however, that very few scholars in the administrative sciences have in fact contributed to the integration of ethics and spirituality in management.

Chester I. Barnard's suggestion that such integration is a question for philosophy and religion reminds us of the significance and the responsibility that the three letters "Ph.D." imply. Ph.D., *Philosophiae Doctor* in Latin or "Doctor in philosophy," was introduced in 1140 by the University of Bologna in Italy. The notion of philosophy referred to its Greek etymological root, meaning to be a "friend of wisdom," in other words, using wisdom in daily action; also, the term "Doctor" refers specifically to the title, "Doctor of theology." It seems imperative to remember that since its origin, the title "Ph.D." has been associated with the knowledge and practice of philosophy and theology. Today, we are far removed from this tradition. I do hope, however, in the future, that more Ph.D.s in administrative sciences will work in collaboration with managers and employees to integrate ethical and spiritual values in organizations, in honor of the etymology of their title. I hope to meet them at a future Forum on International Management, Ethics, and Spirituality, or the new interest group formed at the Academy of Management—Management, Spirituality, and Religion—or events organized by the Integral Institute in business, or still in other gatherings, for our world and we all are in great need of their vocation.[77]

Notes

INTRODUCTION

1. See T. C. Pauchant and Associates, *In search of meaning*, 1995.

2. See T. C. Pauchant and Associates, *In search of meaning*, 1995, for a detailed presentation of these factors.

3. On this subject see W. Wolman and A. Colamosca, *The Judas economy*, 1997 or P. Seguin, *En attendant l'emploi*, 1996. It is noteworthy that these critiques of the market economy do not stem from an ideology opposed to the market economy but from the proponents of this same economic system: William Wolman is the chief economist at *Business Week* and Philippe Seguin is a Gaulist leader in France.

4. See C. Taylor, *The malaise of modernity*, 1991.

5. See T. C. Pauchant and I. I. Mitroff, *Transforming the crisis-prone organization*, 1992.

6. See E. M. Morin, *Enantiodromia and crisis management*, 1993.

7. See D. Miller, *The icarus paradox*, 1990.

8. These two strategies, amplification and escape, have been discussed differently by Wilfred Bion who refers to "fight" and "flight." See W. R. Bion, *Experiences in group*, 1959.

9. On this subject see A. Maslow, *The farther reaches of human nature*, 1971, and T. C. Pauchant, *Healing health*, 2002.

10. See P. Tillich, *The courage to be*, 1952, and R. May, *The courage to create*, 1975.

11. See P. J. Palmer, *The courage to teach*, 1998.

12. See C. I. Barnard, *Elementary conditions of business morals*, 1958.

13. Conference Board of Canada, *Competency profiles*, 1998.

14. On this topic see W. Bennis and J. Goldsmith, *Learning to lead*, 1994; C. Handy, *The age of paradox*, 1994; and D. Yankelovich, *Got to give to get*, 1997.

15. See, for example, in Britain, *Business Ethics*; in Canada, *Ethica*; in the United States, *Business Ethics Quarterly* and *Journal of Business Ethics*; and in France, *Entreprise Ethique*.

16. See S. P. Sethi, *Ethical behavior*, 1998.

17. Quoted from Dalla Costa, *The ethical imperative*, 1998, p. 6.

18. For a list of these issues, see B. J. White and R. R. Montgomery, *Corporate codes of conduct*, 1980; and Ethics Resource Center, *Ethics policies and programs in American business*, 1990.

19. See *Finding faith*, 1999 for these statistics.

20. Cited by J. A. Conger, *Spirit at work*, 1994, p. 203.

21. For these statistics, see M. Doggan, Le déclin des croyances religieuses, 1995.

22. See M. Doggan, Le déclin des croyances religieuses, 1995, who presents a synthesis of three international studies dating from the early 1990s. These trends are confirmed by other studies from the mid-1990s.

23. Expression taken from a report in *Le Nouvel Observateur* in 1996.

24. See F. Popcorn, *Clicking*, 1996.

25. See P. H. Ray, *The integral culture survey*, 1996.

26. See F. Turner, *The culture of hope*, 1995.

27. On this spiritual view of science, see, for example, K. Wilber, *Quantum questions*, 1984, or S. Weil, *On science*, 1968.

28. See, for example, K. Wilber, J. Engler, and D. P. Brown, *Transformation of consciousness*, 1986, for a comparison of traditional contemplative practices and more modern approaches in psychology and psychiatry.

29. On this thesis, see J. O. Gollub, *The decade matrix*, 1991.

30. See F. Michelin, *Et pourquoi pas?* 1998; J. W. Marriott, *The spirit to serve Marriott's way*, 1997; and R. Österberg, *Corporate renaissance*, 1993.

31. Based on articles in newspapers and magazines such as M. Nichols, Does new age business have a message for managers? 1994; The search for the sacred, 1994; Companies hit the road less travelled, 1995; Business with a soul, 1997; Soul surfaces, 1998; *Le Devoir*, 1998; and M. Conlin, Religion in the workplace, 1999. See also K. E. Goodpaster and T. E. Holloran, Anatomy of corporate and social awareness, 1999, and P. H. Mirvis, *Soul work in organizations*, 1997.

32. See on this topic S. Inoue, *Putting Buddhism to work*, 1997.

33. D. N. Elkins, Spirituality: Why we need it, 1999.

34. On these ads, see T. Stein, How advertising has co-opted spirituality, 1999.

35. See F. Capra, *The turning point*, 1982, and M. Ferguson, *The aquarian conspiracy*, 1980. These two books have had a great impact having sold millions of copies in several languages.

36. See D. Zohar, *The quantum self*, 1990 and *Rewiring the corporate brain*, 1997; D. Zohar and I. Marshall, *The quantum society*, 1994; M. J. Wheatley, *Leadership and the new science*, 1994; and M. Wheatley and P. Chödron, It starts with uncertainty, 1999.

37. For a general introduction to this "new science" see for example, G. Bateson, *A sacred unity*, 1991; J. Gleick, *Chaos*, 1987; R. Lewin, *Complexity*, 1993; H. R.

Maturana and F. J. Varela, *The tree of knowledge*, 1992; I. Prigogine and I. Stengers, *Order out of chaos*, 1984; or M. M. Waldrop, *Complexity*, 1992. For applications in management and leadership, see, for example, S. Kelly and M. A. Allison, *The complexity advantage*, 1999; M. Maruyama, *Mindscapes in management*, 1994; W. McWhinney, *Paths of change*, 1992; I. I. Mitroff and H. A. Linstone, *The unbounded mind*, 1993; G. Paquet, *Governance through social learning*, 1999; T. C. Pauchant and I. I. Miroff, *Transforming the crisis-prone organization*, 1992; P. M. Senge, C. Roberts, R. B. Ross, B. J. Smith, and A. Kleiner, *The fifth discipline fieldbook*, 1994; P. Senge, A. Kleiner, C. Roberts, R. Ross, G. Roth, and B. Smith, *The dance of change*, 1999; or R. D. Stacey, *Managing the unknowable*, 1992.

38. See M. Ferguson, *The aquarian conspiracy*, 1980, pp. 419–420.

39. See K. Wilber, *Eye to eye*, 1983, chap. 7.

40. I can only succinctly present here part of the complex process described by Ken Wilber referring only to the prepersonal, personal, and transpersonal stages of consciousness. As the author reminds us constantly in his work, this synthesis is an abusive and dangerous simplification. I can only counsel the reader to consult Wilber's work itself. This being quite a huge work, I suggest to start with the book *A brief history of everything* for a not too technical presentation of his work.

41. Even while saying this, I do not consider a newborn to be a simple vegetating larva strictly determined by the laws of nature. Based on my personal experience, as a father of three, I am convinced that even a newborn exhibits singular personality traits and a spiritual nature.

42. See American Psychiatric Association, *DSM-IV*, 1995.

43. See M.F.R. Kets de Vries and D. Miller, *The neurotic organization*, 1984; H. S. Schwartz, *Narcissistic process and corporate decay*, 1990; R. B. Denhardt, *In the shadow of organization*, 1981; and T. C. Pauchant and I. I. Mitroff, *Transforming the crisis-prone organization*, 1992.

44. On these critiques of humanism, see, for example, J. Carroll, *Humanism*, 1993. See also C. Taylor on the modern development of the self in *Sources of the self*, 1989.

45. On these metapathologies see A. Maslow, *The farther reaches of human nature*, 1971, pp. 316–322.

46. Quoted from A. Maslow, *Toward a psychology of being*, 1968, pp. iii–iv. Similar views have also been expressed by Carl Rogers, another founder of the humanist movement. See *On becoming a person*, 1961.

47. Quoted from W. Bennis, Preface to *A spiritual audit*, by I. I. Mitroff and E. A. Denton, 1999, p. xi.

48. These are only two of many examples.

49. For these approaches, see J. O'Toole, *The executive compass*, 1993.

50. For a description of these levels, see Wilber, *The Atman project*, 1980; *Eye to eye*, 1983; and *A brief history of everything*, 1996.

51. On Maslow's and Kohlberg's theories, see Maslow, *Toward a psychology of being*, 1968 and *The farther reaches of human nature*, 1971; on Kohlberg see *Development of moral character*, 1964 and *The philosophy of moral development*, 1981. On the relations between these theories and the levels of consciousness, see Wilber, *The Atman project*, 1980, pp. 180–181 and *A brief history of everything*, 1996, p. 146. Also, even though Kolhberg and Maslow's theories have been criticized and need some fine tuning, this does not invalidate the general conclusions drawn here.

For these critiques see C. Levine, L. Kohlberg, and A. Hewer, *The current formulation of Kohlberg's theory*, 1985 and E. Hoffman, *The right to be human*, 1988.

52. See A. H. Maslow, *Motivation and personality*, 1970, and *The farther reaches of human nature*, 1971, more particularly pt. VII.

53. Quoted from A. H. Maslow, *Motivation and personality*, 1970, p. 29.

54. Quoted from A. H. Maslow, *Motivation and personality*, 1970, p. 55.

55. In addition to the relationship with L. Kohlberg and A. Maslow's works, K. Wilber's model has much in common with those proposed by R. Assagioli, T. d'Avila, S. Aurobindo, integral yoga, Skandha Buddhism, E. Fromm, J. Habermas, J. Loevinger, J. Piaget, and Pierre Teilharde de Chardin. For these relations, see K. Wilber, *The Atman project*, 1980; *Sex, ecology, spirituality*, 1995; and *Integral psychology*, 2000.

CHAPTER 1

1. How entrepreneurs are reshaping the economy, 1993.

CHAPTER 2

1. I. I. Mitroff and E. A. Denton, *A spiritual audit of corporate America*, 1999.

2. See T. C. Pauchant and Associates, *In search of meaning*, 1995.

3. See T. C. Pauchant and I. I. Mitroff, *Transforming the crisis-prone organization*, 1992, or I. I.Mitroff and H. A. Linstone, *The unbounded mind*, 1993.

4. On this subject see I. I. Mitroff and E. A. Denton, *A spiritual audit of corporate America*, 1999.

5. See in particular L. Bolman and T. E. Deal, *Leading with soul*, 1996; A Briskin, *The stirring of soul in the workplace*, 1996; T. Chappel, *The soul of a business*, 1994; B. Cohen and J. Greenfield, *Ben & Jerry's double-dip*, 1997; J. A. Conger, *Spirit at work*, 1994; B. DeFoore and J. Ronesh, *Rediscovering the soul of business*, 1995; M. Novak, *Business as a calling*, 1996; J. K. Salkin, *Being God's partner*, 1994.

CHAPTER 3

1. Quote from S. Connolly, Soul surfaces, 1998, p. B21.

2. I .I. Mitroff and E. A. Denton, *A spiritual audit of corporate America*, 1999.

3. T. C. Pauchant and Associates, *In search of meaning*, 1995, p. 13.

4. We should underline that in our interviews with people of all ages, the definition of ethics embodied the value of respect. This expresses the deep workings of the conscience which senses that without respect there are no values possible. Respect is at the base of all philosophies of individual or collective life. Through interviews and contacts with a variety of milieus, this call to respect appears as a counterpoint to the many ways in which the other politics professionals and institutions have been made banal and is in opposition to the mistrust which imbues social relationships: "I respect this; I will not go beyond this limit; and so forth." In reference to this historical approach to values, I refer to the first chapter in *Le défi des générations* by J. Grand'Maison, L. Baroni, and J-M. Gauthier, 1995.

5. Quote from Pope John XXIII, *Mater et magistra, #83*, 1961 encyclical on

Christianity and social progress.

6. Quote from J. T. Godbout, *L'esprit du don*, 1992, p. 309.

7. See H. Cox, *Religion and technology*, 1962, p. 79, where the author considers religion as culture's highest component, as a symbolic system that guides the values and orientations of a society.

8. Quote from G. Vahanian, *Dieu et l'utopie*, 1977.

9. Ibid, 1977.

10. In terms of his analysis, Daniele Hervieu-Leger defines secularization in the following manner: "the process of permanent reorganization of the work of religion in a society that is structurally powerless in order to fulfill the expectations which it must elicit to exist." See *Vers un nouveau christianisme?*, 1986, p. 29.

11. See *Sectes, le défi de l'irrationnel*, 1997.

12. Quote from T. Todorov, *La vie commune*, 1995, p. 15.

13. Ibid, p. 17.

CHAPTER 4

1. On the subject of dialogue in organizations, see M. Cayer, *An inquiry into the experience of Bohm's dialogue*, 1996; W. Isaacs, *Dialogue and the art of thinking together*, 1999; P. M. Senge, *The fifth discipline*, 1990; or D. Zohar, *Rewiring the corporate brain*, 1997.

2. See J. Campbell, *The hero with a thousand faces*, 1949. For the female version of this experience, see M. Murdock, *The heroine's journey workbook*, 1998.

3. See L.H.K. Secretan, *Reclaiming higher ground*, 1996.

4. See L. Freeman, *Christian meditation*, 2001.

5. See K. Wilber, *A brief history of everything*, 1996.

6. See G. Soros, *Soros on Soros*, 1995.

7. I. I. Mitroff, R. Mason, and C. Pearson, *Frame break*, 1994.

CHAPTER 5

1. On the history of the Desjardin movement see P. Poulin, *Histoire du mouvement Desjardins*, 1990–1998.

2. For an example of these criticisms see the editorial Claude Béland, 1999.

3. See C. Béland *Inquiétude et espoir*, 1998.

CHAPTER 7

1. For examples of the use of systems thinking in management, see R. E. Freeman, The politics of stakeholder theory, 1994; C. Hampden-Turner, *Charting the corporate mind*, 1990; W. McWhinney, *Paths of change*, 1992; T. C. Pauchant and I. I. Mitroff, *Transforming the crisis-prone organization*, 1992; R. Tannenbaum, N. Margulies, and F. Massarik, *Human systems development*, 1985; E. Trist, F. Emery, and H. Murray, *The social engagement of social science*, 1997; or P. Senge, *The fifth discipline*, 1990.

2. See P. Preville, *For God's sake*, 1999.

3. J.-R. Ouimet, *De nouveaux outils de gestion pour l'entreprise*, 1998.

4. A. Rich, *Éthique économique*, 1994.

CHAPTER 8

1. H. Arendt, *The human condition*, 1958.

2. See E. Hamilton and H. Cairns, *The collected dialogues of Plato*, 1963, book VIII.

3. Quotation by J. M. Keynes, *The collected writings*, 1972, pp. 326–331.

CHAPTER 9

1. For studies conducted at Harvard, see K. Wilber, J. Engler, and D. P. Brown, *Transformations of consciousness*, 1986; and for those done at Yale, B. S. Siegel, *Love, medicine and miracles*, 1986, a book that was on the *New York Times* best-sellers list for many years. See also a synthesis on this subject in Faith and healing, 1996; and H. G. Koenig, *The healing power of faith*, 1999.

2. The Anna-Laberge Healthcare Center is a short-term general and specialized healthcare center with 250 beds, located in Châteauguay, on the south shore of Montreal.

3. This experience was conducted at Charles-LeMoyne Hospital, a short-term general and specialized healthcare center with 468 beds affiliated with Sherbrooke University. I was then assistant general director of this hospital and responsible for the Quality and Performance Challenge Program.

4. The healthcare network has many management information systems through which performance indicators can help us in terms of comparison and evolution: the DRG (diagnostic related groups), the MED–ECHO (a system of archives based on diagnosis), the SOFI (system of comparative financial data), and so on.

5. The validation of these objectives was done in the centers where I worked during 1998 and in accord with the views of representatives of the University Health centers of Quebec and Montreal with whom I was in communication.

6. This survey was done with 100 people in the area of Quebec by the regional pastoral healthcare.

7. For a recent review of this literature, see H. G. Koening, *The healing power of faith*, 1999. See also H. G. Koening, ed., *Handbook of religion and mental health*, 1998; H. G. Koening and A. Futterman, Religion and health outcomes, 1995.

8. Concerning these results, see R. B. Byrd, Positive therapeutic effects of intercessory prayer in a coronary care unit population, 1988; J. W. Dwyer, L. L. Clarke, and M. K. Miller, The effect of religious concentration and affiliation on county cancer mortality rates, 1990; Y. Friedlander, J. D. Kark, and Y. Stein, Religious orthodoxy and myocardial infraction in Jerusalem, 1986; K. S. Kendler, C. C. Gardner, and C. A. Prescott, Religion, psychopathology and substance use and abuse, 1997; H. G. Koening and A. Futterman, *Religion and health outcomes*, 1995; H. G. Koening, Use of acute hospital services and mortality among religious and non-religious copers with medical illness, 1995; T. E. Oxman and others, Lack of social participation or religious strength and comfort as risk factors for death after cardiac surgery in the elderly, 1995.

9. Concerning these studies, see M. Galanter and P. Buckley, *Evangelical religion and meditation*, 1978; H. G. Koening, K. I. Pargament, and J. Nielsen, Religious coping and health status in medically ill hospitalized older adults, 1998; K. Wilber, J. Engler, and D. P. Brown, *Transformations of consciousness*, 1986.

10. See H. G. Koening, L. K. George, and J. C. Siegler, The use of religion and other emotion-regulative coping strategies among older adults, 1988; J. S. Levin,

D. B. Larson, and C. M. Puchalski, Religion and spirituality in medicine, 1987; I. K. Mation, The stress-buffering role of spiritual support, 1989; E. McSherry, Pastoral care departments, 1986.

11. See H. G. Koening, *The healing power of faith*, 1999.

12. See J. Desy et al., Âme, médecine et spiritualité, 1998.

CHAPTER 10

1. For discussing this issue, see, for example, E. E. Whitehead, and J. D. Whitehead, *Christian life patterns*, 1982.

2. For the ideas briefly discussed at this point we are particularly indebted to the thought of Parker Palmer, a Quaker educator. See P. J. Palmer, *To know as we are known—a spirituality of education*, 1983. See also his more recent work, *The courage to teach*, 1998.

3. We define a containing space as the space allowing for that conversation between the self and others, both internal and external, through which we define ourselves and, eventually, find the courage to be. The concept both derives from and is similar in intent to D. W. Winnicott's notion of the holding environment. For further discussion, see J. Applegate and J. Bonovitz, *The facilitating partnership: A Winnicottian approach for social workers and other helping professions*, 1995. We propose that such space allows for deep and transforming listening to take place within the person, the organization, the community, and the nation. The provision of such space is essential in any approach requiring development, change, and transformation. Without the opportunity to experience this space, human development, ethically and spiritually, can become only a superficial act of conformity. Our particular concern is how to provide this space in management education, and in the factors that both inhibit and foster the provision and use of such conversational space.

4. For a fuller description of the program and issues in its implementation, see C. Morley and J. Priest, *RMIT reflects on its DBA programme*, 1998.

5. For a discussion of experiential learning, see D. A. Kolb, *Experiential learning: Experience as a source of learning and development*, 1984. For the orientation of experimental learning to the issue of integrity in management, see D. A. Kolb, Integrity, advanced professional development, and learning, 1988.

6. These authors elaborate their notion of Model 1 and Model 2 modes of learning and of professional education in general in C. Argyris, *Overcoming organizational defenses*, 1990; and in C. Argyris and D. A. Schon, *Theory in practice: Increasing professional effectiveness*, 1974.

7. J. W. Fowler, *Becoming adult, becoming Christian*, 1984.

8. On this notion derived from "containing environments" of D. W. Winnicott, see J. Applegate and J. Bonovitz, *The facilitating partnership*, 1995.

9. For a discussion of the notion of vocation and its relationship to work see M. Fox, *The reinvention of work*, 1994; also J. C. Raines and D. C. Day-Lower, *Modern work and human meaning*, 1986.

10. Religious Society of Friends, *Christian faith and practice in the experience of the Society of Friends*, Section 40.

11. See F. Thorsen, *Through quiet processes and small circles*, 1997. We are also grateful to Frances Thorsen for pointing us to the work of D. W. Winnicott and the concept of the "holding environment."

12. E. Fromm, *The art of loving*, 1957.

13. See J. Milton, *Paradise lost*, 1987, book XII: 565–569.

CHAPTER 11

1. See I. Illich, *Deschooling society*, 1971.

CHAPTER 12

1. For three beautiful biographies of Simone Weil, see H. Bouchardeau, *Simone Weil*, 1995; R. Coles, *Simone Weil*, 1987; and D. McLellan, *Utopian pessimist*, 1990.

2. See J-M. Perrin, *Mon dialogue avec Simone Weil*, 1984.

3. This refers to the philosopher Gustave Thibon for Weil's *Gravity and grace*, 1952; to the Dominican priest Joseph-Marie Perrin for many works including *Waiting for God*, 1950 and *Intuitions prechretiennes*, 1951; to the union activist Albertine Thevenon for *La Condition ouvrière*, 1951; and to Anne Reynaud-Guerithault, one of her students, for *Leçons de philosophie*, 1959.

4. Regarding this, M.-M. Davy, for instance, compared Simone Weil to the ancient philosopher Heraclitus of Ephesus who also eludes all classifications. According to her, both are like "a fabulous butterfly whose species is not possible to determine. See M.-M. Davy, *Simone Weil*, 1966, p. 30.

5. See J. Grenier, *Albert Camus*, 1968, p. 142.

6. Quote from A. Camus, *Oeuvres complétes*, 1967, p. 392.

7. See M. Schumann, *La mort née de leur propre vie*, 1974.

8. Quote from J. Guitton, in S. Weil, *Leçons de philosophie*, 1959, preface.

9. Quotes from T. Merton, Pacifism and resistance in Simone Weil, 1968, pp. 76–77.

10. Concerning this influence, see D. McLellan, *Utopian pessimist*, 1990.

11. Quote from G. Steiner, Bad Friday, 1992, p. 86.

12. Concerning these influences, see D. McLellan, *Utopian pessimist*, 1990, p. 268.

13. See H. Bouchardeau, *Simone Weil*, 1995, and M. Serres, *Eclaircissements*, 1992, p. 33.

14. See R. Coles, *Simone Weil*, 1987.

15. Quote from S. Weil, *The need for roots*, 1987, pp. 93–94.

16. Quote from S. Weil, Science et perception dans Descartes, 1988, pp. 208–209.

17. Quote from S. Weil, *Gravity and grace*, 1952, p. 1.

18. See I. I. Mitroff and E. A. Denton, *A spiritual audit of corporate America,* 1999.

19. Quote from S. Weil, *The need for roots*, 1987, pp. 285–286.

20. Ibid., 89–90.

21. See also T. C. Pauchant, Simone Weil et l'organisation actuelle du travail, 1998.

22. Quote from S. Weil, *Oppression and liberty*, 1973, pp. 67–68.

23. See, for example, the Group of Lisbon, *Limits to competition*, 1995.

24. Quote from S. Weil, *The need for roots*, 1987, p. 272.

25. See S. Greenspsan and G. H. Pollock, *The course of life*, vol. 4, *Adolescence*, 1991, or E. H. Erikson, *Chilhood and society*, 1963. For a synthesis of the studies on this subject, see T. C. Pauchant, *Healing health*, 2002.

26. Quote from S. Weil, *Oppression and liberty*, 1973, p. 54.

27. Ibid.

28. Ibid.

29. See, for example, A. Jacquard, *J'accuse l'économie triomphante*, 1995.

30. Quote from S. Weil, *Oppression and liberty*, 1958.

31. Quote from S. Weil, *The need for roots*, 1987, pp. 90–91.

32. Quote from S. Weil, *Oppression and liberty*, 1958, pp. 109–110.

33. Ibid., 60, 82, 98.

34. Ibid., 93–94.

35. Ibid., 113, 116.

36. Ibid., 105, 124.

37. For a similar call, as formulated during the same period in 1933, see Alfred North Whitehead, *Adventures of ideas*, 1967, a book that is still poorly understood today.

38. Quote from S. Weil, *La connaissance surnaturelle*, 1950, pp. 92–93.

39. See C. I. Barnard, *The functions of the executive*, 1982; A. H. Maslow, *Eupsychian management*, 1965; M. Parker Follet, *Prophet of management*, 1995; H. Hesse, *Siddhartha*, 1951 or *The glass bead game*, 1969; E. F. Schumacher, *Good work*, 1979; and Hildegard von Bingen, *Hildegarde von Bingen's books*, 1987.

40. Quote from T. S. Eliot in the preface to S. Weil, *The need for roots*, 1952, pp. vi–xii.

CHAPTER 13

1. See R. Berthouzoz, R. Papini, C. J. Pinto de Oliveira, and R. Sugranyes de Franch (eds.), *Économie et développement*, 1997.

2. The Gospel according to St. Mark, 8, 36.

3. Quote from Gandhi, in Küng, *A global ethics*, 1993, p. 348.

4. See P. Ricoeur, *Soi-même comme un autre*, 1990.

5. See N. Luhmann, *Social systems*, 1995.

6. See H. R. Maturana and F. J. Varela, *Autopoesis and cognition*, 1980, and *The tree of knowledge*, 1992.

7. In this observation, Nikklas Luhmann proposes a criticism of the sociological and philosophical approach of Jürgen Habermas described in *Moral consciousness and communicative action*, 1992. Luhmann was able to show that Habermas, in his theory of communicational action, envisaged only one particular case of social operation or communication, that of forming a consensus.

8. On this subject, see R. Solomon and K. R. Hanson, *It's a good business*, 1985, or P. Ulrich, *Integrative Wirtschaftsethik*, 1997.

9. See J. Pasquier-Dorthe and C.-J. Pinto de Oliveira, *La gestion, carrefour de l'économie et de l'éthique*, 1990, and *Réussir les affaires et accomplir l'homme*, 1997.

10. M. Weber, *The theory of social and economic organization*, 1947.

11. For a first outline of this model, see R. Berthouzoz, *Dimensions éthiques et théologiques des droits et devoirs des minorités*, 1995.

12. On this subject, see L. Lavelle, *De l'intimité spirituelle*, 1955, and P. Ricoeur, *Soi-même comme un autre*, 1990.

13. M. Friedman, *Capitalism and freedom*, 1962; F. A. Hayek, *Droit, législation et liberté*, 1985.

14. See also on this subject R. Pétrella, *le bien commun*, 1996.

15. See CIDRESOC, *Charte des responsabilités communes dans l'activité économique*, 1998.

16. On charters of economical ethics, see M. Borghi and M. Meyer-Bish (eds.), *Ethique économique et droits de l'homme*, 1998, and P. Spicher, *Les droits de l'homme dans les chartes d'éthique économique*, 1996.

17. See on codes of ethics for business, for example, V. Averos, *L'éthique dans l'entreprise*, 1997.

CHAPTER 14

1. See M. Weber, *The sociology of religion*, 1963.

2. See British–North American Research Association, *An interfaith declaration*, 1993.

3. See Leviticus 25, 14; 25, 36.

4. See, in particular, Matthew 6, 25, 31–33; 20, 25–26; 25, 31–46; Luke 11, 41; Mark 8, 2; Acts 20, 35.

5. See Koran, Sourates IV, 2; VI, 153, VII, 31; VIII, 27; IX, 34.

6. Deuteronomy 23, 15; Baba Bathra, chap. 2, Mishnah 9.

7. See Genesis 1, 27–28; 3, 17–19; Matthew 5, 3; 2.

8. See Koran, Sourates II, 30, 256; VII, 54, 166; XII, 40.

9. See Talmud Bavli, Baba Bathra, 21b.

10. Pie XI, Quadragesima anno, 15 ami 1931, nos. 95, 109, 137; Paul VI, Populorum progressio, March 26, 1967, nos. 58–59; Jean-Paul II, Centesimus annus, May 1, 1991, nos. 33–34.

11. See Koran, Sourates V, 3; LIX, 7.

12. See Exodus 22, 25–26; Deuteronomy 24, 10–13.

13. Pie XI, Quadragesima anno, no. 50; Paul VI, Populorum progressio no. 19, 22–23, 49; Jean-Paul II, Centesimus annus, no. 43; Thomas Aquinus, Somme theologique, II, q. 66, a.1–2, q. 134; Jean Chrysostome, Homily on the Gospel according to Saint Matthew, homily 50.

14. See Koran, Sourates LI, 19; LVII, 20; LIX, 7.

15. Baba Metzia, chap. 7, Mishnah 1; Talmud Bavli, Baba Bathra, 8b; Mishneh Torah, book 13, chap. 13, 6.3.

16. See Thomas Aquinas, Somme theologique, II, q. 61, a.1, ad.2; Thomas Aquinas, De regimine principum, part I, chap. 15; Le XIII, Rerum novarum, nos. 12, 26–27; Pie XI, Quadragesimo anno, no. 54; Jean XXIII, Mater et magistra, p. 17, 154; Paul VI, Populorum progressio, no. 29; John-Paul II, Centesimus annus, nos. 15, 48.

17. See Koran, Sourates II, 29, 276, 278; III, 110; V, 92; XXVI, 181–183.

18. Deuteronomy 24, 15; Talmud Bavli, Baba Metzia, 10a, 76a, 111a, 112a; Mishneh Torah, book 12, chap. 11, 1, 2.1, 2.2; Baba Metzia, chap. 9, Mishnah 11–12.

19. See Acts 5, 29; Romans 13, 2.

20. See Koran, Sourates VI, 132; LXII, 10.

21. See Deuteronomy 23, 15.

22. See Genesis 1, 27–28; 3, 17–19; Matthew 5, 3; 2 Corinthians 8, 9.

23. See Koran, Sourates XI, 86; XCIX, 7–8.

CHAPTER 15

1. Matthew 25, 14–30.
2. See E. M. Morin, M. Gindon, and E. Boulianne, *Les indicateurs de performance*, 1996.
3. See B. Brault, *Exercer la saine gestion*, 1999.

CHAPTER 16

1. For systemic thinking, see, for example, P. Checkland, *Systems thinking, systems practice*, 1981; C. W. Churchman, *The systems approach*, 1968; T. C. Pauchant and I. I. Mitroff, *Transforming the crisis-prone organization*, 1992; P. Senge, *The fifth discipline*, 1990; or L. von Bertalanffy, *General system theory*, 1968.
2. See R. Freeman, *Strategic management*, 1984, and The politics of stakeholder theory, 1994.
3. On the notion of "pluriverse" see W. James, *The writings of William James*, 1965, pp. 405–417.
4. A. De Tocqueville, *Democracy in America*, 1956; see also R. N. Bellah, R. Madsen, W. M. Sullivan, A. Swidler, and S. M. Tipton, *Habits of the heart*, for a contemporary analysis of American personality and culture.
5. See R. Ashby, *Introduction to cybernetics*, 1956. As related to more general economic thought, see also E. F. Schumacher, *A guide for the perplexed*, 1977, chaps. 4, 5.
6. On this subject see W. Bennis, *On becoming a leader*, 1989, chap. 3.
7. For this example see T. C. Pauchant and I. I. Mitroff, *Transforming the crisis-prone organization*, 1992, chap. 1.
8. See C. I. Barnard, Elementary conditions for business morals, 1958.
9. For these authors, see Hamilton and Cairns (eds.), *The collected dialogues of Plato*, 1963; Aristotle, *The ethics of Aristotle*, 1955; Thomas Aquinas, *On the virtues in general*, 1951; E. Kant, *Critique of pure reason*, 1996; W. Windelband, *History of philosophy*, 1958; K. Gibran, *The prophet*, 1982; J. Dewey, *Logic*, 1938; A. Arendt, *The human condition*, 1958; P. Teilhard de Chardin, *Hymn of the universe*, 1955; S. Weil, *The need for roots*, 1948. For research on truth, goodness, and beauty and its links to different levels of consciousness as discussed in this book, see K. Wilber, *A brief history of everything*, 1996, chap. 8, pp. 120–134.
10. See C. Taylor, *Hegel*, 1975, and *Sources of the self*, 1989.
11. Citation from C. Taylor, *The malaise of modernity*, 1991, pp. 3, 5–6.
12. K. Wilber dealt with this question of the integration of truth, goodness, and beauty. See *A brief history of everything*, 1996, chap. 8.
13. In my opinion, in philosophy, it is the pragmatists who best tackled this issue. Pragmatism, one of the most recent philosophies of the century, is often wrongly associated with a utilitarian and instrumental vision of things, or trivialized as having only a practical meaning. On the other hand, authors such as William James or John Dewey proposed that an ethic based on esthetics was in fact the basis of truth. Students of organizational sciences, as well as managers, would benefit from having a better knowledge of pragmatism.

14. On the issue of "rejection of the false," see P. H. Ray, *The integral culture survey*, 1996; C. Spretnak, *The resurgence of the real*, 1997; Reclaiming real life, 1997.

15. See P. H. Ray, *The integral culture survey*, 1996, and his description of the social group called the "transmodernists."

16. See D. C. Korten, *When corporations rule the world*, 1995, or the Group of Lisbon, *Limits to competition*, 1995.

17. See C. I. Barnard, *The functions of the executive*, 1968, p. 4.

18. See Between nations and the world, 1993.

19. Citation from R. N. Bellah et al., *Habits of the heart*, 1985, pp. 43, 66.

20. See J. Keeble, *Out of the channel*, 1991, on the effects of the Exxon–Valdez crisis.

21. These statistics come from several different sources: E. Chivian, M. McCally, H. Hu, and A. Haines, *Critical conditions*, 1993; E. Goldsmith, R. Bunyard, H. Hildyard, and P. McCully, *Imperiled planet*, 1990; Group of Lisbon, *Limits to competition*, 1995; D. C. Korten, *When corporations rule the world*, 1995; G. Lean and D. Hinrichsen, *Atlas of the environment*, 1992; D. H. Meadows, D. L. Meadows, and J. Randers, *Beyond the limits*, 1992; C. W. Montgomery, *Environmental geology*, 1992; T. C. Pauchant and associates, *In search of meaning*, 1995; J. Rifkin, *The end of work*, 1995; and D. Smith, *Business and the environment*, 1993.

22. Citation from M. Serres, Nous entrons dans une période oú la morale devient objective, 1994, pp. 95–96.

23. Citation from M. Serres, *Atlas*, 1994, p. 244.

24. See D. C. Korten, *When corporations rule the world*, 1995.

25. See the Council on Economic Priorities, *Shopping for a better world*, 1998. The council also publishes a guide, *Rating America's corporate conscience*.

26. B. W. Karrh, Du Pont and corporate environmentalism, 1990, pp. 74–76.

27. Group of Lisbon, *Limits to competition*, 1995.

28. Adapted from I. I. Mitroff and E. A. Denton, *A spiritual audit of corporate America*, 1999, chap. 3.

29. The modernsists form a majority within our society as seen in the opening chapter in this book.

30. See H. Cox, *The market as God*, 1999.

31. As we have seen in the introduction of the book, the modernists, who embrace market values, actually represent the dominant belief.

32. See J. Macy, *Mutual causality in Buddhism and general systems theory*, 1991.

33. See L. von Bertalanffy, *General system theory*, 1968, pp. 10–13.

34. See M. Doggan, *Le déclin des croyances religieuses en Europe occidentale*, 1995.

35. See W. Pauck and M. Pauck, *Paul Tillich*, 1989, pp. 273–274.

36. Citation from P. Tillich, The ambiguity of perfection, 1963, p. 53.

37. See P. Abbé, *Testament*, 1994; Dalai Lama, *Freedom in exile*, 1990; E. Erickson, *Gandhi's truth*, 1969; V. Havel, *Disturbing the peace*, 1990; M. L. King, *I have a dream*, 1992; N. Mandela, *Long walk to freedom*, 1994; and Mother Theresa, *No greater love*, 1997. A recent and very interesting book on leadership compares two of these leaders, Martin Luther King and Mahatma Gandhi, to others, such as Alfred P. Sloan, Jean XXIII, Eleanor Roosevelt, and Margaret Thatcher. See H. Gardner, *Leading minds*, 1995.

38. See T. C. Pauchant and I. Fortier, *Anthropocentric ethics in organizations*, 1990.

39. See W. Isaacs, *Dialogue*, 1999, pp. 310–317; D. Zohar, *Rewiring the corporate brain*, 1997, chap. 8.

40. On the dialogic of ethics, that is ethics derived from a deep dialogue with oneself and with others, see C. Rogers, *On encounter groups*, 1970; J. Habermas, *Communication and the evolution of society*, 1979, and *Moral consciousness and communicative action*, 1990; and M. Buber, *Pointing the way*, 1990. See also on this subject, T. C. Pauchant and associates, *Healing health*, 2002.

41. M. Buber, *I and thou*, 1958.

42. Citation from P. Tillich, *Existentialism and psychotherapy*, 1990, p. 46.

43. For these dialogues, see P. Abbé and A. Jacquard, *Absolu*, 1994; Dalai Lama, *The good heart*, 1996; U. Eco and C. M. Martini, *Croire en quoi?*, 1998; J. Krishnamurti and D. Bohm, *The future of humanity*, 1986; J-F. Revel and M. Ricard, *Le moine et le philosophe*, 1999; and A.Toynbee and D. Ikeda, *The Toynbee–Ikeda dialogue: Man himself must choose*, 1976.

44. Citations from U. Eco and C. M. Martini, *Croire en quoi*, 1998, pp. 48, 49, 50, 65.

45. See A. Huxley, *The perrenial philosophy*, 1944.

46. See Küng, *A global ethic*, 1993.

47. See M. Martin, *The decline and the fall of the Roman church*, 1981, final chap.

48. Citation from H. Küng, *A global ethic*, 1993, pp. 18, 19, 20.

49. Citation from M. Serres, *Statues*, 1989, pp. 30, 33, 34.

50. See O. Germain-Thomas, *Les yeux fertiles d'Andre Malraux*, 1996, p. 57.

51. Citations from Andre Malraux, in Ibid., 57.

52. For these recent developments in the work of Ken Wilber, see *Sex, ecology and spirituality*, 1995; *A brief history of everything*, 1996 (which presents the material in a nontechnical format); and *The marriage of sense and soul*, 1999.

53. On this new Institute, see < http://wwww.Wilber.shambala.com >.

54. The description of these levels, as suggested in the introduction to this book, was undertaken by many people from a variety of very different cultures. As an example, Pierre Teilhard de Chardin proposed the notions of "lithosphere" (inert matter), "biosphere" (organic matter), "noosphere" (mental), and "christosphere" (spiritual)—see P. Teilhard de Chardin, *The human phenomenon*, 1955.

55. On the notion of coevolution, see, for example, G. Bateson, *A sacred unity*, 1991.

56. For this matter on the individual level, see A. H. Maslow, *The farther reaches of human nature*, 1971, pp. 317–319.

57. On the fragmentation of spirituality, see D. N. Elkins, Spirituality: Why we need it, 1999.

58. See K. Wilber, *A brief history of everything*, 1996, chap. 8.

59. For a definition, see M. Friedman, *Capitalism and freedom*, 1962.

60. On these numerous cases, see T. C. Pauchant and I. I. Mitroff, *Transforming the crisis-prone organization*, 1992.

61. For this definition of beauty by certain computer analysts, see S. Turkle, *The second self*, 1984.

62. Once again, Ken Wilber is not the only one to express this view, based on a geological notion of time—meaning measured in thousands of years. To use an example, Pierre Teilhard de Chardin, a paleontologist and believer, also adheres to

this paleontological vision of time, and was surprised that people could be impatient with the slow evolution of the world. See *The human phenomenon*, 1955, book 4, chap. 2.

63. See F. I. Herzberg, The four questions of life, 1995.

64. Citation from F. I. Herzberg, The four questions of life, 1995, p. 251.

65. See J. O'Toole, Do good, do well, 1991.

66. See A. H. Maslow, *Eupsychian management*, 1965, pp. 236–246.

67. On this array of strategies, see H. Mintzberg, *The rise and fall of strategic planning*, 1994; H. Mintzberg, B. Ahlstrand, and J. Lampel, *Strategic safari*, 1998; J. B. Quinn, H. Mintzberg, and R. M. James, *The strategy process*, 1988.

68. For this subject, see W. Bennis and P. Ward Biederman, *Organizing genius*, 1996.

69. See J. Abrams and C. Zweig, *Meeting the shadow*, 1991; for a personal point of view, see N. L. Quenk, *Beside ourselves*, 1993; for an organizational point of view, see R. B. Denhardt, *In the shadow of organization*, 1981; and G. Egan, *Working the shadow side*, 1994; and for the notion of work "via negativa," see M. Fox, *The reinvention of work*, 1994.

70. See E. Goffman, *Asylums*, 1961.

71. See W. Bennis, *On becoming a leader*, 1989; F. Friedlander and L. D. Brown, *Organization development*, 1974; I. I. Mitroff, *Stakeholders of the organizational mind*, 1983, or A. Zaleznik, *The managerial mystique*, 1989.

72. For a list of these programs, see Common Boundaries, *Graduate education guide*, 1994.

73. See P. Senge, *The fifth discipline*, 1990.

74. On the spiritual potential of dialogue, see M. Cayer, *An inquiry into the experience of Bohm's dialogue*, 1996; P. Hawkins, *The spiritual dimension of the learning organization*, 1991; W. Isaacs, *Taking flight*, 1993 and *Dialogue and the art of thinking together*, 1999; or D. Zohar, *Rewiring the corporate brain*, 1997, chap. 8; M. Buber, *Pointing the way*, 1990; D. Bohm and M. Edwards, *Changing consciousness*, 1991; or J. Mouttapa, *Dieu et la revolutiondeu dialogue*, 1996.

75. A more elaborate analysis of this material is in the process of being done. See K. Aarup, D. Cauchon, and T. C. Pauchant, *Integrating ethics and spirituality in management: A content analysis of some major challenges and paradoxes*, 2000.

76. For examples of exceptions, we can refer to H. Fayol, *General and industrial management*, 1949, or A. P. Sloan, *My years with General Motors*, 1990.

77. Information on FIMES can be found at < http://www.hec.ca/fimes >. For further information on the Academy of Management's new group, Management, Religion, and Spirituality is available at < http://www.aom.pace.edu/msr >. For events at the Integral Institute go to < http://www.wilber.shambala.com >.

References

Aarup, K., Cauchon, D., and Pauchant, T. C. (2000). *Integrating ethics and spirituality in management: A content analysis of some major challenges and paradoxes*. Paper presented at FIMES, HEC Montreal.

Abbé, P. (1994). *Testament*. Paris: Bayard Éditions.

Abbé P., and Jacquard, A. (1994). *Absolu*. Paris: Éditions du Seuil.

Abrams, J., and Zweig, C. (Eds.). (1991). *Meeting the shadow: The hidden power of the dark side of human nature*. Los Angeles: Jeremy P. Tarcher.

Alford, H. J., and Naughton, M. J. (2001). *Managing as if faith mattered*. Notre Dame, IN: University of Notre Dame Press.

American Psychiatric Association. (1995). *DSM-IV: Diagnostic and statistical manual of mental disorders*. Washington, DC: American Psychiatric Press.

Applegate, J., and Bonovitz, J. (1995). *The facilitating partnership: A Winnicottian approach for social workers and other helping professions*. London: Jason Aronson.

Aquinas, T. (1951). *On the virtues in general* (J. P. Reid, trans.). Providence, RI: Providence College Press.

Arendt, H. (1958). *The human condition*. Chicago: University of Chicago Press.

Argyris, C. (1990). *Overcoming organizational defenses*. Boston: Allyn and Bacon.

Argyris, C., and Schon, D. A. (1974). *Theory in practice: Increasing professional effectiveness*. San Francisco: Jossey-Bass.

Aristotle. (1955). *The ethics of Aristotle: The Nicomachean ethics* (J.A.K. Thomson, trans.). New York: Penguin Books.

Ashby, R. (1956). *Introduction to cybernetics*. London: Chapman Hall.

Aurobino, S. (1987). *The life divine*. Pondicherry: Centenary Library.

Averos, V. (1997). L'éthique dans l'entreprise: Le lien problématique entre la pratique et la théorie. *Revue d'Éthique et de Théologie Morale, 202*, 182–194.

Barnard, C. I. (1958). Elementary conditions for business morals. *California Management Review, 1* (1), 1–13.

Barnard, C. I. (1982). *The functions of the executive*. Cambridge: Harvard University Press (original work published 1938).

Barrett, R. (1998). *Liberating the corporate soul: Building the visionary organization*. Cambridge, MA: Butterworth-Heinemann.

Bateson, G. (1991). *A sacred unity: Further steps to an ecology of mind* (R. E. Donaldson, ed.). New York: HarperCollins.

Béland, C. (1998). *Inquiétude et espoir*. Montreal, Quebec: Éditions Quebec-Amérique.

Bellah, R. N., Madsen, R., Sullivan, W. M., Swidler, A., and Tipton, S. M. (1985). *Habits of the heart: Individualism and commitment in American life*. Berkeley and Los Angeles: University of California Press.

Bennis, W. (1989). *On becoming a leader*. Reading, MA: Addison-Wesley.

Bennis, W. (1999). Foreword. In I. I. Mitroff and E. A. Denton, *A spiritual audit of corporate America* (pp. xi–xii). San Francisco: Jossey-Bass.

Bennis, W., and Goldsmith, J. (1994). *Learning to lead: A workbook on becoming a leader*. Reading, MA: Addison-Wesley.

Bennis, W., and Biederman, P. Ward. (1996). *Organizing genius: The secret of creative collaboration*. Reading, MA: Addison-Wesley.

Benson, H.M.D. (1997). *Timeless healing: The power of biology and belief*. New York: Simon and Schuster.

Bernard, H. F. (1995, March). The role of psychological factors in cancer incidence and prognosis. *Oncology*, pp. 245–253.

Bertalanfy, L. von (1968). *General system theory: Foundations, development, applications*. New York: George Braziller.

Berthouzoz, R. (1995). Dimensions éthiques et théologiques des droits et devoirs des minorités. *Revue d'Éthique et de Théologie Morale, 195*, 77–81.

Berthouzoz, R., Papini, R., Pinto de Oliveira, C. J., and Sugranyes de Franch, R. (Eds.). (1997). *Économie et développement: Répertoire des documents épiscaux des cinq continents (1891–1991)*. Fribourg, Switzerland: Éditions Universitaires; and Paris: Éditions du Cerf.

Between nations and the world. (1993, September 11). *The Economist*, pp. 51–54.

Biberman, J., and Whitty, M. D. (Eds.). (2000). *Work and spirit: A reader of new spiritual paradigms for organizations*. Scranton, NY: University of Scranton Press.

Bion, W. R. (1959). *Experiences in groups*. New York: Basic Books.

Boa, K., and Burnett, G. (2000). *Wisdom at work: A Biblical approach to the workplace*. Colorado Springs, CO: Navpress.

Bohm, D., and Edwards, M. (1991). *Changing consciousness: Exploring the hidden source of the social, political and environmental crises facing our world*. San Francisco: Harper.

Bolman, L., and Deal, T. E. (1996). *Leading with soul: An uncommon journey of spirit*. New York: Random House.

Borghi, M., and Meyer-Bish, M. (Eds.). (1998). *Éthique économique et droits de l'homme: La responsabilité commune*. University of Fribourg, Switzerland.

Bouchardeau, H. (1995). *Simone Weil: Au fil des textes et de sa vie*. Paris: Éditions Julliard.

Bouddhisme. Le triomphe d'une religion sans Dieu. (1998, August 5). *L'Express*, pp. 26–33.

Bracey, H., Rosemblaum, J., Sanford, A., and Trueblood, R. (1990). *Managing from the heart*. New York: Dell.

Brault, B. (1999). *Exercer la saine gestion: Théorie appliquée à l'audite de saine gestion* (2d ed.). Montreal, Quebec: Publications CCH Ltée.

Briskin, A. (1996). *The stirring of soul in the workplace*. San Francisco: Jossey-Bass.

British–North American Research Association. (1993). *An interfaith declaration: A code of ethics on international business for Christians, Muslims and Jews*. London: Grosvenor Gardens House.

Bryson, J. M., and Crosby, B. C. (1992). *Leadership for the common good: Tackling public problems in a shared-power world*. San Francisco: Jossey-Bass.

Buber, M. (1958). *I and thou* (2d ed., R. G. Smith, trans.). New York: Scriber.

Buber, M. (1990). *Pointing the way* (M. Friedman, ed.). Atlantic Highlands, NJ: Humanity Press International.

Business with a Soul. (1997, August). *Mother Jones*, pp. 49–63.

Byrd, R. B. (1988). Positive therapeutic effects of intercessory prayer in a coronary care unit population. *Southern Medical Journal, 81*, 826–829.

Campbell, J. (1949). *The hero with a thousand faces*. Princeton, NJ: Princeton University Press.

Camus, A. (1967). *Œuvres complètes*. Paris: Éditions de la Pléiade.

Canfield, J., Hansen, M. V., Rogerson, M., Rutte, M., and Clauss, T. (1996). *Chicken soup for the soul at work: 101 stories of courage, compassion and creativity in the workplace*. Deerfield Beach, FL: Health Communications.

Capra, F. (1982). *The turning point: Science, society and the rising culture*. New York: Bantam Books.

Carroll, J. (1993). *Humanism: The wreck of Western culture*. New York: HarperCollins.

Carter, J. (1997). *Sources of strength: Meditations on scriptures for a living faith*. New York: Times Books.

Cayer, M. (1996). *An inquiry into the experience of Bohm's dialogue*. Untitled Ph.D. diss., Saybrook Institute, California.

Chatterjee, D. (1998). *Leading consciously: A pilgrimage toward self-mastery*. Boston: Butterworth-Heinemann.

Champion, F. (1993). *Le fait religieux aujourd'hui*. Paris: Fayard.

Chappell, T. (1994). *The soul of a business: Managing for profit and the common good*. New York: Bantam Books.

Chappell, T. (1999). *Managing up-sidedown*. New York: William Morrow.

Checkland, P. (1981). *Systems thinking, systems practice*. New York: John Wiley and Sons.

Chewning, R. C., Eby, J. W., and Roels, Shirley J. (1990). *Business through the eyes of faith*. San Francisco: Harper and Row.

Chivian, E., McCally, M., Hu, H., and Haines, A. (1993). *Critical conditions: Human health and the environment*. Cambridge, MA: MIT Press.

Churchman, C. W. (1968). *The systems approach*. New York: Laurel.

CIDRESOC (Centre internationel de documentation et de rechech en éthique sociale chrètiènne). (1998). Chartre de resbasabilités communes deus l'activité économique. University of Fribourg, Switzerland.

Cohen, B., and Greenfield, J. (1997). *Ben & Jerry's double-dip: Lead with values and make money too*. New York: Simon and Schuster.

Coles, R. (1987). *Simone Weil: A modern pilgrimage*. Reading, MA: Addison-Wesley.

Common Boundaries. (1994). Graduate education guide: Holistic programs and resources integrating spirituality and psychology. *Common Boundaries* (C.H. Simpkinson, D.A. Wengell, and M.J.A. Casavant, eds.). Besthesda, MD: Common Boundaries.

Companies hit the road less travelled. (1995, June 5). *Business Week*, pp. 82–83.

Conference Board of Canada. (1998, January). *Competency profiles for employment*. Available at: <http://www.conferenceboard.ca/nbc>.

Conger, J. A., and Associates. (1994). *Spirit at work: Discovering the spirituality in leadership*. San Francisco: Jossey-Bass.

Conlin, M. (1999, November 1). Religion in the workplace: The growing presence of spirituality in corporate America. *Business Week*, pp. 51–56.

Connolly, S. (1998, May 22). Soul surfaces in the office canyons. *The Globe and Mail*, p. B21.

Coombs A., and Raycheba, M. E. (2001). *The living workplace: Soul, spirit and success in the 21st century*. Toronto, Ontario: HarperCollins.

Cordelier, J., and Gollifu, C. (2000, March 31). Quand les patron croient en Dieu. *Le Point*, no. 1437.

Council on Economic Priorities. (1998). *Shopping for a better world: A quick and easy guide to socially responsible supermarket shopping*. New York: Council on Economic Priorities and Ballantine Books.

Cox, H. (1962). *Religion and technology: A study of the influence of religion on attitudes toward technology with special reference to the writings of Paul Tillich and Gabriel Marcel*. Unpublished Ph.D. diss., Harvard University, Massachusetts.

Cox, H. (1999, March). The market as God: Living in the new dispensation. *The Atlantic Monthly*, pp. 18–23.

Dalai Lama. (1990). *Freedom in exile*. New York: Hodder and Stoughton.

Dalai Lama. (1994). *The good heart*. Boston, MA: Wisdom.

Dalla Costa, J. (1998). *The ethical imperative: Why moral leadership is good business*. New York: HarperBusiness.

Daly, H. E., and Cobb, J. B., Jr. (1994). *For the common good: Redirecting the economy toward community, the environment, and a sustainable future* (2d ed.). Boston: Beacon.

D'Aquin, Thomas. (1982). *St. Thomas Aquinas: Theological texts* (T. Gilby, ed.). London: Durham Editions.

Davy, M.-M. (1966). *Simone Weil: Sa vie, son œuvre avec un exposé de sa philosophie*. Paris: Presses Universitaires de France.

De Loyola, I. (1986). *Excercises spirituels*. Paris: Desclée de Boouweer (original published 1544).

De Tocqueville, A. (1956). *Democracy in America*. New York: New American Library.

De Vleeschauwer, P. (1962). *The development of Kantian thought* (A. R. Duncan, trans.). London: T. Nelson.

DeFoore, B., and Ronesh, J. (1995). *Rediscovering the soul of business: A renaissance of values*. San Francisco: NewLeaders.

Delbecq, A. L., Thomas, J., and McCarthy, K. L. (1999, January). Spirituality for executive leadership: Reporting on a pilot course. *Third International Symposium on Catholic Social Thought and Management Education*, Goa, India.

Denhardt, R. B. (1981). *In the shadow of organization*. Kansas: Regent Press of Kansas.

Des Rivières, P., and Pichette, J. (1999, October 4). L'éducation, ça donne quoi? *Le Devoir*, pp. A1, A4.

Désy, J., Cencig, A., Deshaies, L., Tétu de Labsade, F., Gaumond, M., and Drouin, J. (1998). Âme, médecine et spiritualité. *Le Médecin du Québec, 33* (4), 37–84.

Dewey, J. (1938). *Logic: The theory of inquiry*. New York: Henry Holt.

Dillbeck, M. C., and Bronson, E. C. (1981). Short-term longitudinal effects of the Transcendental Meditation technique on EEG power and coherence. *International Journal of Neurosciences, 14*, 147–151.

Dion, M. (1994). *L'éthique de l'entreprise*. Montreal, Quebec: FIDES.

Doggan, M. (1995, September). Le déclin des croyances religieuses en Europe occidentale. *Revue Internationale des Sciences Sociales, 145*, 465–475.

Donaldson, T. (1989). *The ethics of international business*. New York: Oxford University Press.

Dreher, D. (1997). *The Tao of personal leadership*. New York: HarperBusiness.

Drucker, P. F. (1993). *Post-capitalist society*. New York: HarperBusiness.

Dwyer, J. W., Clarke, L. L., and Miller, M. K. (1990). The effect of religious concentration and affiliation on county cancer mortality rates. *Journal of Health and Social Behavior, 31*, 185–202.

Eco, U., and Martini, C. M. (1998). *Croire en quoi?* Paris: Rivages Poche.

Éditorial: Claude Béland. Relancer Desjardins. Entrevue avec S. Dugas and P. Duhamel. (1999, August). *Revue Commerce*, pp. 20–24.

Egan, G. (1994). *Working the shadow side: A guide to positive behind-the-scenes management*. San Francisco: Jossey-Bass.

Elkins, D. N. (1999, October). Spirituality: Why we need it. *Psychology Today*, pp. 45–48.

Ellison, C. G. (1995, March). Religious involvement and subjective well being. *Journal of Health and Social Behavior, 32*, p. 90.

Enderle, G. (1997, July). Five views of international business ethics: An introduction. *Business Ethics Quarterly, 7*, 1–4.

Erickson, E. (1969). *Gandhi's truth: On the origins of militant nonviolence*. New York: W. W. Norton.

Erikson, E. H. (1963). *Childhood and society*. New York: W. W. Norton.

Ethics Resource Center. (1990). Ethics policies and programs in American business. *Report of a landmark survey of US corporations*. Washington, DC: Ethics Resource Center.

Etzioni, A. (1988). *The moral dimension*. New York: The Free Press.

Faith and healing. Can spirituality promote health? (1996, June 24). *Time Magazine*, pp. 34–44.

Fayol, H. (1949). *General and industrial management* (C. Storrs, trans.). London: Pitman (original published 1916).

Ferguson, M. (1980). *The aquarian conspiracy: Personal and social transformation in the 1980s*. Los Angeles: Jeremy P. Tarcher.

Finding faith. (1999, April). *The Globe and Mail*, p. D3.

Fleuré, E. (1978). Une camarade pas comme les autres . . . Simone Weil vue par ses compagnons de travail. *Cahiers Simone Weil, 1* (3), 34–50.

Fowler, J. W. (1984). *Becoming adult, becoming Christian*. New York: Harper and Row.

Fox, M. (1994). *The reinvention of work: A new vision of livelihood for our time*. New York: Harper.

Freeman, L. (2001). *Light within*. New York: Crossroad.

Freeman, R. E. (1984). *Strategic management: A stakeholder approach*. Boston: Pitman.

Freeman, R. E. (1994). The politics of stakeholder theory. *Business Ethics Quarterly, 4* (4), 409–421.

Friedlander, F., and Brown, L. D. (1974). Organization development. *Annual Review of Psychology, 25*, 313–342.

Friedlander, Y., Kark, J. D., and Stein, Y. (1986). Religious orthodoxy and myocardinal infraction in Jerusalem: A case control study. *International Journal of Cardiology, 10*, 33–41.

Friedman, M. (1962). *Capitalism and freedom*. Chicago: University of Chicago Press.

Fromm, E. (1957). *The art of loving*. London: Unwin Paperbacks.

Gaarder, J. (1996). *Sophie's world: A novel about the history of philosophy*. New York: Farrar, Straus and Giroux.

Galanter, M., and Buckley, P. (1978). Evangelical religion and meditation: Psychotherapeutic effects. *Journal of Nervous and Mental Disease, 166* (4), 685–691.

Gardner, H. (1983). *Frames of mind: The theory of multiple intelligences*. New York: Basic Books.

Gardner, H. (1995). *Leading minds: An anatomy of leadership*. New York: Basic Books.

Germain-Thomas, O. (1996). Les yeux fertiles d'André Malraux. *Le Nouvel Observateur*, Hors Série, La soif de Dieu. Voyage au cœur des religions, *2803*, 57.

Gibran, K. (1982). *The prophet*. New York: Alfred A. Knopf.

Gill, E. (1983). *A holy tradition of working: Passages from the writing of Eric Gill*. West Stockbridge, MA: Lindisfarne Press.

Gilson, E. (1953). *La philosophie de saint Bonaventure*. Paris: J. Vrin.

Gleick, J. (1987). *Chaos: Making a new science*. New York: Viking.

Godbout, J. T. (1992). *L'esprit du don*. Montreal, Quebec: Éditions Boréal.

Goffman, E. (1961). *Asylums: Essays on the social situations of mental patients and other inmates*. Garden City, NY: Anchor Books.

Goldsmith, E., Bunyard, P., Hildyard, N., and McCully, P. (1990). *Imperiled planet: Restoring our endangered ecosystems*. Cambridge, MA: MIT Press.

Goleman, D. (1998). *Working with emotional intelligence*. New York: Bantam Books.

Goleman, D., and Thurnman, R.A.F. (Eds.). (1991). *Mind science: An East West dialogue: The Dalai Lama and participants in the Harvard Mind Science Symposium*. Boston: Wisdom.

Gollub, J. O. (1991). *The decade matrix: Why the decade you were born into made you what you are today*. Reading, MA: Addison-Wesley.

Goodpaster, K. E., and Holloran, T. E. (1999, January). Anatomy of corporate and social awareness: The case of Medtronic, Inc. *Third International Symposium on Catholic Social Thought and Management Education*, Goa, India.

Gore, A. (1993). *Earth in the balance: Ecology and the human spirit*. New York: Plume Books.

Grand'Maison J., Baroni, L., and Gauthier, J-M. (Eds.). (1995). *Le Défi des générations*. Montreal, Quebec: Éditions Fides.

Greenspan, S. I., and Pollock, G. H. (Eds.). (1991). *The course of life*, vol. 4: *Adolescence*. Madison, CT: International University Press.

Grenier, J. (1968). *Albert Camus: Souvenirs*. Paris: Gallimard.

Group of Lisbon. (1995). *Limits to competition*. Cambridge, MA: MIT Press.

Habermas, J. (1979). *Communication and the evolution of society*. Boston: Beacon Press.

Habermas, J. (1992). *Moral consciousness and communicative action*. Cambridge, MA: MIT Press.

Hamilton, E., and Cairns, H. (Eds.). (1963). *The collected dialogues of Plato*. Bolligen Series. Princeton, NJ: Princeton University Press.

Hampden-Turner, C. (1990). *Charting the corporate mind*. New York: The Free Press.

Handy, C. (1994). *The age of paradox*. Boston: Harvard Business School Press.

Harman, W., and Rheingold, H. (1984). *Higher creativity: Liberating the unconscious for breakthrough insights*. Los Angeles: Jeremy P. Tarcher.

Harrison, R. (1995). *Consultant's journey: A dance of work and spirit*. San Francisco: Jossey-Bass.

Havel, V. (1990). *Disturbing the peace*. New York: Alfred A. Knopf.

Hawken, P. (1993). *The ecology of commerce: A declaration of sustainability*. New York: HarperBusiness.

Hawkins, P. (1991). The spiritual dimension of the learning organization. *Management Education and Development, 22*, 172–187.

Hawley, J. (1993). *Reawakening the spirit in work: The power of dharmic management*. San Francisco: Berrett-Koehler.

Hayek, F. A. (1985). *Droit, législation et liberté: Une nouvelle formulation des principes libéraux de justice et d'économie politique, Tomme II: Le mirage de la justice sociale*. Paris: Éditions P.U.F.

Heider, J. (1985). *The Tao of leadership*. New York: Bantam Books.

Hervieu-Léger, D. (1986). *Vers un nouveau christianisme? Introduction à la sociologie du christianisme occidental*. Paris: Édition du Cerf.

Herzberg, F. I. (1995). The four questions of life. In T. C. Pauchant and Associates, *In search of meaning*. San Francisco: Jossey-Bass.

Hesse, H. (1951). *Siddhartha*. New York: Bantam Books.

Hesse, H. (1969). *The glass bead game* (Magister Ludi). New York: Holt, Rinehart and Winston.

Hock, D. (1999). *Birth of the chaordic age*. San Francisco: Berrett-Koehler.

Hoffman, E. (1988). *The right to be human: A biography of Abraham Maslow*. Los Angeles: Jeremy P. Tarcher.

How entrepreneurs are reshaping the economy and what can big companies learn. (1993, Special Issue). *Business Week*, pp. 10–18.

Huxley, A. (1944). *The perennial philosophy*. New York: Harper and Row.

Ibrahim, N. A., Rue, L. W., McDougall, P. P., and Greene, G. R. (1991). Characteristics and pratices of "Christian-based" companies. *Journal of Business Ethics, 10*, 123–132.

Illich, I. (1971). *Deschooling society*. New York: Harper and Row.

Inoue, S. (1997). *Putting Buddhism to work: A new approach to management and business*. New York: Kodansha International.

Isaacs, W. (1993). Taking flight: Dialogue, collective thinking and organizational learning. *Organizational Dynamics, 22*, 24–39.

Issacs, W. (1999). *Dialogue and the art of thinking together*. New York: DoubledayCurrency.

Jacquard, A. (1995). *J'accuse l'économie triomphante*. Paris: Calmann-Lévy.

James, W. (1958). *The varieties of religious experience*. New York: New America Library (original published 1902).

James, W. (1965). *The writings of William James* (J. J. McDermott, ed.). New York: Modern Library.

James, W. (1974). *Pragmatism*. New York: New American Library (original published 1907).

Jantsch, E. (1980). *The self-organizing universe*. Oxford: Pergamon Press.

John XXIII. (1961). *Mater et magistra: Encyclical letter of his holiness Pope John XXIII on christianity and social progress* (W. J. Gibbons, trans.). New York: Paulist Press.

Jung, C. G. (1964). *Man and his symbols*. Garden City, NY: Doubleday.

Kant, E. (1965). *Critique of pure reason* (N. Kemp Smith, trans.). New York: St. Martin's Press.

Kant, E. (1996). *Critique of pure reason* (W. Pluhar, trans.). Indianapolis, IN: Hackett.

Karrh, B. W. (1990). Du Pont and corporate environmentalism. In W. M. Hoffman, R. Frederick, and E. S. Pery (Eds.), *The corporation, ethics and the environment* (pp. 69–76). New York: Quorum Books.

Kaye, L. (1996). *Zen at work: A Zen teacher's 30 year journey into corporate America*. New York: Three Rivers Press.

Kazuo, I. (1997). *For people and for profit: A business philosophy for the 21st century*. Tokyo: Kodansha International.

Keeble, J. (1991). *Out of the channel: The Exxon–Valdez oil spill in Prince William Sound*. New York: HarperCollins.

Kelly, S., and Allison, M. A. (1999). *The complexity advantage*. New York: McGraw-Hill.

Kendler, K. S., Gardner, C. O., and Prescott, C. A. (1997). Religion, psychotherapy and substance use and abuse: A multi-measure, genetic-epidemiological study. *American Journal of Psychiatry, 154* (3), 322.

Kernaghan, I. (1996). *The ethics era in Canadian public administration*. Ottawa: Canadian Centre for Management Development.

Kets de Vries, M.F.R., and Miller, D. (1984). *The neurotic organization: Diagnosing and changing counterproductive styles in management*. San Francisco: Jossey-Bass.

Keynes, J. M. (1972). *Collected writings*, vol. 9. New York: Macmillan.

King, M. L. (1992). *I have a dream: Writings and speeches that change the world.* San Francisco: Harper.

Koenig, H. G. (1994). *Ageing and God.* Bingham, NY: Hawthorn Press.

Koenig, H. G. (1995) Use of acute hospital services and mortality among religious and non-religious copers with medical illness. *Journal of Religious Gerontology, 9* (3), 1–22.

Koenig, H. G. (1999). *The healing power of faith: Science explores medicine's last great frontier.* New York: Simon and Schuster.

Koenig, H. G. (Ed.). (1998). *Handbook of religion and mental health.* San Diego: Academic Press.

Koenig, H. G., and Futterman, A. (1995, March 16–17). Religion and outcomes: A review and synthesis of the literature. Paper presented to the *Conference on Methodological Approaches to the Study of Religion, Ageing, and Health,* organized by the National Institute of Ageing.

Koenig, H. G., George, L. K., and Siegler, I. C. (1988). The use of religion and other emotion-regulating coping strategies among older adults. *Gerontologist, 28* (3), 303–310.

Koenig, H. G., Pargament, K. I., and Nielsen, J. (1998). Religious coping and health status in medically ill hospitalized older adults. *Journal of Nervous and Mental Disorders, 186,* 513–521.

Kohlberg, L. (1964). Development of moral character and moral ideology. In M. Hoffman and L. Hoffman (Eds.), *Review of child development research,* vol. 1. New York: Russell Sage.

Kohlberg, L. (1981). *The philosophy of moral development.* San Francisco: Harper and Row.

Kolb, D. A. (1984). *Experiential learning: Experience as a source of learning and development.* Englewood Cliffs, NJ: Prentice Hall.

Kolb, D. A. (1988). Integrity, advanced professional development, and learning. In S. Srivastava and Associates, *Executive integrity: The search for human values in organizational life* (pp. 68–87). San Francisco: Jossey-Bass.

Korten, D. C. (1995). *When corporations rule the world.* San Francisco: Berrett-Koehler.

Krishnamurti, J., and Bohm, D. (1986). *The future of humanity: A conversation.* New York: Harper and Row.

Küng, H. (1993). *A global ethic: The declaration of the parliament of the world's religions.* London: SCM Press.

Laforge, P. G. (1999, January). Cultivating three ethical relationships through mediation. *Third International Symposium on Catholic Social Thought and Management Education,* Goa, India.

Lardeur, T. (1999). *Les sectes dans l'entreprise.* Paris: Éditions d'Organisation.

La soif de Dieu. Voyage au cœur des religions. *Le Nouvel Observateur, 2802,* 100 pages.

Lavelle, L. (1955). *De l'intimité spirituelle.* Paris: Aubier.

Lean, G., and Hinrichsen, D. (1992). *Atlas of the environment.* London: Helicon.

Lecourt, V. (2000). *La contribution de la spiritualité Ignacienne à l'évolution du management des organisations,* memoire de maîtrise, unpublished masters thesis, HEC Montreal.

Levin, J. S., Larson, D. B., and Puchalski, C. M. (1997). Religion and spirituality in medicine: Research and education. *Journal of the American Medical Association, 278* (9), 792–793.

Levine, C. L., Kolhberg, L., and Hewer, A. (1985). The current formulation of Kolhberg's theory and a response to critics. *Human Development, 28,* 94–100.

Lewin, R. (1993). *Complexity: Life at the edge of chaos.* New York: Macmillan.

Liebig, J. E. (1994). *Merchants of vision: People bringing new purpose and values to business.* San Francisco: Jossey-Bass.

Low, A. (1976). *Zen and creative management.* Rutland, VT: Charles E. Tuttle.

Luhmann, N. (1977). *Die gesellschaft der gesellschaft.* Frankfurt, Germany: AM University Press.

Luhmann, N. (1995). *Social systems.* Stanford, CA: Stanford University Press.

Macy, J. (1983). *Dharma and development.* New Hartford, CT: Kumarian Press.

Macy, J. (1991). *Mutual causality in Buddhism and general systems theory.* Albany: State University of New York Press.

Mandela, N. (1994). *Long walk to freedom.* Boston: Little, Brown.

Mariott, J. W. (1997). *The spirit to serve Marriott's way.* New York: HarperCollins.

Martin, M. (1981). *The decline and fall of the Roman church.* New York: Putnam.

Maslow, A. H. (1964). *Religions, values, and peak-experiences.* Columbus: Ohio State University Press.

Maslow, A. H. (1965). *Eupsychian management: A journal.* Homewood, IL: Richard D. Irwin.

Maslow, A. H. (1968). *Toward a psychology of being* (2d ed.). New York: Van Nostrand Reinholt.

Maslow, A. H. (1970). *Motivation and personality.* New York: Harper and Row.

Maslow, A. H. (1971). *The farther reaches of human nature.* New York: Viking Press.

Mation, K. I. (1989). The stress-buffering role of spiritual support: Cross-sectorial and prospective investigation. *Journal for the Scientific Study of Religion, 28* (3), 310–323.

Matthews, D. A., Larson, D. B., and Barry, C. P. (1993). *The faith factor: An annotated bibliography of clinical research on spiritual subjects,* vol. 1. Rockville, MD: National Institute for Healthcare Research.

Maturana, H. R., and Varela, F. J. (1980). *Autopoiesis and cognition: The realization of the living.* Boston: D. Reisel.

Maturana, H. R., and Varela, F. J. (1992). *The tree of knowledge: The biological roots of human understanding.* Boston: Shambhala.

May, R. (1969). *Love and will.* New York: Dell.

May, R. (1975). *The courage to create.* New York: W. W. Norton.

Mayor, R. (1990). Pour une éthique planétaire. Special edition, A soif de dieu. *Le Nouvel Observateur.*

Mayurama, M. (1994). *Mindscapes in management.* Brookfield, VT: Dartmouth.

McLellan, D. (1990). *Utopian pessimist: The life and thought of Simone Weil.* New York: Poseidon Press.

McSherry, E. (1986). Pastoral care departments: More necessary in the DRG era? *Health Care Management Review, 11* (1), 58.

McWhinney, W. (1992). *Paths of change: Strategic choices for organizations and society.* Newbury Park, CA: Sage.

Meadows, D. H., Meadows, D. L., and Randers, J. (1992). *Beyond the limits*. Toronto, Ontario: McClelland and Stewart.

Merton, T. (1968). Pacifism and resistance in Simone Weil. In T. Merton, *Faith and violence: Christian teaching and Christian practice* (pp. 76–84). Notre Dame, IN: University of Notre Dame Press.

Merton, T. (1985). *Love and living* (N. B. Stone and P. Hart, eds.). New York: Harcourt Brace Jovanovich.

Michelin, F. (1998). *Et pourquoi pas?* Paris: Éditions Grasset.

Miller, D. (1990). *The Icarus paradox: How exceptional companies bring about their own downfall*. New York: HarperBusiness.

Milton, J. (1987). *Paradise lost*. New York: Chelsea House.

Mintzberg, H. (1994). *The rise and fall of strategic planning: Reconceiving roles for planning, plans, planners*. New York: The Free Press.

Mintzberg, H., Ahlstrand, B., and Lampel, J. (1998). *Strategic safari: A guided tour through the wilds of strategic management*. New York: The Free Press.

Mirvis, P. H. (1997). Soul work in organizations. *Organization Science, 8* (2), 193–206.

Mitroff, I. I. (1983). *Stakeholders of the organizational mind*. San Francisco: Jossey-Bass.

Mitroff, I. I., and Denton, E. A. (1999). *A spiritual audit of corporate America: A hard look at spirituality, religion, and values in the workplace*. (A Warren Bennis Book). San Francisco: Jossey-Bass.

Mitroff, I. I., Mason, R., and Pearson, C. (1994). *Frame break*. San Francisco: Jossey-Bass.

Mitroff, I. I., and Linstone, H. A. (1993). *The unbounded mind: Breaking the chains of traditional business thinking*. New York: Oxford University Press.

Montgomery, C. W. (1992). *Environmental geology* (3d ed.). Dubuque, IA: W. C. Brown.

Moore, T. (1998). *Spiritual investments: Wall Street wisdom from the career of Sir John Templeton*. Philadelphia, PA: Templeton Foundation Press.

Moore, T. (1992). *Care of the soul: A guide for cultivating depth and sacredness in everyday life*. New York: HarperCollins.

Morin, E. M. (1993). Enantiodromia crisis management: A Jungian perspective. *Industrial and Environmental Crisis Quarterly, 7* (2), 91–114.

Morin, E. M., Savoie, A., and Beaudion, G. (1994). *L'efficacité de l'organisation: Théories, représentations et mesures*. Montreal, Quebec: Gaëtan Morin Éditeur.

Morin, E. M., Guidon, M., and Boulianne, E. (1996). *Les indicateurs de performance*, Ordre des comptables généraux licenciés du Québec. Montreal, Quebec: Éditions Guérin.

Morley, C., and Priest, J. (1998, September). *RMIT reflects on its DBA programme*. Unpublished paper presented at the *Innovations in Teaching & Research Conference*, Coffs Harbour, N.S.W., Australia.

Mother Teresa. (1997). *No greater love*. New York: New World Library.

Mouttapa, J. (1996). *Dieu et perévolution du dialogue*. Paris: Albin Michel.

Moxley, R. S. (2000). *Leadership and spirit: Breathing new vitality and energy into individuals and organizations*. San Francisco: Jossey-Bass.

Murdock, M. (1998). *The heroine's journey workbook*. Boston: Shambhala.

Neal, J. A. (1997). Spirituality in management education: A guide to resources. *Journal of Management Education, 21* (1), 121–139.

The new spirituality: Mainstream North America searches for meaning in life. (1994, October 10). *Maclean's*, pp. 44–54.

Nichols, M. (1994, March–April). Does new age business have a message for managers? *Harvard Business Review, 58*, 52–60.

Novak, M. (1996). *Business as a calling: Work and the examined life*. New York: The Free Press.

Olive, D. (1987). *Just rewards: The case for ethical reform in business*. Toronto, Ontario: Key Porter Books.

Osborn, C. M. (2000). *Inner excellence at work: The path to meaning, spirit and success*. New York: Amacom.

Österberg, R. (1993). *Corporate renaissance: Business as an adventure in human development*. Mill Valley, CA: Nataraj.

O'Toole, J. (1991). Do good, do well: The business enterprise award. *California Management Review, 33*, 19–25.

O'Toole, J. (1993). *The executive compass: Business and the good society*. New York: Oxford University Press.

O'Toole, J. (1996). *Leading change: The argument for values-based leadership*. New York: Ballantine Books.

Ouimet, J-R. (1998). *De nouveaux outils de gestion pour l'entreprise: Apports au bonheur humain et à la profitabilité*. Unpublished Ph.D. diss., Faculty of Economic and Social Sciences, University of Fribourg, Switzerland.

Owen, H. (1999). *The spirit of leadership: Liberating the leader in each of us*. San Francisco: Berrett-Koehler.

Oxman, T. E. et al. (1995). Lack of social participation or religious strength and comfort as risk factors for death after cardiac surgery in the elderly. *Psychosomatic Medicine, 57*, 5–15.

Palmer, P. J. (1983). *To know as we are known—A spirituality of education*. San Francisco: Harper and Row.

Palmer, P. J. (1998). *The courage to teach*. San Francisco: Jossey-Bass.

Paquet, G. (1999). *Governance through social learning*. Ottawa, Ontario: University of Ottawa Press.

Pargament, K. I. (1997). *The psychology of religion and coping*. New York: Guilford Press.

Parker Follet, M. (1995). *Prophet of management* (P. Graham, ed.). Boston: Harvard Business School Press.

Pascarella, P. (1999). *Christ-centered leadership: Thriving in business by putting God in charge*. Rocklin, CA: Prima.

Pasquero, J. (1997, May). *L'éthique des affaires: Fondements théoriques et implications*. Congrès de l'Institut Supérieur de Gestion de Tunis. Paper available at UQAM, École des Sciences de la Gestion, Montreal.

Pasquier-Dorthe, J., and Pinto de Oliveira, C.-J. (1997). Réussir les affaires et accomplir l'homme: Enjeux éthiques et économiques de l'entreprise: Responsabilité et rentabilité. *Cahiers ISES*, Fribourg, Switzerland.

Pasquier-Dorthe, J., and Pinto de Oliveira, C.-J. (Eds.). (1990). La gestion, carrefour de l'économie et de l'éthique: Identification et traitement des critères et problèmes éthiques dans la décision d'entreprise. *Cahiers ISES, 35*, Fribourg, Switzerland.

Pauchant, T. C. (1998). Simone Weil et l'organisation actuelle du travail. *Cahiers Simone Weil, 21* (1–2), 111–140.

Pauchant, T.C. (2002) The management of production and counter-production: A call for mature scholars, managers and educators. *Journal of Management Inquiry*, in press.

Pauchant, T. C. and Associates. (1995). *In search of meaning: Managing for the health of our organizations, our communities and the natural world.* San Francisco: Jossey-Bass.

Pauchant, T. C. and Associates. (2002). *Healing health-care: A group dialogue on the meaning of work, ethics and values in the health-care system.* Unpublished document to be published as a book, HEC Montreal.

Pauchant, T. C., and Fortier, I. (1990). Anthropocentric ethics in organizations: Strategic management and the environment: A typology. In P. Shrivastava and R. B. Lamb (Eds.), *Advances in strategic management* (vol. 6, pp. 99–114). Greenwich, CT: JAI Press.

Pauchant, T. C., and Mitroff, I. I. (1992). *Transforming the crisis-prone organization: Preventing individual, organizational and environmental tragedies.* San Francisco: Jossey-Bass.

Pauck, W., and Pauck, M. (1989). *Paul Tillich: His life and thoughts.* San Francisco: Harper and Row.

Peck, Scott M. (1978). *The road less travelled: A new psychology of love, traditional values and spiritual growth.* New York: A Touchstone Book.

Perrin, J-M. (1984). *Mon dialogue avec Simone Weil.* Paris: Nouvelle Cité.

Petrella, R. (1996). *Le bien commun: Éloge de la solidarité.* Bruxelles: Labor.

Pirsig, R. M. (1974). *Zen and the art of motorcycle maintenance.* New York: William Morrow.

Play and work. (1996, November). *Parabola, 21,* 4.

Popcorn, F. (1996). *Clicking.* New York: HarperCollins.

Pope John XXIII. (1961). Mater et magistra, #83, encyclical on christianity and social progress, Roma.

Poulin, P. (1990–1998). *Histoire du mouvement Desjardins*, Tomes I, II, III. Montreal: Éditions Québec-Amérique.

Preville, P. (1999, June 25–July 9). For God's sake: Montreal canned-food magnate J.-Robert Ouimet thinks he's found the way to make his employees happier and more productive. *Canadian Business*, pp. 58–61.

Prigogine, I., and Stengers, I. (1984). *Order out of chaos: Man's dialogue with nature.* New York: Bantam Books.

Quenk, N. L. (1993). *Beside ourselves: Our hidden personality in everyday life.* Palo Alto, CA: Davies-Black.

Quinn, J. B., Mintzberg, H., and James, R. M. (1988). *The strategy process: Concepts, contexts, and cases.* Englewood Cliffs, NJ: Prentice Hall.

Raines, J. C., and Day-Lower, D. C. (1986). *Modern work and human meaning.* Philadelphia, PA: Westminster Press.

Ray, P. H. (1996). *The integral culture survey: A study of the emergence of transformational values in America.* Sausalito, CA: Institute of Noetic Sciences.

Reclaiming real life. (1997, August). *Utne Reader*, pp. 49–65.

Reder, A. (1994). *In pursuit of principle and profit: Business success through social responsibility.* New York: G. P. Putman's Sons.

Religious Society of Friends. (1960). *Christian faith and practice in the experience of the society of friends*. Annual meeting held in London, section 40.

Renesh, J. (Ed.). (1992). *New tradition in business: Spirit and leadership in the 21st century*. San Francisco: Berrett-Koehler.

Revel, J-F., and Ricard, M. (1999). *Le moine et le philosophe* (2d ed.). Paris: NIL Éditions.

Rich, A. (1994). *Éthipce économique*. Geneve: Labor et Fides.

Richmond, L. (1999). *Work as a spiritual practice: A practical Buddhist approach to inner growth and satisfaction on the job*. New York: Broadway Books.

Ricoeur, P. (1990). *Soi-même comme un autre*. Paris: Éditions du Seuil.

Rifkin, J. (1995). *The end of work*. New York: G. P. Putman's Sons.

Roddick, A. (1990). *Body and soul: Profits with principles*. New York: Crown.

Roddick, A. (2000). *Business as unusual: The triumph of Anita Roddick*. London: Thorsons.

Rogers, C. R. (1961). *On becoming a person*. Boston: Houghton Mifflin.

Rogers, C. R. (1970). *On encounter groups*. New York: Harper and Row.

Salkin, J. K. (1994). *Being God's partner: How to find the hidden link between spirituality and your work*. Woodstock, VT: Jewish Lights.

Saudia, T. L., Kinnery, M. R., Brown, K. C., and Young-Ward, L. (1991). Health locus of control and helpfulness of prayer. *Heart and Lung, 20,* 60–65.

Saul, J. (1992). *Voltaire's bastards: The dictatorship of reason in the West*. New York: The Free Press.

Schumacher, E. F. (1977). *A guide for the perplexed*. New York: Harper and Row.

Schumacher, E. F. (1979). *Good work*. New York: Harper and Row.

Schumann, M. (1974). *La mort née de leur propre vie: Gandhi, Péguy, Simone Weil*. Paris: Éditions Fayard.

Schwartz, H. S. (1990). *Narcissistic process and corporate decay: The theory of the organizational ideal*. New York: New York University Press.

The search for the sacred: America's quest for spiritual meaning. (1994, November 28). *Newsweek*, pp. 52–62.

Secretan, L.H.K. (1996). *Reclaiming higher ground: Creating organizations that inspire the soul*. Toronto, Ontario: Macmillan Canada.

Sectes, le défi de l'irrationnel, Série Dossiers et Documents. (1997, Décembre). *Le Monde*, pp. 40–61.

Seed, J., Fleming, P., Macy, J., and Naess, A. (1988). *Thinking like a mountain*. Philadelphia, PA: New Society.

Seglin, J. L. (2000). *The good, the bad and your business*. New York: John Wiley and Sons.

Seguin, P. (1996). *En attendant l'emploi*. Paris: Éditions du Seuil.

Selznick, P. (1992). *The moral commonwealth: Social theory and the promise of community*. Berkeley and Los Angeles: University of California Press.

Sen, A. (1999). *L'économie est une science morale*. Paris: Éditions La Découverte.

Senge, P. M. (1990). *The fifth discipline: The art and practice of the learning organization*. New York: DoubledayCurrency.

Senge, P. M., Kleiner, A., Roberts, C., Ross, R., Roth, G., and Smith, B. (1999). *The dance of change: The challenge to sustaining momentum in learning organizations*. New York: DoubledayCurrency.

Senge, P.M., Roberts, C., Ross, R. B., Smith, B. J., and Kleiner, A. (1994). *The fifth discipline fieldbook*. New York: DoubledayCurrency.

Serres, M. (1989). *Statues*. Paris: Flammarion.

Serres, M. (1990). *Le contrat naturel*. Paris: Éditions François Bourin.

Serres, M. (1992). *Éclaircissements: Cinq entretiens avec Bruno Latour*. Paris: Éditions François Bourin.

Serres, M. (1994). Nous entrons dans une période où la morale devient objective. In *Les grands entretiens du monde*, Tome II (pp. 89–97). Paris: Le Monde Éditions.

Serres, M. (1994). *Atlas*. Paris: Éditions Julliard.

Sethi, S. P. (1998). Ethical behavior as a strategic choice by large corporations: The interactive effect of the marketplace competition, industry structure and firm resources. *Business Ethics Quarterly, 8* (1), 85–104.

Shrivastava, P. (1996). *Greening business: Profiting the corporation and the environment*. Cincinnati, OH: Thomson Executive Press.

Siegel, B. S. (1986). *Love, medicine and miracles: Lessons learned about self-healing from a surgeon's experience with exceptional patients*. New York: Harper and Row.

Sloan, A. P. (1990). *My years with General Motors*. New York: DoubledayCurrency (original published 1963).

Smith, D. (1999). *Work with what you have: Ways to creative and meaningful livelihood*. Boston: Shambhala.

Smith, D. (Ed.). (1993). *Business and the environment: Implications of the new enviromentalism*. London: Paul Chapman.

Snell, R. S. (1998). Obedience to authority and ethical dilemmas in Hong Kong companies. *Business Ethics Quarterly, 9* (3), 507–526.

Solomon, R., and Hanson, K. R. (1985). *It's good business*. New York: Atheneum.

Soros, G. (1995). *Soros on Soros*. New York: John Wiley and Sons.

Soul surfaces in the office canyons. (1998, May). *The Globe and Mail*, pp. B21, 22.

Spicher, P. (1996). *Les droits de l'homme dans les chartes d'éthique économique*. Fribourg, Switzerland.

Spretnak, C. (1997). *The resurgence of the real: Body, nature and place in a hypermodern world*. New York: Addison-Wesley.

Stacey, R. D. (1992). *Managing the unknowable: Strategic boundaries between order and chaos in organizations*. San Francisco: Jossey-Bass.

Stein, T. (1999, November). How advertising has co-opted spirituality. *Shambhala Sun*, pp. 36–41.

Steiner, G. (1992, March 2). Bad Friday. *The New Yorker*, pp. 86–90.

Tannenbaum, R., Margulies, N., Massarik, F., and Associates. (1985). *Human systems development: New perspectives on people and organizations*. San Francisco: Jossey-Bass.

Taylor, C. (1975). *Hegel*. Cambridge, MA: Cambridge University Press.

Taylor, C. (1989). *Sources of the self*. Cambridge, MA: Harvard University Press.

Taylor, C. (1991). *The malaise of modernity*. Toronto, Ontario: Stoddart.

Teilhard de Chardin, P. (1955). *Hymn of the universe*. New York: Harper and Row.

Thorsen, F. (1997). *Through quiet processes and small circles*. Unpublished paper, Fifth International Symposium for Psychologists for Peace, October, New York.

Tillich, P. (1952). *The courage to be*. New Haven, CT: Yale University Press.

Tillich, P. (1963, May 17). The ambiguity of perfection. *Time Magazine*, p. 53.

Tillich, P. (1990). Existentialism and psychotherapy. In K. Hoeller (Ed.), Readings in existential psychology and psychiatry, special edition, *Review of Existential Psychology and Psychiatry, 20* (1–3), 39–47.

Todorov, T. (1995). *La vie commune: Essai d'anthropologie générale*. Paris: Éditions du Seuil.

Toffler, A. (1971). *Future shock*. New York: Bantam Books.

Torbert, W. R. (1991). *The power of balance: Transforming self, society, and scientific inquiry*. Newbury Park, CA: Sage.

Toulouse, J-M. (1998, September 9). Présentation aux professeurs adjoints, agrégés et titulaires lors de la réunion de l'Assemblée des professeurs. Montreal: Internal Document HEC.

Toynbee, A. J., and Ikeda, D. (1976). *The Toynbee–Ikeda dialogue: Man himself must choose*. New York: Kodasha International.

Trist, E., Emery, F., and Murray, H. (Eds.). (1997). *The social engagement of social science: A Tavistock anthology*. Vol. 3: *The socio-ecological perspective*. Philadelphia: University of Pennsylvania Press.

Turkle, S. (1984). *The second self: Computers and the human spirit*. New York: Simon and Schuster.

Turner, F. (1995). *The culture of hope: A new birth of the classical spirit*. New York: The Free Press.

Ulrich, P. (1997). *Integrative wirtschaftsethik: Grundlagen einer lebensdienlichen Ökonomie*. Bern: University of Bern Press.

Vahanian, G. (1977). *Dieu et l'utopie*. Paris: Édition du Cerf.

Vaill, P. (1998). *Spirited leading and learning*. San Francisco: Jossey-Bass.

Velasquez, M. G. (1982). *Business ethics*. Englewood Cliffs, NJ: Prentice Hall.

von Bingen, H. (1987). *Hildegard von Bingen's books* (M. Fox, ed.). Santa Fe, NM: Bear.

Waldrop, M. M. (1992). *Complexity: The emerging science at the edge of order and chaos*. New York: Simon and Schuster.

Weber, M. (1947). *The theory of social and economic organization*. New York: Oxford University Press (original published 1924).

Weber, M. (1963). *The sociology of religion*. Boston, MA: Beacon Press.

Weil, S. (1950). *La connaissance surnaiurelle*. Paris: Gallimard.

Weil, S. (1952). *Gravity and grace*. London: Routledge and Kegan Paul (original published 1947).

Weil, S. (1957). *Intimations of Christianity among the ancient Greeks*. London: Routledge and Kegan Paul (original published 1951).

Weil, S. (1959). *Leçons de philosophie*. (Présentées par A. Reynaud-Guérithault). Paris: Plon.

Weil, S. (1966). *Waiting for God*. New York: G. P. Putman's Sons.

Weil, S. (1968). *On science, necessity, and the love of God*. London, New York: Oxford University Press (original published 1951).

Weil, S. (1970). *First and last notebooks*. New York: Oxford University Press (original published 1950).

Weil, S. (1973). *Oppression and liberty*. Amherst: University of Massachussetts Press (original published 1955).

Weil, S. (1987). *The need for roots: Prelude to a declaration of duties towards mankind*. New York: Ark Paperbacks (original published 1949).

Weil, S. (1988). Science et perception dans Descartes. *Oeuvres complètes, Premiers écrits philosophiques, Tome I* (pp. 159–221) (A .A. Devaux and F. de Lussy, eds.). Paris: Éditions Gallimard.

Wheatley, M., and Chödrön, P. (1999, November). It starts with uncertainty. *Shambhala Sun*, pp. 58–62.

Wheatley, M. J. (1994). *Leadership and the new science: Learning about organization from an orderly universe*. San Francisco: Berrett-Koehler.

White, B. J., and Montgomery, R. R. (1980). Corporate codes of conduct. *California Management Review, 23* (2), 80–87.

Whitehead, A. N. (1967). *Adventures of ideas*. New York: The Free Press (original published 1933).

Whitehead, E. E., and Whitehead, J. D. (1982). *Christian life patterns*. New York: Image Books.

Whyte, D. (1994). *The heart aroused: Poetry and preservation of soul in corporate America*. New York: DoubledayCurrency.

Wilber, K. (1980). *The Atman project: A transpersonal view of human development*. Wheaton, IL: Theosophical Publishing House.

Wilber, K. (1983). *Eye to eye: The quest for the new paradigm*. New York: Anchor Books.

Wilber, K. (Ed.). (1984). *Quantum questions: Mystical writings of the world's great physicists*. Boston: Shambhala.

Wilber, K. (1995). *Sex, ecology, spirituality: The spirit of evolution*. Boston: Shambhala.

Wilber, K. (1996). *A brief history of everything*. Boston: Shambhala.

Wilber, K. (1999). *The marriage of sense and soul*. New York: Broadway Books.

Wilber, K. (2000). *Integral psychology*. Boston: Shambhala.

Wilber, K., Engler, J., and Brown, D. P. (1986). *Transformations of consciousness: Conventional and contemplative perspectives on development*. Boston: Shambhala.

Windelband, W. (1958). *History of philosophy* (J. H. Tufts, trans.). New York: Harper (original published 1901).

Wolman, W., and Colamosca, A. (1997). *The Judas economy: The triumph of capital and the betrayal of work*. Reading, MA: Addison-Wesley.

Wu, X. (1999). Business and ethical perceptions of business people in east China: An empirical study. *Business Ethics Quarterly, 9* (3), 541–558.

Yankelovich, D. (1997, August). Got to give to get. *Mother Jones*, pp. 61–63.

Zaleznik, A. (1989). *The managerial mystique*. New York: Harper and Row.

Zohar, D. (1990). *The quantum self: Human nature and consciousness defined by the new physics*. New York: William Morrow.

Zohar, D. (1997). *Rewiring the corporate brain: Using new science to rethink how we structure and lead organizations*. San Francisco: Berrett-Koehler.

Index

About the Editor and Contributors

Claude Beland was called to the bar in 1956 and practiced in a law firm before joining the cooperative movement in 1971. Reelected on two occasions, he was the president of *Mouvement Desjardins* from 1987 to 1999, which employs more than 40,000 people and manages assets worth more than $70 billion. Mr. Beland actively participates in Quebec society as a board member for many organizations and institutions, as a leader of certain social and economic forums, and through his support for a number of causes. He also plays an active role in the international cooperative world, and since 1995 has been the president of the International Association of Cooperative Banks. He recently published the book entitled *Inquietude et espoir*.

Yves Benoît has worked in healthcare for the past twenty years. With a bachelor of commerce, he completed his postgraduate work with a masters in health administration from the medical faculty of the University of Montreal. From the public health domain he went on to hold a number of executive positions in hospital administration. Currently he is the director general of the Anna-Laberge Healthcare Center, a general and specialized healthcare facility with 250 beds. At the time of the forum he was the assistant director of Charles Lemoyne Hospital. In addition to his numerous professional activities, his personal values find expression in his involvement with pedagogical foundations and associations.

Roger Berthouzoz is author of a number of scientific articles and books, a Dominican, and a professor of ethics and moral theology at the University of Fribourg in Switzerland. He has recently published a directory of Episcopal documents written during the century (1891–1991) on the theme of justice, work, the economy, and spiritual values entitled *Economie et developpement*. Working on these themes for a number of years, he founded the Center for Documentation and Research on Christian Social Teaching (CIDRESOC) at the University of Fribourg where he is the director of the Institute of Moral Theology.

Vera Danyluk is president of the executive committee of the Montreal Urban Community, which regroups twenty municipalities and more than 1.8 million people, and reelected for a second term, Mrs. Danyluk is also a member of a number of boards of directors including the Canadian Federation of Municipalities and is the vice president of the National Strategy for Community Safety and Crime Prevention. Formerly the mayor of the town of Mount Royal, Mrs. Danyluk has a bachelors in education and has completed her studies for a masters in moral and religious education at McGill University.

Michel Dion is trained as a lawyer and theologian at the doctoral level, and is a professor of ethics with the faculty of theology, ethics, and philosophy at the University of Sherbrooke in Canada. He founded and directs the Southeast Asian–Canadian Consortium for Business and Human Rights, which works in collaboration with university institutions and nongovernmental agencies in Indonesia, Malaysia, the Philippines, and Thailand. He also directs the Research Group in Governmental Ethics. Professor Dion has published numerous scientific articles and many books on the subject of ethics and religion.

James Hurley is a professor emeritus of management at the Graduate School of Business Administration, Royal Melbourne Institute of Technology (RMIT) in Melbourne, Australia. An author of many publications and consultant, Mr. Hurley was one of the mainsprings in the conception and the administration of the DBA program (doctor of business administration) offered at RMIT to executives from Australia, Hong Kong, India, Malaysia, and Singapore. This innovative program attempted to integrate a process of personal development as well as ethical and spiritual values into managerial practice.

Solange Lefebvre has a bachelor of music (piano) from the Quebec Conservatory of Music in Montreal, a doctorate in theology from the University of Montreal, and doctoral diploma in social anthropology from L'Ecole des Hautes Etudes en Sciences Sociales of Paris. She is a professor with the faculty of theology at the University of Montreal. She works on questions of values and spirituality as well as intergenerational relationships. Currently she directs a research project on transition in the workplace and is a contributor to *Le Devoir* newspaper on religious issues.

J.-Robert Ouimet is sole shareholder in a medium-size company in the food industry, and president and chief executive officer of Ouimet Cordon Bleu Inc. in Canada. He is a member of the Order of Canada, the Order of Quebec L'orde des Gardiens du Mont-Sion et du Saint-Sepulcre in Jerusalem, as well as sitting on a number of boards. Mr. Ouimet has a degree from HEC, a degree in political science from the University of Fribourg, an MBA from Columbia University, and has recently obtained a doctorate of economic and social science from the University of Fribourg. In his thesis, Mr. Ouimet proposed that the concurrent development of economic, ethical, and spiritual wealth is possible in a market economy.

Thierry C. Pauchant is author of more than 130 publications including eight books, *In Search for Meaning* among them, former manager in the tourism industry and consultant (M.Sc. Pantheon-Sorbonne, MBA, UCLA, Ph.D. Administration, USC), and holds the chair in Ethical Management of Organizations at HEC Montreal. He has cofounded many organizations where he holds or has held executive positions, and he is a member of several boards of directors. His research and consulting activities in Canada, the United States, and France aim to promote the ethical management of complex systems, which integrate the psychological, economical, social, ecological, and spiritual dimensions.

Ian I. Mitroff is author of more than 250 scientific publications and twenty books, and holds the Harold Quinton Chair in General Policy and Strategic Management at the Marshall School of Business, University of Southern California in Los Angeles. Much in demand as a consultant for Fortune 500 enterprises and public and government institutions, he is a regular contributor to the *Los Angeles Times* and is a fellow of the Academy of Management. He is also the president of the consulting firm Comprehensive Crisis Management. His latest books include *Transforming the Crisis-Prone Organization* with Thierry Pauchant, *The Unbounded Mind* with Harold Linstone, *Frame Break* with Richard Mason and Chris Pearson, and *A Spiritual Audit of Corporate America*, one of the first systematic surveys on spirituality in the workplace, with Elisabeth Denton.

Peter Sheldrake was the executive director of the Graduate School of Business Administration, Royal Melbourne Institute of Technology in Australia. The RMIT is one of the most important business schools in the world with over 500 employees and 10,000 students, and offers graduate and postgraduate degrees in administration, in cooperation with many international management associations in Singapore, Malaysia, Hong Kong, and India. A professor of management and author of a number of publications and consultant, Mr. Sheldrake was involved in the administration of the DBA offered at his institution, an innovative program that tried to integrate ethical and spiritual values in administrative education.

Jean-Marie Toulouse is trained in social psychology and administration, and is pursuing his second term as director of HEC Montreal, the oldest, largest, and one of the most prestigious business schools in Canada. Author of a number of scientific articles and books, the work of Mr. Toulouse on entrepreneurship, business strategy, and organizational dynamics is particularly well-known. Before being elected director, he occupied the Maclean Hunter Chair of Entrepreneurship. He was recently elected as a member of the Royal Academy of Science of Canada and sits on a number of boards of directors.

> To contact us:
> FIMES
> HEC
> 3000 Cote–Sainte–Catherine
> Montreal (Quebec) H3T 2A7, Canada
> Telephone: (514) 340–7145
> Fax: (514) 340–7146
> Web site: http://www.hec.ca/fimes
> e-mail: fimes@hec.ca